Ferri's book is an engaging one-stop storehouse of knowledge on index funds. It is a vital roadmap for those seeking higher returns and lower risk. Worth its weight in gold!

—William Bernstein
Investment advisor,
author of *The Intelligent Asset Allocator*

It is said that there is no one more religious than a convert. So when a former stockbroker comes to believe that owning the entire stock market through an index fund is the key to investment success, he presents his case with passion. And Ferri is right! This book tells you why, and how to get started.

—John C. Bogle
Founder and former chairman,
The Vanguard Group

All About Index Funds clearly explains why investing in index mutual funds is the only reliable winning strategy. Ferri compares and contrasts active mutual funds with index funds in a way that even a novice will have no trouble navigating. Once you read this book, you will no longer listen to the hype from Wall Street stockbrokers and their analysts who are paid to make money from you, not for you.

—Larry Swedroe
Investment advisor,
author of *What Wall Street Doessn't Want You to Know*

OTHER TITLES IN THE "ALL ABOUT..." FINANCE SERIES

All About Stocks, 2nd edition
by Esme Faerber

All About Bonds and Bond Mutual Funds, 2nd edition
by Esme Faerber

All About Options, 2nd edition
by Thomas McCafferty

All About Futures, 2nd edition
by Russell Wasendorf

All About Commodities
by Thomas McCafferty and Russell Wasendorf

All About Mutual Funds, 2nd edition
By Bruce Jacobs

All About Real Estate Investing, 2nd edition
by William Benke and Joseph M. Fowler

All About Your 401K Plan
by Ellie Williams Clinton and Diane Pearl

All About Variable Annuities
by Bruce Wells

All About DRIPs and DSPs
by George C. Fisher

ALL ABOUT INDEX FUNDS

The Easy Way to Get Started

RICHARD A. FERRI, CFA

McGraw-Hill

New York   Chicago   San Francisco   Lisbon   London
Madrid   Mexico City   Milan   New Delhi   San Juan
Seoul   Singapore   Sydney   Toronto

To my children,
Thomas, Nicholas, and Ashley

So that you may invest wisely
and someday spend your own money.

The **McGraw·Hill** Companies

Library of Congress Cataloging-in-Publication Data

Ferri, Richard A.
　All about index funds : the easy way to get started / Richard A. Ferri.
　　p.　cm.
Includes bibliographical references and index.
　ISBN 0-07-138705-6
　1. Index mutual funds.　2. Index mutual funds—United States.　I. Title.
　HG4530 .F427　2002
　332.63'27—dc21

2002002663

1 2 3 4 5 6 7 8 9 0　DOC/DOC　098765432

ISBN 0-07-138705-6

This publication is designed to provide accurate and authoritative information in regard to the subject matter covered. It is sold with the understanding that the publisher is not engaged in rendering legal, accounting, or other professional service. If legal advice or other expert assistance is required, the services of a competent professional person should be sought.

　　　　　　　　—From a declaration of principles jointly adopted by a committee of the
　　　　　　　　American Bar Association and a committee of publishers.

This book is printed on recycled, acid-free paper containing a minimum of 50% recycled, de-inked fiber.

McGraw-Hill books are available at special quantity discounts to use as premiums and sales promotions, or for use in corporate training programs. For more information, please write to the Director of Special Sales, Professional Publishing, McGraw-Hill, Two Penn Plaza, New York, NY 10121-2298. Or contact your local bookstore.

CONTENTS

PART THREE

MANAGING YOUR PORTFOLIO OF INDEX FUNDS

APPENDIXES

Welcome to the new and evolving world of index mutual funds. By the time you finish reading this book, you will be well versed on the many types of index funds available in the marketplace and how to utilize them in your investment accounts. *All About Index Funds* is loaded with good advice that you can use to manage small accounts and large accounts. The strategies put forth are simple, straightforward, and will lead to greater wealth and personal satisfaction.

Index mutual funds use a "passive" investment methodology. The funds simply hold the same stocks or bonds as one of the popular market indexes, such as the Dow Jones Industrial Average. Although a portfolio manager is responsible for the actual mechanics of running an index fund, a computer does most of the work. This means the cost of management is much less than traditional "actively managed" mutual funds, where large research staffs are employed to pick and choose individual stocks and bonds. There are several types of stock and bond index funds available, and this book will help you select the right mix of funds for your needs.

Besides earning more money, an investment in index funds saves time and reduces stress. No longer will you waste away the hours sifting through thousands of stocks, bonds, and active mutual funds trying to find meaning in it all. No longer will you make hasty investment decisions based on incomplete or incomprehensible marketing brochures. By investing a little of your time today to learn about this marketplace, you will save weeks of time and torment in your life. Indexing is a simple, clean, and cost-effective solution to your investment needs.

Make no mistake about it, embracing the concept of using index mutual funds can be a life-altering event. It is somewhat like switching religions. When you were young you may have been taught the beliefs of one specific religion, but as you got older, those teachings did not work for you. So you searched for deeper meaning and discovered a better alternative, a better religion. The same goes for indexing. All your life you read the popular financial press, listened to market experts on TV, and went with a few of your stock-broker's recommendations. But the more experience you gained, the less that method of investing made sense. This book introduces you to an alternative style of investing that is based on sound logic and is easy to comprehend. Once you discover the many benefits of index mutual funds, your beliefs on investing will change forever.

MY PERSONAL JOURNEY

As a young, impressionable man in my early twenties, I held the im-pression that stockbrokers and other financial advisers were skilled professionals. Clearly, they must have had superior training in the areas of accounting and economics and knew things about the mar-kets that common folk did not know. Because of their deep knowl-edge, these people made a lot of money for their clients as well as for themselves. So, when I was hired as a stockbroker in 1988, I fol-lowed the advice and recommendations of experienced stockbro-kers in my office as well as the analysts at my firm. I knew by doing this I was going to do very well for my clients and for myself.

Well, it didn't take long to realize that the investment ideas turned out by my firm were no better than those pulled out of the air, and many times they were much worse. Soon I understood why our recommendations were mediocre at best. The fact is many ana-lysts and brokers have an ulterior motive for recommending certain investments. Specifically, they were doing so to generate commis-sions and fees. To make matters worse, these people apparently had little personal belief in the ideas they were selling. The bottom of their paycheck was the top priority. This revelation created a dilem-ma in my life. I had hoped to build a successful business by follow-ing the guiding light of expert recommendations, but it wasn't go-ing to happen.

Luckily, our firm had an "investment consulting" division that included access to top investment adviser firms and proprietary mutual fund research. Private investment advisers and mutual fund managers are not paid a commission for managing portfolios. In-stead, they are compensated based on a percentage of the money that they manage. The incentive here was to grow the accounts us-ing their superior investment skill so they could collect a higher management fee. This seemed like a win, win, win situation. My clients made money through growth, the managers made money through fees, and I got paid a cut of the fee or a commission on the mutual fund. Surely it was a recipe for success.

Alas, investment consulting, too, was an illusion. As a group, professional money managers were no more capable of achieving high returns than a bunch of monkeys throwing darts at the stock pages of *The Wall Street Journal*. A small number of managers did achieve respectable returns, but they were far and few between, and it was impossible to pick the winners in advance. Overall, the investment consulting idea was a disappointment, so it was time to move on.

My next brainstorm was totally different. If success could not be found in the stock market, perhaps the futures and commodities pits would prove more fruitful. Trying to make sense of the oil, grain, and currency markets was like rocket science, and therefore, the futures industry attracted an extraordinary group of scientists. Mathematicians and physicists that designed Star Wars weaponry during the Cold War were now working for Wall Street firms designing money machines. They sat in large trading rooms filled with computers, measuring every wiggle in the financial markets, looking for profitable trading opportunities. These smart people could be hired through a "pooled" account to manage money for my clients. This strategy was certain to lead us all to wealth.

Well, there were certainly a lot of wiggles generated in those investment pools, and some people actually made money. My firm made money, the rocket scientists made money, and I made money, but my clients didn't make much money. The high fees and expenses of commodity pools and hedge funds wiped out most of the gains. It became obvious that commodities was not the place to be.

Frustrated, I decided to do it myself. If the analysts, mutual fund mangers, and rocket scientists could not beat the markets, surely there was someone who could, and that someone might as well be me. I realized I needed more education, which took me back to academia. Over a 7-year period I achieved a chartered financial analyst (CFA) designation and Master of Science in finance degree. In addition I read dozens of books, scanned hundreds of research reports, and did a significant amount of personal research, with the goal of finding the secret to superior returns. During this period I continued to work full time as a stockbroker and started writing my first book on investment principles, *Serious Money, Straight Talk About Investing for Retirement.*

The educational barrage began to pay off when I realized I was searching for a false prophet. My idea was to find a strategy that "beat the market," but that was a flawed idea. The more I studied, the clearer it became that no such strategy exists, at least not with enough consistency for the average Joe to benefit. In fact most of the academic studies I read came to the same conclusion. The more investors moved their money around into strategies they thought would lead to superior returns, the further behind they fell. I learned what Charles D. Ellis pointed out years ago in his classic book, *Investment Policy:* Trying to beat the market was a loser's game.

It is clear that a vast majority of investors would be better off if they simply bought the *entire* stock market and held on rather than trying to find some superior method to beat the market. The best way to buy the market is through *index mutual funds.* Index funds are designed to track the performance of a stock or bond market rather than trying to beat it. These funds operate the same way as any other mutual fund you may have invested in. The difference is that index funds perform better than average over the long-term because they are lower in cost and follow a consistent strategy.

To finish the story, I ultimately resigned from the brokerage industry and opened an independent investment firm. Our company is dedicated to managing portfolios using low-cost passive strategies that include many of the index funds mentioned in this book.

THE GENERAL OUTLINE OF THE BOOK

All About Index Funds is divided into three parts. All three sections are written to help investors at all levels of experience. The sections can be read independently of each other or flow from one to the other.

Part I (Chapters 1–5) explains what a market index is and how index mutual funds work. There is a short history of the index fund industry, including a chapter devoted to new exchange-traded funds (ETFs). Part I also highlights the performance advantages that index funds have over other types of investments.

Part II (Chapters 6–11) categorizes the broad spectrum of index funds based on type and style. Many people are aware of the big index funds, such as S&P 500®1 index funds, but don't know that there are hundreds of index funds covering a variety of markets. There are funds tracking the bond market, international stock and bond markets, technology and energy sectors, and the socially responsible index. New index funds are formed every month, and the number of funds barely touches the number of market indexes that are available to index.

Part III (Chapters 12–16) is all about using index funds in your portfolio. To help with this decision, there are chapters on forecasting market returns, asset allocation, risk control, and retirement planning. Several model portfolios are introduced.

A GUIDE FOR ALL

All About Index Funds is a guidebook for new index investors and a reference for more experienced investors. The book was written to provide more than enough information to build and manage a quality index fund portfolio. There are a few words of caution before we proceed. Converting to an index fund portfolio does not guarantee positive returns every year. No viable investment strategy can do that. You must be patient. In the long-term a well-diversified index fund portfolio will make you more money with less risk that any other popular investment method. This is a guarantee. Index funds cost far less than other types of mutual funds, so eventually the laws of economics will take over, and index funds will deliver higher returns.

There is one other important point to remember. For any indexing strategy to be truly effective, you must build the right mix of index funds for your needs and wait patiently for the markets to do their magic. If you stick with a well-managed strategy for several years, the fruits of the marketplace will come to you. It is in the long run that index funds truly shine.

All About Index Funds is all about a simple and effective investment strategy that just plain works.

ACKNOWLEDGMENTS

Special thanks for the great comments and editing by J. Parsons, Tony Rochte, and Morgan Lee of Barclays Global Investors; William J.

Bernstein of Efficient Frontier Advisors; and Larry Swedroe of Buckingham Asset Management. Many thanks for the contributions of John Bogle, founder and former chairman of The Vanguard Group, and Jim Wiandt and Will McClatchy, editors of Indexfunds.com. This book was only possible with the patience and support of my wife, Daria, and my business partner, Scott Salaske. Finally, I would like to give special thanks to Dr. Howard Green, who has been a great friend and mentor during this project and throughout my career in the investment industry.

NOTES

1. S&P is the registered trademark of Standard & Poor's, a McGraw-Hill company.

PART ONE

Index Funds Basics

CHAPTER 1

What Are Index Funds?

Key Concepts

- There is a difference between an index and a market.
- Indexes are used as benchmarks.
- What are mutual funds and investment accounts?
- Index funds differ from other funds.

Common sense, simplicity, and perseverance are ideals we strive for in life. Yet, when we tackle the subject of investing, the guiding principles are often overshadowed by ambiguity, complexity, and irrationality. *All About Index Funds* focuses on getting back to investment basics. It is an instruction guide that will help you invest for the rest of your life.

Many books, magazines, and TV shows lead you to believe that there are undiscovered riches in the financial markets waiting for you to exploit. They attempt to gain your attention and your dollars by appealing to your greed. This book avoids such deceit. *All About Index Funds* deals with common sense. Investing is a part of life, like eating, working, and paying taxes. If your habits are poor, then there will be serious consequences.

Whether you are a novice investor or have been at it for a while, this book will help you bring your portfolio in line with the laws of economics. After carefully reading this book, you will be able to develop a sound portfolio of index mutual funds that is simple, practical, and tailored to your personal financial goal.

This chapter provides definitions and general background information on the concept of index mutual funds. It explains what market indexes are and what they are used for. We will also review the idea behind mutual funds in general and how they are managed. Finally, we will look at how mutual fund companies have linked market indexes and mutual funds together, creating *index funds.*

UNDERSTANDING INDEXES

"How's the market?" This simple question is asked millions of times a day by millions of people around the globe. In the United States, the market that people typically quote is the Dow Jones Industrial Average (DJIA), better known as the *Dow.*[1] For better or worse the Dow is the most widely quoted stock market index in the United States, if not the world. Why is the index so popular? Over 100 years ago, people on Wall Street found it difficult to discern whether the general stock prices were rising or falling. There was no published index to measure a composite of stock prices against. So when Charles Dow first unveiled his industrial stock average in 1896, it was considered the bellwether benchmark, more so because it was published every day in a tip sheet called *The Wall Street Journal* (a Dow Jones & Co. publication). People began to view the Dow as though it were a line in the sand and measured the tide of all stock prices against it.

The computation of the Dow Jones Industrial Average was quite simple 100 years ago, and it remains that way today. Starting in the late 1800s, at the end of each trading day, Charles Dow added up the prices of 12 large industrial stocks listed on the New York Stock Exchange. That was the index, pure and simple.

As time marched on, Charles Dow found that keeping the index current was not an easy task. Some companies merged or went out of business, and others split their stock thereby reducing the price. Still others paid cash dividends, whereas some paid stock dividends or no dividends at all. Thus, a whole range of calculation problems developed. Dow figured out how to adjust the index for all these changes, thereby keeping the index consistent. Over the years the number of stocks in the Dow gradually increased to 20 in 1916 and again to 30 in 1928, where it remains today.

Dow methodology is simple, but the index has some major setbacks. A movement in the DJIA average is based on point movements in individual stocks in the index rather than on percentage movements of those stocks. That means a $1 gain in a $5 stock has the same effect in the DJIA as a $1 gain in a $100 stock. Intuitively, that leads to distortion between the index price and market values. For example, assume there are only two companies in the Dow index, Company A and Company B. Assume Company A has a total market value of $100 billion, and its stock is trading at $10 per share. Company B has a total market value of $100 billion, and its stock is trading at $100 per share. According to the Dow pricing methodology, the price level of our two-stock index is 110 (calculated as $100 + $10). Recall that the total value of both companies is $200 billion ($100 billion + $100 billion). Let's say that over a 1-year period the price of Company A stock doubles from $10 to $20, which means the total value of the company doubled from $100 billion to $200 billion. During the same period the price of Company B stock stayed at $100, so the total value of the company stayed at $100 billion. Here is the Dow methodology flaw: Although the combined total value of both companies increased from $200 billion to $300 billion (a 50 percent increase), the value of the Dow methodology index increased from $110 to $120 (a 9 percent gain). The methodology on which the DJIA is based does not capture the value movements of companies, only their price movements, which distorts reality. In addition to its methodology flaws, the DJIA consists of only 30 stocks and does not reflect the movement of the entire stock market, which consists of more than 7000 liquid stocks.

Despite its outdated pricing methodology and other flaws, the DJIA still plays a key role in the U.S. economy. It is the main barometer of the stock market activity used by the media and the public. The Dow is the most widely quoted stock index in the world, and most people seem to be aware of its approximate level and general direction. From a practical standpoint the Dow is of limited use to professionals. Broader measures of stock market performance are used when a more accurate index is needed.

The Standard & Poor's 500 Index is a *market weighted* index of 500 leading U.S. companies from a broad range of industries. Market weighting means that larger companies have a greater bearing on the index value than small companies. For example, if the stock price of a very large company like General Electric goes up by 10 percent, it will affect the value of the S&P 500 Index more than if the price of a much smaller company like Tiffany's went up by 10 percent. Both companies are members of the S&P 500 Index, but GE has more market weight. Market weighting allows the true dollar value of the entire index to be measured.

Most indexes used on Wall Street today are market weighted, and there are plenty of them to choose from. There are hundreds of U.S. stock indexes covering all corners of the market. There are very large indexes that track nearly all U.S. companies, such as the Wilshire 5000 Index®, the Russell 3000 Index®, and the Dow Jones Total Market Index®. There are indexes that track a certain market sector such as large companies, small companies, value companies, and growth companies. There are indexes that track industrial sectors, including new economy technology industries and old economy brick-and-mortar industries. There are even indexes that track socially responsible companies. Each of these indexes can include hundreds, if not thousands, of stocks. Many of these indexes are discussed in Part Two of this book.

The United States is not the only country that has multiple stock indexes. Countries around the globe have developed their own set of indexes that track their own stock market. For example, Japan is a highly developed country. The Nikkei Stock Average is an index of 225 leading stocks that trade on the Tokyo Stock Exchange. There is also a Nikkei small company index that tracks smaller Japanese companies.

Foreign markets are commonly divided into two types: developed markets and emerging markets. A developed market has a higher per capita income (over $10,000 U.S.), and an emerging market has a lower per capita income. Grouping countries together creates the opportunity for a composite index of developed markets and a composite index of emerging markets. There are also regional indexes based on geographic location such as Europe or the Pacific Rim. The major providers of foreign index data are Morgan Stanley Dean Witter, Dow Jones, Salomon Smith Barney, and Bloomberg.

So far we have only discussed stock indexes, but we forget the largest market in the world: the bond market. Bond markets are also referred to as credit markets and fixed-income markets. Popular bond indexes include the U.S. Treasury bonds, corporate bonds, high-yield bonds, convertible bonds, mortgages, tax-exempt bonds, and foreign bonds. Some of the leading providers of bond indexes are Lehman Brothers, Salomon Smith Barney, and Merrill Lynch.

There are large differences between bond indexes. Junk bonds have a higher risk of default than Treasury bonds, so they pay a higher interest rate. The difference between the interest rate on junk bonds and the interest rate on Treasury bonds is called a *credit spread*. You can track credit spreads between various bond indexes to view the historic changes in the perceived risk between market segments. A larger spread means higher risk is present in that bond market segment, and a smaller spread means less risk is perceived by investors. More information on index spreads is available in Chapter 9.

As you may have guessed, an index can be created for any group of stocks or bonds. I think it is safe to say that if you cannot find an index that covers a particular type of investment, wait a month or so and one will likely be created.

THE DIFFERENCE BETWEEN INDEXES AND MARKETS

It is important to understand the difference between a stock market and an index. The Dow Jones Industrial Average is an index. The New York Stock Exchange (NYSE) is a market. The S&P 500 is an index. The NASDAQ is a market. A market is the place where stocks and bonds trade, either a physical location or in cyberspace. An index tracks a broad range of security prices wherever they trade. An example of a market is the NYSE. It is physically located on Wall Street in New York City, where approximately 2650 stocks trade. Although the NYSE is a market, the owners of the exchange have created their own quasi-indexes that cover only stocks that trade on that exchange. A few of these proprietary indexes include the NYSE Financials Index, the NYSE Transportation Index, and the New York Composite Index.

Although exchanges create their own indexes, they are not the best choice for an index because they do not cover the entire stock market. Exchange-created indexes hold only those stocks that trade on that particular exchange. For example, the NYSE Composite Index holds General Electric (GE) because it trades on the NYSE; however, it does not hold Microsoft (MSFT) because that stock trades on the NASDAQ, which is a competing exchange. MSFT stock will not be found in any NYSE or AMEX indexes even though it is one of the largest companies in the country.

Many people believe the NASDAQ is an index, but it is not an index; it is a market. NASDAQ is an acronym for the National Association of Security Dealers Automated Quote System, which is owned by the National Association of Securities Dealers. The NASDAQ is a computerized market system that links brokers and dealers together who trade stocks *over the counter*. Although the NASDAQ is not at a physical location like the NYSE, it is a major competitor to the NYSE.

The NASDAQ has created a number of incomplete (and over-hyped) indexes, which cover only stocks traded over the counter. There is a fallacy in the mass media that the NASDAQ indexes best represent the "new" economy. This is not true. Some of the largest new economy companies are listed on the NYSE and therefore are not represented in NASDAQ indexes. For example, the NASDAQ Computer Index does not include International Business Machines (IBM) or Electronic Data Systems (EDS). Those companies trade on the NYSE.

One popular NASDAQ index fund that is greatly misunderstood is the NASDAQ-100 Tracking Stock, better known as QQQ. The objective of this fund is to provide investment results that generally correspond to the price and yield performance of the largest 100 stocks that trade on the NASDAQ. This index fund accomplishes its mission but is not a good proxy for the new economy because the NASDAQ-100 Index excludes several important new economy companies that trade on the NYSE.

A complete market index does not have exchange bias. It cuts across all markets and is not restricted to one exchange or another. All of the Standard & Poor's, Russell, and Wilshire indexes are unbiased. They represent stocks listed on the NYSE, NASDAQ, AMEX, and a few small regional stock exchanges. We will concentrate only on complete indexes in this book.

INDEXES AS PORTFOLIO BENCHMARKS

Indexes are useful in a variety of ways. They can be used to gauge the general wealth of a nation. They can be used to track the mood of consumers, which may help economists forecast sales and profits. They can be compared to one another, and the spread may indicate a possible trading opportunity. In this book we are going to ignore what the indexes may be forecasting and concentrate on what we actually know. Our use of market indexes is focused on *benchmarking*.

Benchmarking uses a market index as a milestone to measure the performance of an investment portfolio. If you own a portfolio of individual stocks that went up by 10 percent last year, you might think that it was a good return. Maybe it was and maybe it wasn't. It is hard to say without comparing it to an appropriate market benchmark. If your portfolio was made up of mostly large U.S. stocks, the S&P 500 may be the right index to measure the portfolio against. If the S&P 500 gained 5 percent during the year, your 10 percent return was outstanding. On the other hand, if the S&P 500 gained 20 percent, your 10 percent return was dismal.

Benchmarking is an important element in managing any investment portfolio. A comparison should be made on a quarterly basis. Most mutual funds benchmark their portfolios monthly. If a mutual fund manager is not keeping up with his or her benchmark, it may be time to look for a new manager. Many portfolio managers have lost their jobs because the accounts they managed failed to keep up with their predesignated market benchmark. We discuss the benchmarking of mutual funds throughout this book, but first let's review what a mutual fund is.

MUTUAL FUNDS AND INVESTMENT ACCOUNTS

There is so much misunderstanding about the difference between a mutual fund and an investment account that review is warranted. Consider this conversation that I have had with many people over the years:

> "Rick, should I invest in index funds or put my money in an IRA account?"
> *"You should buy index funds in an IRA account."*
> "I don't understand. What's the difference?"
> *"An IRA is a type of account, just like a savings account or a checking account. Once you open an IRA and put money into it, then you can buy index funds as an investment."*

Before you buy an index fund, you must open an account. The account will have a title, such as an IRA, Living Trust, UGMA, or 401(k). In fact, mutual funds make wonderful investments. After you fund the account with money, you can then buy index funds.

How Mutual Funds Work

Mutual funds are a wonderful investment idea. They offer diversification, ease of management, and tax simplification, all at a reasonable fee. The general concept behind all *open-end* mutual funds is as follows: A large group of investors pool their money in an account that is held at a bank trust department. A professional money manager is hired to pick stocks or bonds that go into the account. The trust is divided into shares, and each investor owns shares based on the amount of money he or she put into the trust. If investors want to sell shares, they can sell back to the trust at the end of each trading day at the valuation price, also known as the net asset value (NAV). At that time the fund manager will sell stocks or bonds to raise the cash needed to pay off the investors. If a new investor wants to buy shares, or old investors want to buy more shares, money is deposited in the trust, new shares are created, and the portfolio manager uses the money to buy more securities.

The manager of a mutual fund has the right to buy and sell stocks or bonds as they see fit as long they follow the strict guidelines that are laid out in the fund *prospectus*. This legal document explains in nauseating detail how the money in the trust account will be allocated among various securities. For example, the prospectus of a large U.S. stock fund may dictate that the manager can buy only the stock in U.S. companies worth $20 billion or more and restricts the manager from placing any more than 10 percent of the fund in one industry group, such as technology. Some funds forbid managers to have less than 95 percent of the money invested in stocks, regardless of how badly the manager thinks the stock market may perform in the future.

The prospectus is free to all investors, even if they do not own or are considering buying a mutual fund. It should be read prior to purchase because it will give you a detailed description as to how your money will be managed. An annual update of the prospectus is mailed to all shareholders. The board of directors must approve major changes to the fund. Sometimes those changes need the approval of a majority of shareholders. All of this information is available to the general public free of charge, and most are filed in electronic format with the Securities and Exchange Commission (www.sec.gov).

To simplify accounting, the mutual fund sends investors a Form 1099 at the end of each year, which summarizes the fund's cash distributions and tax liability. The securities in a mutual fund may pay dividends or interest during the year, and the buying and selling of securities within the fund may create capital gains or capital losses. Form 1099 is a standardized document that lists all of these items and makes year-end tax preparation very simple.

Are Mutual Funds Safe?

If you own shares of a stock mutual fund, you own partial shares of many different stocks. So, let's make it clear that mutual funds do not offer protection from a bad stock market. A rising market lifts most funds, and a falling market sinks them. Mutual funds do not offer protection in a bad market regardless of what an advertisement in the newspaper may infer.

Some mutual fund managers have the authority to reduce the amount of stock in a fund if they think a bear market is coming, but most fund managers are reluctant to act on that hunch. The ability to successfully identify the tops and bottoms of the market is a rare trait indeed. Mutual fund managers who are wrong on their predictions can cost shareholders a lot of money, and that may cost them a job. As a result, stock mutual funds managers generally remain invested during all market conditions, which means the fund will go down when the market goes kaput.

Three Good Reasons to Own Mutual Funds

If mutual funds offer no protection when the stock market goes down, why do people invest in them? There are three good reasons to own mutual funds:

1. diversification
2. professional management
3. convenience

"A little knowledge about the markets is a dangerous thing," says Jeremy Siegel of the Wharton School of Business.[2] Most people do not have the time or expertise to fully investigate the merits of each stock or bond they buy, so diversification among many securities is mandatory. An investor gets instant diversification by investing in a mutual fund. The average stock mutual fund contains about 145 securities according to Morningstar Principia®.

The second reason to buy mutual funds is professional management. For the most part mutual fund managers are well educated in the fields of economics and corporate finance. Many hold advanced college degrees, and about half have earned the prestigious title of Chartered Financial Analyst (CFA®).[3] There is no guarantee a mutual fund manager will earn a decent return because they have a lot of education, but they have a better chance at it.

Besides the diversification benefits and professional management, there is one compelling reason to own mutual funds in your portfolio: *your time.* Who has time to sift through 7000 stocks, read all the financial publications, listen to analysts' research calls, and tune into CNN on an ongoing basis? Who wants to spend hours accounting for individual stock gains and losses to meet the April 15 tax deadline or pay an accountant to do the tedious work for you? Let someone else do the dirty work. Mutual funds are one of the most convenient investments a person can make from an accounting point of view. They offer a clean and simple solution. The only problem is there are so many mutual funds to choose from, it is difficult to pick the best ones. Index funds narrow the search.

ALL ABOUT INDEX FUNDS

An index fund is a mutual fund just like those that have been described. The difference between an index fund and any other mutual fund is the way the portfolio manager selects stocks or bonds for the portfolio. An index fund manager has far less discretion as to the individual investments that go into a fund.

Recall our discussion about traditional mutual funds. We said that the manager of a traditional fund has the right to buy and sell stocks or bonds as they see fit as long as they follow the guidelines laid out in the mutual fund prospectus. This means the portfolio manager has the right to buy General Motors (GM) and sell Citi-

Group (C) if they feel GM has better profit potential in the near future. The prospectus may even allow the portfolio manager to reduce the overall stock position in the fund if they believe the prospects for the stock market look dim. This style of management is called *active* investing. The portfolio manager takes an active role in the fund in an attempt to beat the stock market.

Index funds are different. The prospectus of a stock index fund does not allow the portfolio manager to use his or her own judgment to decide which stocks will go into the fund and which ones will not. Index fund managers must follow the benchmark composition as closely as possible, which means holding a proportionate share of each stock held in the benchmark index. The prospectus does not allow the portfolio manager to "time" the market by moving in or out of stocks based on a market forecast. They must be 100 percent invested 100 percent of the time.

Since index funds are not meant to beat a benchmark, merely to mirror one, how do you judge how well a manager is performing? Index funds are graded based on how closely they perform to a predetermined benchmark. This difference in performance between an index fund and its benchmark is called *tracking error*. The ideal index fund has a zero tracking error, which means the fund is performing lock step with the benchmark. However, zero tracking error is nearly impossible to achieve because of several costs, including management fees and commissions, as well as the operational inefficiencies that occur as a result of cash inflows and outflows. An index fund tracking error of approximately 0.25 percent per year below the benchmark is generally accepted.

An Example

The best way to illustrate the mechanics of an index fund is to provide an example. The Vanguard 500 Index Fund is the oldest and largest index fund available to the public today. It began operations in August 1976 with a few million dollars under management. At first, asset growth was slow. It took the fund over 10 years to reach $1 billion in assets. But since late 1986 the fund has grown to over $80 billion in assets and is now one of the largest mutual funds on the market (Figure 1-1).

The Vanguard 500 Index Fund is *benchmarked* to the S&P 500 In-

FIGURE 1–1

The Growth of Assets in the Vanguard 500 Fund

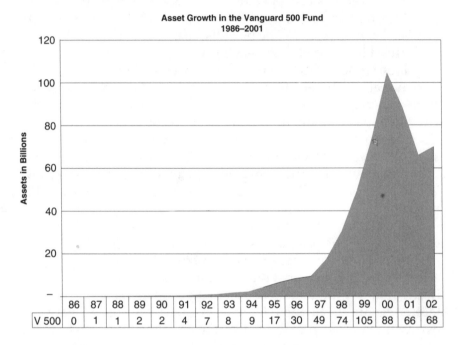

Asset Growth in the Vanguard 500 Fund
1986–2001

	86	87	88	89	90	91	92	93	94	95	96	97	98	99	00	01	02
V 500	0	1	1	2	2	4	7	8	9	17	30	49	74	105	88	66	68

(y-axis: Assets in Billions, marked at 20, 40, 60, 80, 100, 120)

dex. Vanguard attempts to replicate the S&P 500 Index by investing substantially all of its assets in the stocks that make up that index. Each stock is represented in proportion to its market value. Since Standard & Poor's maintains the benchmark, the investment committee at S&P decides which changes will take place in the index. Corporate mergers and acquisitions play a key role in many of those changes. If a stock is taken out of the index, another is added. For example, John Hancock Financial Services, Inc. was added in June 2001 when a slot was created by the merger of two other financial firms in the index.

The portfolio management team at Vanguard is responsible for adjusting the holdings of the Vanguard 500 Index Fund to match the new index. However, these adjustments may occur over a number of days, and possibly weeks, to ensure the market impact of their

FIGURE 1-2

The Growth of Index Funds in the United States

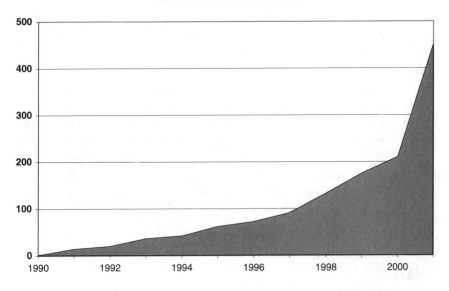

The Number of Index Funds Available to
Individual Investors in the United States

trading is minimal. These gradual adjustments may create some tracking error in the fund, but that is better than bidding up the price of a new stock for the sake of filling the allocation quickly.

All index funds benchmarked to the S&P 500 Index pay a licensing fee to Standard & Poor's for use of the name and access to detailed index data. As indexing has grown over the years, index licensing has become an important source of revenue for Standard & Poor's and other index providers. As a result of this newfound revenue stream, there has been a proliferation of new indexes coming from several different research companies searching for licensing fees.

Many of the new indexes created by competing firms can be redundant and confusing. This book focuses on only the major indexes that you should consider when building an index fund portfolio.

CHAPTER SUMMARY

> The greatest results in life are usually attained by simple means and
> the exercise of ordinary qualities. These may for the most part be
> summed up in two—common sense and perseverance.
>
> *Owen Flethman*

In this chapter you learned there is a big difference between a market and an index. A market is an exchange where trading is conducted. A good index measures the value of a group of stocks or bonds and is not specific to any particular market. Indexes have a variety of useful purposes. In this book indexes are used as benchmarks for the formation and evaluation of index funds. The closer an index fund comes to its benchmark, the better the fund manager. There are hundreds of indexes measuring the performance of stocks and bonds around the globe. As of this writing, there were more than 450 index funds benchmarked to various indexes. This is a small number compared to over 10,000 traditional mutual funds; however, the revolution is just beginning.

NOTES

1. The Dow Jones Industrial Average is a registered trademark of Dow Jones & Co., New York.
2. For a long-term prospective on the U.S. stock market, read Jeremy Siegel's *Stocks for the Long Run* (2d ed.), New York: McGraw-Hill.
3. The Chartered Financial Analyst (CFA) program is a globally recognized standard for measuring the competence and integrity of financial analysts and portfolio managers. It is administered by the Association for Investment Management and Research, Charlottesville, Virginia.

CHAPTER 2

Why Index Funds Work

Key Concepts
- Searching for superior active funds is an inferior strategy.
- In the long run, index funds beat most active funds.
- The index fund advantage extends to all markets.
- Low costs are critical in all mutual fund investing.

Index funds are based on a simple concept. Each fund attempts to replicate, as closely as possible, the securities and structure of a market benchmark, such as the S&P 500. In line with this goal, index funds are expected to earn a return equal to their benchmark, less a small fee for administrative and management costs. There is nothing mysterious or complex about index fund investing, and there should be no surprises in performance. When the S&P 500 index goes up, index funds benchmarked to that index should go up by the same amount, and vice versa. Since index funds are designed to mirror the movement of a market, they are evaluated based on *tracking error,* or how closely a fund matches its benchmark. The smaller the tracking error with the benchmark, the more reliable the index fund.

Index funds are an easy concept to understand and can be easily added to an existing investment portfolio. While these are good reasons to own index funds, the best reason is consistent performance. Index funds achieve higher returns than a vast majority of actively managed funds that try to beat a benchmark. Why is this true? The cost to manage an index fund is far lower than the cost to manage an active fund. For example, the average cost of an S&P 500 Index fund is about 0.3 percent per year compared to over an average 2.0 percent cost for a large-cap active mutual fund.[1] The lower cost of an index fund gives it a significant performance advantage. Although active fund managers may be able to conduct research that enables them to select stocks that outperform the market, they cannot do it with enough consistency to make up the higher fee, let alone exceed the index. In the final analysis, trying to beat the stock market is a loser's game.

Bond index funds also beat most actively managed bond mutual funds because of lower costs. Bond index funds also cost about 0.3 percent per year, and actively managed bond funds cost about 1.2 percent. An active bond manager must consistently earn 0.9 percent in fees each year just to match the return of an index fund. That is extremely difficult to do in the bond markets. Since it is not likely that the cost of active management will come down significantly over the next 25 years, index funds should continue to earn higher returns than a vast majority of active mutual funds.

SEARCHING FOR SUPERIOR ACTIVE FUNDS IS AN INFERIOR STRATEGY

Actively managed mutual funds have a very difficult time beating the performance of index funds. There are just not enough talented mutual fund managers to go around. To make this point clear, imagine if there were 5000 professional baseball teams. The fact that there are 5000 teams does not mean there are 5000 great pitchers in professional baseball. The number of great pitchers is small and does not increase with an increase in the number of teams. The same holds true for mutual funds managers. There are only a few great managers out there, and increasing the number of mutual funds from 1000 to 10,000 does not mean there will be 10 times the number of great managers. Granted, there will always be a few new managers that beat the market each year. Unfortunately, the only way to profit from this is to know the winners in advance, which is impossible to know.

Every year different fund managers become stars, mostly by

chance. Nevertheless, a great majority of these rising stars quickly become falling stars as the market turns in another direction. Despite the facts surrounding mutual fund managers, and the clear mediocrity of their average performance, over the years an entire industry has evolved around selling "research" about mutual funds and their manager that is supposed to help people pick the winners. Don't be misled by this hype. Most of the information you hear or read about predicting performance of a mutual fund is pure nonsense. There is no academic evidence that any system of selecting actively managed mutual funds works. You shouldn't waste your time or money, especially because the alternative does work. That alternative is buying and holding a diversified portfolio of low-cost index funds.

Top universities and academic researchers have been searching for years trying to find a quantitative method for picking next year's top performing mutual funds. The best and the brightest financial researchers from colleges across the country have sliced and diced a seemingly endless number of mutual fund factors looking for clues to future performance. All of this research has lead to two conclusive facts. First, mutual funds that will beat the market next year cannot be identified in advance. Second, mutual funds with lower fees have a greater likelihood of beating mutual funds with high fees.

If you read academic reports, you get the truth about mutual funds and their managers, but if you read the marketing information published by mutual funds companies and listen to the marketers of mutual funds, you get a completely different picture. The investment story you hear from the sales side is that their selected fund exhibits impressive growth, rock solid stability, and that the fund manager is a wise decision maker. But there is rarely substance behind these claims. Most sales literature points to past performance and "star" ratings, although sometimes the brochures and ads have to go far back to find a time when the fund actually did beat something. Regardless of the past history of a fund, it is the future we are concerned about, and neither fund companies, magazines, nor financial TV networks can tell us anything about the future of a mutual fund. Hence, we are inundated with irrelevant data and useless trivia.

In addition to the media hype, many misinformed and undertrained financial advisers claim to be able to provide you with the names of future winning funds, for a nominal fee or commission, of course. Most of the information these quasi-researchers have gathered is far less robust than the data academics have compiled, and that is why the academics have proven the salespeople wrong time and again. Despite the obvious flaws in their "research," it does not matter to a financial adviser who is looking for a paycheck. If past performance and irrelevant data are an easy sell to the public, then that is what is sold. The Securities and Exchange Commission requires sales literature to state that "past performance is not an indication of future results," but many times that part of the presentation is overlooked.

COMPARING ACTIVE FUNDS TO INDEX FUNDS

> I would rather be certain of a good return than hopeful of a great one.
>
> *Warren Buffett*

The best way to prove that index funds perform better than active funds is with actual results. However, it is important to note that while index funds are consistently good performers, they are rarely the best performing mutual fund in any given category. There has always been, and will always be, actively managed mutual funds that beat the return of index funds. But that is irrelevant. You should not be looking for the highest return. You should seek a consistent return. By delivering consistently good returns, index funds become the long-term winner. Over time the cream floats to the top.

The Vanguard 500 Index Fund

In August 1976 the Vanguard 500 Index Fund became the first index fund available to the general public. The Vanguard 500 Index Fund is benchmarked to the S&P 500®, a broadly diversified index of mostly large U.S. companies. Vanguard set the management fee very low in comparison to active funds, and as a result they did not have much money available for marketing. At first the new index fund struggled, and Vanguard was ridiculed in the media. After all, "who would want a fund that just produced average returns?" Nevertheless, the concept stuck, and due to its superior performance over the past 25 years, the Vanguard 500 Index Fund has become one of the largest and most successful mutual funds in history.

We will begin our analysis of index fund performance by comparing the returns of the Vanguard 500 Index Fund to actively managed mutual funds that invest in the same types of stocks. A quick scan of the Morningstar Principia database generates a list of U.S. stock mutual funds that invest in the same type of group of stocks as the Vanguard 500 and have been around for 20 years or more. The Principia search turned up 57 funds, which include mostly large growth, growth and income, and equity income styles. Ironically, when Vanguard started the Vanguard 500 Index Fund in 1976, there were 211 general U.S. equity funds on the market. Most of those funds are no longer in business due to poor performance. Table 2-1 compares 57 of the surviving funds to the Vanguard 500 Index Fund. The *annualized return* is the average return of all 57 funds, and the *load adjusted* return takes into consideration added commissions and other sales charges that may have been paid to purchase those actively managed funds. The Vanguard 500 Index Fund is a pure no-load mutual fund, which means there is no commission charge to buy shares.

The Vanguard 500 Index Fund beat the average actively managed fund by 2.4 percent per year after adjusting for all commissions and fees. A $10,000 investment in the Vanguard 500 Index in December 1981 would have grown to $162,531 in 20 years, over 50 percent more money than the active funds returned. If we included the

TABLE 2-1

Performance of Vanguard 500 Versus Peer Group

20 Years Ending 2001	Vanguard 500 Fund	57 Other Large-Cap Blend Category	Vanguard 500 Rank in Group
Annualized return	15.0%	12.6%	9 of 58
Load adjusted (after commissions)	15.0%	12.5%	8 of 58
Growth of $10,000 load adjusted	$162,531	$106,998	
Source: Morningstar Principia			

FIGURE   2-1

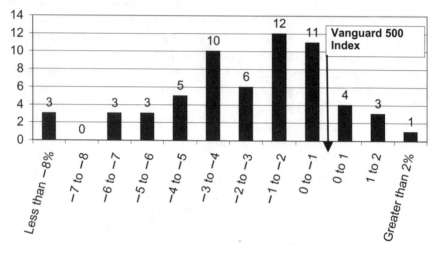

57 Large-Cap Active Funds Versus the Vanguard 500
20 Years Ending December 31, 2001

Source: Morningstar Principia

performance of the nonsurviving funds in the table for the period
that they existed, the average active fund performance would have
been about 3.5 percent less than the Vanguard 500 Index Fund.[2]

Figure 2-1 is a histogram that gives a clear picture of the dis-
persion the 57 funds around the Vanguard 500 Index. Overall, Vanguard was tied for seventh in the group. Eight of the active funds
performed better than the Vanguard 500 Index by an average of 1.2
percent, one fund tied, and the 48 fell short by an average of 2.9 percent. Fund number 28, which is the median, or middle of the group,
performed 1.7 percent less than the Vanguard 500. You can clearly
see that there were several big losing funds, with three falling over
8 percent short of the Vanguard 500 Index Fund. It was very difficult for active managers to beat the return of this index fund.

A second screening of the Principia database was conducted to
look at a list of 57 for the 10 most "successful" active funds over the
years. These popular funds have a long track record of success and

have gathered at least $10 billion in assets. Many of the funds are considered cornerstones in the mutual fund industry. The largest and most successful actively managed mutual fund is the Fidelity Magellan Fund. It boasts nearly $80 billion in assets and has over 1 million shareholders.

It is interesting to compare how the Vanguard 500 Fund stacked up against these icons because in aggregate this is where much of America's mutual fund money is currently invested. These "big 10" funds have been the long-term winners in the last 20 years. Several hundred potential candidates have come and gone over the years, and there is no telling which new fund will be a star in the future and which old fund will flame out. Table 2-2 looks at the performance of these winning funds over the last 5 years, 10 years, and 20 years and compares it to the performance of the Vanguard 500 Index Fund.

Even if you picked one of these winner funds 20 years ago, unless you picked the top funds, there was not much advantage. Eight

TABLE 2-2

Vanguard 500 Index vs. Big 10 Funds Load Adjusted Returns Through 2001	Billions in the Fund	20-year Return	10-year Return	5-year Return
Fidelity Magellan	79,515	18.0	12.6	10.3
Amer. Funds Invmt. Co. America A	54,008	15.5	12.5	11.7
Amer. Funds Washington Mutual A	48,135	16.0	13.5	10.9
Fidelity Contra Fund	32,321	16.0	14.0	9.8
Fidelity Equity-Income	21,831	14.9	13.7	10.1
Amer. Funds Fundamental A	19,100	15.8	13.3	10.4
Putnam Fund for Growth & Inc. A	19,023	13.8	11.3	6.6
Vanguard Windsor	16,027	16.6	14.4	11.0
Fidelity Fund	12,452	15.0	13.5	11.2
AXP New Dimensions A	12,946	16.0	11.6	8.8
Average for the top active funds	31,536	15.8	13.0	10.1
Vanguard 500 Index Fund return	73,150	15.0	12.8	10.7
Vanguard 500 Index rank out of 11 funds	2	9	7	5

Source: Morningstar Principia

TABLE 2-3

Mutual Fund Expenses on the 57 Surviving Funds

Statistics	Surviving 57 Funds	Biggest Funds	Vanguard 500
Expense ratio	0.95%	0.63%	0.18%
12b-1 fee	0.10%	0.17%	0%
Front end load (commission)	2.2%	2.9%	0%
Cost of fees (over 5 years)	1.45%	1.30%	0.18%
Average cash position	5%	5%	0%
Cost of holding cash (estimate)	0.15%	0.10%	0%
Average number of holdings	113	208	500
Average turnover of stocks	78%	46%	6%
Cost to trade stocks (estimate)	0.70%	0.40%	0.05%
The total cost of funds	2.40%	1.80%	0.23%

Source: Morningstar Principia

of the successful active funds beat the Vanguard 500 Index Fund over the 20 years, but only two funds beat it by more than 1.5 percent, and that advantage does not seem to be available to new investors. On average investors in the 10 successful funds have basically matched the performance of the Vanguard 500 Index Fund over the last 10 years and underperformed by 0.6 percent over the last 5 years.

As you look at the data in Table 2-3, it is evident that higher fees and expenses were the likely cause for the average performance shortfall of the 57 surviving funds and may have begun to affect the big 10 funds. It is tough to beat an index fund that starts each year with a 1.5 percent cost advantage.

It is very difficult for large mutual fund managers to beat the stock market. In aggregate they can only perform as well as the market, less fees and commissions. Real-world operating costs of active funds drag down portfolio performance to the point where talented fund managers cannot make up the difference. It is not surprising that the Vanguard 500 Index Fund beat the average large-cap mutual fund by more than 2 percent over the last 20 years because that is almost exactly the combined cost of fees, commissions, cash drag, and trading. In the long run costs matter.

FIGHT for $15

END student poverty

FIGHT for $15

END student poverty

Trolley Caravan to SDSU
Wednesday, April 15, 2015
Meet at Park & B @ 2pm
SDSU Scripps Cottage Lawn @ 4pm

$15 and a union!

F I G H T

Live Music - Free Food Trucks - March - Rally

☆ Students shouldn't have to quit school to work!

☆ People who work should be able to live not just survive!

☆ When more workers have money in their pockets, they spend it which improves the economy for all (not just the 1%)!

☆ Since 2008, the minimum wage hasn't increased while housing and food has almost doubled!

☆ This fight is about raising the living standard & giving a voice to all workers

DON'T JUST STUDY HISTORY,
MAKE HISTORY!

THE INDEX FUND ADVANTAGE EXTENDS TO ALL MARKETS

The advantage of low-cost indexing extends to other categories of the U.S. stock and bond markets and to international markets as well. This fact is based on two assumptions:

1. In the aggregate the performance of all mutual funds within a category will equal the benchmark index, less costs.
2. Mutual funds with the lowest overall costs will ultimately outperform the category average.

With the exception of the Vanguard 500 Index Fund, most index funds are less than 10 years old. As a result, there is not a lot of actual index fund performance data to look at. In certain cases I will make assumptions about the future return of index funds relative to active returns without the benefit of historic numbers (Figure 2–2). The performance of index funds may not turn out to be exactly as predicted. However, I am certain that low-cost index funds will beat the average active fund in each category over the long term.

FIGURE 2-2

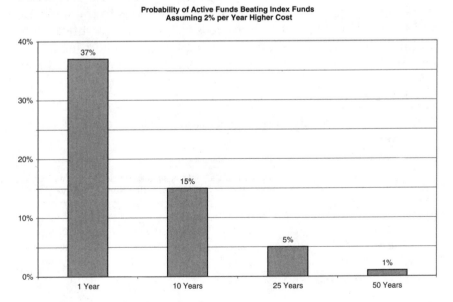

Probability of Active Funds Beating Index Funds
Assuming 2% per Year Higher Cost

Source: Bogle Financial Markets Research Center®

To be fair to active fund managers, the average fee and added costs of active funds in the following tables include established funds that have been on the market for at least 10 years. The cost of running an established fund tends to be lower than newer funds because they have achieved an economy of scale. All the tables include an expense ratio, which is listed in the prospectus, as well as an estimate of portfolio turnover costs and the cash drag from holding cash. The tables exclude all sales commissions. A detailed explanation of all the funds mentioned in the tables can be found in Part II of this book.

Due to the high cost of managing active small- and mid-cap funds, it will be very difficult for the average actively managed small- and mid-cap fund to beat the market (Table 2-4). The actual performance of index funds over active funds may not be quite as large as the 1.75 percent fee differential suggests. However, based on a very low comparable cost, small- and mid-cap index funds like the Vanguard Extended Market Index can be expected to perform better than the average active small- and mid-cap fund arena.

International stock index funds are also beginning to gain prominence in the mutual fund marketplace, and they are significantly less expensive than actively managed international funds. As Table 2-5 highlights, managing any foreign stock mutual fund is inherently more expensive than managing a U.S. stock fund. Overseas stockbrokers typically charge higher commissions to trade stocks, and banks charge higher custody fees to hold stock certificates. In addition, there are costs due to regulation, taxes, and legal constraints. Certainly, lower operating costs will be a major factor in de-

T A B L E   2–4

Small- and Mid-Cap U.S. Stock Funds with 10 Years of History

Statistics	Active Funds in Category	Vanguard Extended Market Index Fund	Index Fund Advantage
Expense ratio	1.25%	0.25%	1.00%
12b-1 fee	0.15%	0.00%	0.15%
Turnover cost (est.)	0.80%	0.35%	0.45%
Cash drag (est.)	0.15%	0.00%	0.15%
Total cost before commissions	2.35%	0.60%	1.75%

Source: Morningstar Principia

TABLE 2-5

International (Foreign) Stock Funds with 10 Years of History

Statistics	Active Funds in Category	Vanguard Developed Markets Index Fund	Index Fund Advantage
Expense ratio	1.35%	0.31%	1.04%
12b-1 fee	0.15%	0.00%	0.15%
Turnover cost (est.)	1.00%	0.50%	0.50%
Cash drag (est.)	0.15%	0.00%	0.15%
Total cost before commissions	2.65%	0.81%	1.84%

Source: Morningstar Principia

termining the winners in this fund category, and international index funds hold a large cost advantage.

If low fees are important when choosing a stock mutual fund, they are everything when choosing a bond fund (Table 2-6). The return of a bond mutual fund is based nearly 100 percent on the cost of the fund. Low-cost bond funds earn higher returns because they take less in fees than high-cost funds. Managers of high-fee funds can do little to earn higher returns and make up the fee because the bond market is a level playing field. If the current market yield on a 5-year Treasury note is 5 percent, then that is what the yield is regardless of which fund buys it. An active fund manager cannot "do more research" and buy the 5-year Treasury note at a 6 percent yield. The bond market simply does not work that way. In theory there is

TABLE 2-6

Intermediate-Term U.S. Bond Funds with 10 Years of History

Statistics	Active Funds in Category	Index Fund (Simulated)	Index Fund Advantage
Expense ratio	0.95%	0.25%	0.70%
12b-1 fee	0.10%	0.00%	0.10%
Turnover cost (est.)	0.10%	0.05%	0.05%
Cash drag (est.)	0.05%	0.00%	0.05%
Total cost before commissions	1.20%	0.30%	0.90%

Source: Morningstar Principia

a level playing field for all bond managers, so the low-fee funds should always beat the high-fee funds. It follows that the only ingredient that matters when selecting a bond mutual fund is the fee. However, many bond managers try to hide a higher fee by taking on risk in the hope of achieving a higher return. In the long run, the higher risk does show itself in the form of more volatility. There is no such thing as a free lunch on Wall Street. Chapter 9 of this book will explain more about bond investing and help you select the appropriate low-cost bond index fund for your needs.

OUTFOX THE BOX

Over time, low-cost index funds deliver higher returns than most mutual funds but never the best returns. Should you go for the reliability of an index fund or take your chances finding a better performing active mutual fund? If you haven't decided yet, one unique way to answer this question is to play a game called Outfox the Box. Bill Schultheis described this game in his delightful little book, *The Coffeehouse Investor* (Longstreet Press, 1999). Here is the game:

> You visit an investment firm and ask them to invest $10,000 in a mutual fund for your benefit. They comply with your request, and you go about your business. Ten years later you go back to the investment house and ask for the money. An executive leads you into a room and shows you ten boxes arranged on a table. Each box has money inside. The executive gives you a list showing the amount of money contained in each box. The list looks like this:

#1 $16,000	#6 $23,000
#2 $17,000	#7 $24,000
#3 $18,000	#8 $25,000
#4 $20,000	#9 $26,000
#5 $22,000	#10 $30,000

Next, the executive asks you to leave the room, and after about five minutes you are allowed to go back in. The ten boxes are still on the table, but this time only the box with $25,000 is open. The rest of the boxes are closed and the numbers are covered up. The order of the boxes on the table has also been changed. The order now looks like this:

?	?
?	?
?	?
# 8 $25,000	?
?	?

The executive turns to you and says, "None of the money in the boxes has changed. Without opening or touching the boxes, you may choose one box as your investment return. Which box do you choose?"

Did you pick the $25,000 box or did you forfeit the $25,000 and take your chances on the $30,000 box? Let's look at this puzzle mathematically. There are 10 boxes, and one contains $25,000. You have a 2 in 9 chance of bettering yourself by picking either the $26,000 box or the $30,000 box. The average amount in those two boxes is $28,000. That means you have a 22 percent probability of gaining an extra $3000. On the other hand, there is a 7 in 9 chance of picking a box with less money in it. The average amount in those boxes is only $20,000. That means you have a 78 percent probability of earning $5000 less. What would you do?

When I tell this story at seminars, everyone in attendance picks the $25,000 box. Their reasoning is the same. Although it is possible to pick a box that contains more money, the probability of success is low and the payoff for being right is not enough to justify taking the risk. If you went through the same thought pattern and picked the $25,000 box, then you are a perfect candidate for the wonderful world of index fund investing.

CHAPTER SUMMARY

"Great rewards grow from small differences in cost."

John C. Bogle, founder of the Vanguard Group

Index funds perform well relative to actively managed mutual funds because the cost is much lower. Although some actively managed funds will beat index funds every year, those winning funds cannot be identified in advance, and it is costly and time consuming to try. In every market, including U.S. stocks, bonds, and international stocks, index fund costs are considerably less than competing active funds. It is prudent and logical to conclude that in the future, index funds will continue to shine in the marketplace.

In closing this chapter I will leave you with this thought: Do you remember when you were a teenager and dreamed of owning a really cool automobile? You didn't care if the car cost too much and didn't run well, as long as you looked good driving it. Later in life, things changed. You wanted a reliable car that didn't cost you a lot of money. People seem to take the same path with their investment decisions. Early in life they want fast-moving active mutual funds that will beat the market. Later in life experienced investors realize that reliability and economy are the keys to success, and they switch to index funds. In the long run, low costs drive investment performance. Keep your portfolio costs low with index funds.

NOTES

1. The estimated total cost of an active mutual fund includes a 1.3 percent management fee, administrative costs, legal expense, and 0.7 percent for internal trading costs and holding cash. It does not include sales charges such as commission costs (loads) or wrap fees paid to intermediaries such as brokers and commission-based financial advisers.

2. Several research reports have been conducted to isolate the impact of nonsurviving funds on long-term category returns. On average, these studies find that *survivorship bias* in mutual fund composites inflate the return by more than 1 percent.

CHAPTER 3

A History of Index Funds

Key Concepts

- Index funds were not available prior to 1976.
- The Vanguard Group introduced the first index fund.
- There are now over 400 index funds on the market.
- Exchange-traded funds (ETFs) are the newest type.

In 1896 Charles Dow published the first stock market index, and shortly thereafter the Dow Jones Industrial Average became the benchmark for all stock investors. Several competing research firms have established numerous U.S. stock indexes since that time. In 1924 Massachusetts Investors created the first U.S. mutual fund in which people where able to buy and sell shares on a daily basis. Over the next 50 years, hundreds of investment companies established mutual funds. But it was not until 1976, when John Bogle established the Vanguard Group, that the first index fund was available to the public. What took so long?

To understand why it took 80 years to launch the first index fund after the establishment of the Dow, we have to look back at the mutual fund industry since its inception. The mutual fund industry has had a long and often uncomplimentary history in the United States. Fund companies generally provided an important service to society, but Congress has had to write thousands of regulations requiring them to behave in a fair and ethical manner. This chapter takes you on a short history of the mutual fund business. It starts with the inception of mutual funds in the early 1920s and goes through the new era of *exchange-traded funds* that we are in today.

Much of the credit for the success of indexing can be directed to one man, John Bogle, the founder of the Vanguard Group. Bogle's dedication to indexing has done more good for individual investors than any other person in modern finance. He has done so much that many investors refer to him as Saint Jack. Now, I don't know if he is a real saint, but we can thank God for John Bogle.

EARLY MUTUAL FUNDS 1920–1970

In the early 1900s, the U.S. economy was transforming rapidly from an agrarian-based system to an industrial powerhouse. This change was accelerated by the fact that American factories had not been damaged during World War I, while much of Europe's infrastructure lay in shambles. Political decisions in Washington were particularly favorable toward economic growth during the period. "The chief business of the American people is business," President Calvin Coolidge asserted in 1925. The economic boom lead to the most spectacular bull market in history, and one in which the general public was a large and captive participant. The excitement on Wall Street was fueled by the growth of large "investment trusts," which eventually lead to the establishment of a unique investment product called a *mutual fund.*

Investment trusts were a collection of capital from various public and private investors. Anyone with a few hundred dollars could participate. The money was pooled together in an account at a bank and trust company for the purpose of investing in the stock market. Each investor in the trust was issued a pro-rata number of shares representing their portion. After the shares were issued, they could be bought and sold on the stock market in the same way stocks were traded. Since the shares of the trust were a "free-floating" security on the stock market, they could trade at a price premium or discount that was different from the actual value of the investments in the trust. For example, the net asset value of a trust share could be $10 while the market price of a trust share was only $9.

Investment trusts had been around in some form since the late 1800s and had developed a bad name on Wall Street by the 1920s.

Many investment trusts were established for a specific purpose, such as the monopolization of an industry or as a dumping ground for unwanted investments. Banks were particularly notorious for establishing investment trusts and using them as a waste disposal for stocks in the banks' private portfolios that went sour. To add insult to injury, many banks encouraged the public to borrow money to invest in these trusts, and the banks extended up to 90 percent credit. After collecting a pool of capital, many of the trusts borrowed more money internally, thus leveraging the investors even further. Securities and antitrust laws were virtually nonexistent in the early part of the century, so unchecked speculation and shady financing among trusts were common. If word got out about questionable dealings in a trust, there was a mad rush to sell shares on the open market, and that caused the market value to collapse. Some of these rumors were falsely started by people trying to manipulate the price of a trust for personal gain.

The First Mutual Funds

By 1923 a new idea was buzzing around Wall Street. There needed to be a way to keep the market value of a trust in line with its net asset value, so the share price would not collapse on false rumors. The answer was an *open-end* trust. This pooled investment differed from traditional trusts in three critical ways. First, it would invest only in publicly traded common stock, so investors could accurately track the value of the fund on a daily basis. Second, it would not borrow money to leverage the portfolio holdings, so the cumulative value of the underlying stocks were the true net asset value of the fund. Third, shares would be redeemed by the trust itself at the net asset value rather than having shares trade at a discount or premium in the open market.

In March 1924 the first "mutual fund" was established using the new doctrine. It was called the Massachusetts Investment Trust, also known as MIT. The fund held a diversified portfolio of 46 stocks ranging from insurance companies to railroads. No leverage was used in MIT, and fund shares could be redeemed on demand from the trust at net asset value. MIT was an immediate success.

Within 1 year of the formation of MIT, there were three mutual funds on the marketplace, including Incorporated Investors and

State Street Investment Corporation. All three funds are still in existence today. They are now called the MFS Massachusetts Investment A, Putnam Investors A, and State Street Research Investment S. As a matter of record, all three funds have performed well over the last 75 years. None of the funds beat the stock market, but they did produce a return on par with the market average, less management costs and commissions. That is much better than average investors would have faired on their own.

Early Calls for Indexing

Professional researchers recognized the advantage of an index-type portfolio in the early 1930s, when mutual funds were just getting their start. In 1933 Alfred Cowles published an in-depth report about the futility of using Wall Street research to beat the stock market. He believed the market was much too dynamic for any one person on Wall Street to figure out. The Cowles Commission Index tracked all the stocks that traded on the New York Stock Exchange since 1871, not just the Dow 30. In the 1960s the Cowles Index was reengineered and reintroduced as the Standard & Poor's 500 Index.

Alfred Cowles was not alone in the call for greater prudence on Wall Street. In the 1950s academic researchers began to search for "efficient" portfolios of stocks and found that the most efficient portfolio was the market itself. Efficient portfolios are groups of stocks that earn the highest return per level of risk. Harry Markowitz, Paul Samuelson, Irving Fisher, and A.D. Roy conducted much of the early research on efficient portfolios, and some of these people went on the win the Nobel Prize in Economics for their efforts. All of the research seems to point to the same conclusion. There was little reason to invest in any portfolio except an index portfolio.

Over the next 20 years, extensive work was conducted on the concept of an index fund, but no fund was created. In 1973 Princeton University Professor Burton Malkiel published his classic book, *A Random Walk Down Wall Street* (W.W. Norton, 1973). Malkiel called for "a no-load, minimum management fee mutual fund that simply buys hundreds of stocks making up the stock market averages and does no trading." It was clear to Malkiel and others that active fund managers were not keeping up with the market benchmarks. Charles Ellis highlighted the shortfall of active managers in his widely regarded article, "The Loser's Game" published in *The Financial Analyst Journal*, July/August 1975. Ellis reported that over the prior decade, 85 percent of all institutional investors who tried to beat the stock market had underperformed the S&P 500 Index.

Despite repeated calls by academia for an index fund, there were several operational reasons the first one did not appear until the mid-1970s. First, the concept of an index-based portfolio is a simple idea, but the actual management of an index fund is a sophisticated process. By their nature, index funds hold hundreds of securities, and daily cashflows into and out of the portfolio make daily balancing a complicated process. Needless to say, computers must be at the heart of every index fund, but readily available computing power was prohibitively expensive until the mid-1970s. Thus, index funds had to wait. A second reason index funds did not make an earlier appearance was that they were cost prohibitive. Prior to 1976 Wall Street was on a fixed commission rate system, which means fund managers could not negotiate lower trading costs with brokers. Index funds make a lot of small trades, and a high commission rate would wipe out any advantage. After 1976 commission costs were deregulated and rates came down considerably. Distribution was a third roadblock. For most of the twentieth century, mutual funds were distributed through stockbrokers who where paid an 8 percent commission or more. The very idea of paying a broker a large commission simply to buy an index fund did not fit well with investors. No-load funds first appeared in the late 1970s. The fourth reason index funds did not exist prior to 1976 was the reluctance of the mutual fund industry to accept the idea. Fund company executives wanted to prove their firm could beat the market, and they viewed indexing as a personal insult to their intelligence. In addition, the fund managers did not want to give up their hefty salaries and bonuses. Low-cost index funds simply did not fit the business models of established fund companies.

THE FIRST INDEX FUND

The first attempt to model a stock market index in an actual account dates back to 1971. Wells Fargo Bank constructed a $6 million index account for the pension fund of Samsonite Corporation, the luggage people. The strategy was to buy all the stocks on the New York Stock

Exchange in equal proportions, thus creating the first *equal weighted* index fund. The concept sounded great, but actual execution was a nightmare. Trying to keep the portfolio equally balanced between all stocks was extremely difficult and cost a fortune in commissions. A few years later the strategy was abandoned, and a straight S&P 500 Index Fund style was adopted for the Samsonite account.

The first S&P 500 Index strategy was created by Batterymarch Financial Management. The firm presented the idea at a Harvard Business School seminar in 1971, although they did not attract any institutional clients until 1974.

After a few large pension funds tested the waters in the index fund arena, it became overwhelmingly obvious that a publicly traded index fund was the next step. The question was: Which mutual fund company is going to put their business model on the chopping block? It was not likely to be an established mutual fund company whose fund managers and corporate officers were getting fat on high management fees. What was needed was an entirely new fund company with a mandate of lower management fees, lower trading costs, and direct distribution to the public.

Along Came John

In 1950 undergraduate students at Princeton University were required to write a senior thesis, and John C. Bogle was no exception. Bogle had not given much thought to the fledgling mutual fund industry as a topic until he read an article in the December 1949 issue of *Fortune* magazine. The article was entitled "Big Money in Boston," and it highlighted the "rapidly expanding and somewhat contentious [mutual fund] industry." He knew he had found his topic.[1]

Over the next 18 months, Bogle meticulously researched the mutual fund industry and wrote a thesis entitled "The Economic Role of the Investment Company." A copy of the thesis has been reproduced in *John Bogle on Investing, the First 50 Years* (McGraw-Hill, 2001). In his 100-page senior thesis, Bogle covered the history and dynamics of the fund industry. He also made the following recommendations to fund companies to increase sales: First, explicitly state a fund's objective; second, reduce sales loads and management fees; and third, make no claim to superiority over the market averages. The insight in Bogle's thesis would have been hailed as revolutionary if written by a seasoned veteran in the mutual fund industry, let alone a 21-year-old college student with no prior experience.

In 1975 Bogle had a chance to put all his ideas into action. As the chairman of the newly formed Vanguard Group, Bogle set the ship's course squarely on low-cost investing. His firm was going to be the first company to offer a low-cost index fund to the public. Vanguard was able to follow this mandate because of its unique corporate structure. The company is owned by the shareholders that invest in its mutual funds rather than by a private for-profit investment group. Vanguard operates much like a co-op, where lower fees benefit all investors. This "mutual" mutual fund organization was a novel concept in the fund industry, and Vanguard is still one of the only fund companies that operates in that fashion.

The Vanguard board of directors approved an index-style mutual fund in May 1976 and filed a prospectus with the Securities and Exchange Commission (SEC). The fund was initially called the First Index Investment Trust, although it was changed to the Vanguard 500 Index Trust in 1980. The SEC approved the fund, and an opening date was set for August 31, 1976. The only thing missing from the equation was money. The fund needed an initial outlay of cash to get started.

In 1976 all mutual funds were still being sold through commission brokerage firms. Wall Street had the marketing clout, and Vanguard had no other alternative. Bogle needed a burst of assets to come into the new fund to get it rolling, so Vanguard solicited four large brokerage firms to act as its initial sales force. The goal was to bring in between $50 and $150 million in assets during the preopening road show. The commission to buy the fund was 6 percent.

Vanguard had the support of brokerage firm management, but the brokers themselves were less enthusiastic. Why should they sell a 6 percent commission mutual fund when they could make 8 percent selling another fund? The fact that the Vanguard Fund was a good investment was irrelevant (this attitude still prevails at brokerage firms today). By August 30, 1976, only $11.4 million was raised for the new fund. That was a far cry from $50 million but enough to get started. As an aside, in February 1977, Vanguard dropped all sales agreements with brokerage firms and permanently eliminated all sales loads in their funds.

From $11 Million to $80 Billion

From its meager beginning, assets in the Vanguard 500 Index Fund have grown to over $80 billion today. However, the road to success was not easy. A deluge of critics assaulted the concept, particularly Vanguard's competitors. It was described as "Bogle's Folly" by one fund company executive, and Fidelity Chairman Edward Johnston told the press, "I can't believe that the great mass of investors are going to be satisfied with just receiving average returns." Another competitor put out a flyer calling the fund "un-American," and others asked who would want to do business with an average doctor, an average lawyer, or an average mutual fund. As a stockbroker in the 1980s, if a client brought up the subject of index funds, I was told to say, "Average returns are for average investors. We think our clients are above average."

THE GROWTH OF INDEX FUNDS

After the introduction of the Vanguard 500 Index Fund, 7 years passed before a second index fund was established. In 1984 Wells Fargo introduced the Stagecoach Corporate Stock Fund, which was benchmarked to the S&P 500. Unfortunately, the fund had a 1 percent management fee, so it did not survive in the marketplace. By 1986 nine more index funds were offered by various companies; however, two funds covered obscure international markets, and a third fund was so expensive that it put itself out of business by 1993.

One of the new funds offered in 1986 was the Vanguard Bond Market Fund. It was benchmarked to the Lehman Brothers® Aggregate Bond Index. This was the first index fund devoted exclusively to the bond market, and Bogle was sure it was going to be a success. With a fee of only 0.25 percent per year, the index fund had a great cost advantage over actively managed bond funds that charged an average 1.0 percent per year. Since its inception, the Vanguard Total Bond Market Index Fund (renamed) has grown to over

$11 billion in assets. That is a phenomenal accomplishment for a bond fund.

A third index fund was added to the Vanguard quiver in 1987. The Extended Market Fund was designed to complement the Vanguard 500 Index. It was benchmarked to the Wilshire 4500®, an index of small and medium-sized companies. Since it was not economical for Vanguard to invest in all 4500 stocks, the Extended Market Fund invested in 2000 of the largest companies in the Wilshire 4500 and another 800 small and medium-sized companies based on a statistical sample. The result was a fund that performed very close to the Wilshire 4500 with very low costs. Thus, an investor in both the Vanguard 500 Index and the Extended Market Funds had a full range of market exposure.

The 1990s

Vanguard accelerated the number of index funds in the family in the 1990s. Vanguard added index funds benchmarked to the Russell 2000® Small-Cap Index as well as the Morgan Stanley® Europe and Pacific Basin Indexes. The first competition also came into the marketplace in 1990. That year Fidelity started two index funds, one that modeled the S&P 500 Index and one that modeled the Lehman Brothers Aggregate Bond Index. By the end of 1990, there were 43 index funds available from several mutual fund companies. Most of these funds had little capital, and Vanguard stood as the undisputed leader with nine funds and nearly $5 billion in assets. The average expense ratio for the competitors was 0.5 percent versus 0.2 percent for Vanguard. The fact that competition was trying to imitate Vanguard was a triumph for John Bogle and the Vanguard team.

Through the remainder of the 1990s, Vanguard added 20 more index funds to bring the total at the end of the decade to 29. These funds included a large assortment of stock, bond, balanced, and real estate investment trust index funds. Vanguard was not alone in the growth. Due to a few good years for large-cap U.S. stocks, the popularity of mutual funds indexed to the S&P 500 exploded. The total number of index funds on the market expanded rapidly, from 43 in 1990 to 272 at the end of 1999. From 1997 to 1999 there were 40 new index funds benchmarked to the S&P 500.

It is strange how the world turns. All the major brokerage firms and mutual fund companies now compete against Vanguard with their own version of index funds, albeit at a higher cost. Even Fidelity reluctantly gave in. Most of these firms conceded in a desperate attempt to stop assets from transferring to Vanguard rather than out of a burning desire to serve their customers.

2002 AND BEYOND

The growth of index funds has been phenomenal, and it is just beginning. In 2000 and 2001 there were 80 new index funds formed in the United States, bringing the total at year end 2001 to over 400 funds. The number of new index funds is only limited by the number of new indexes that are created. Collecting index fund royalties has become a big business for the market index providers, such as Standard & Poor's, so it is not likely we will see a slowdown in new indexes occurring anytime soon.

A growing part of the index fund family includes *exchange-traded funds* (ETFs). These special index funds are benchmarked to the same indexes as open-end index funds, but they trade interday on a stock exchange, just like common stock. ETFs have become very popular over the last couple of years, and the number of funds is expanding rapidly. The product is so unique that it warrants a chapter all on its own (see Chapter 4).

CHAPTER SUMMARY

"You can't buy the averages, but it is about time the public could."

Burton Malkiel, Princeton University, 1973

Index funds were born out of necessity. Poor performance by actively managed mutual funds caused an outcry from the academic community for a low-cost market-based solution. Despite the fact that stock and bond indexes have been around for over a century, index funds did not make an appearance until the 1970s. While operational issues were one reason index funds did not debut until later in the century, the reluctance of mutual fund companies to take a cut in pay was likely the main reason.

In 1976 John Bogle ended the wait for public index funds as he steered the new Vanguard Group in a completely different direction. Vanguard's mandate of low investment fees allowed the creation of the first modern index fund. This novel concept revolutionized the investment industry and forced many competitors to create competing products with low fees. Today there are more than 400 index funds traded in the United States, and the list grows longer every year. The newest and most exciting type of index funds are called ETFs, and they are the topic of the next chapter.

NOTES

1. "The First Index Mutual Fund: A History of Vanguard Index Trust and the Vanguard Index Strategy," by John C. Bogle, Bogle Financial Markets Research Center, on-line at www.Vanguard.com.

CHAPTER 4

Exchange-Traded Funds

Key Concepts

- Exchange-traded funds (ETFs) are index funds that trade like stocks.
- You buy ETFs through a brokerage firm over the stock exchange.
- Beware of commissions and trading spreads.
- There are several unique tax features to ETFs.

Exchange-traded funds (ETFs) are the newest phenomenon to hit the index fund industry. Like traditional open-end index funds, ETFs track the performance of a specific market benchmark. Unlike traditional index funds, ETFs can be bought or sold like a stock anytime the market is open. This unique blend between an index fund and a stock has gained rapid acceptance in the marketplace. Trading flexibility is only one of the unique advantages that make ETFs the index fund of choice for many individuals and professional money managers.

CLOSED-END MUTUAL FUNDS

In the early 1990s, before exchange-traded funds appeared on the market, there were two types of mutual funds available to investors: *open-end* and *closed-end*. Each structure has its advantages and disadvantages. Exchange-traded funds were created to combine the best of both worlds.

Most mutual funds on the market today are open-end investment vehicles. This structure allows a fund company to create or redeem shares as necessary based on investor demand. It also means that trading is restricted to one buyer and one seller. The Securities and Exchange Commission (SEC) allows open-end funds to create and redeem its shares only once per day, at the end of the day, based on the market close price. Each day after the markets close, mutual fund companies compute the true underlying value of the stocks and bonds in their funds and determine a fair per-share price for each fund. This amount is called the net asset value (NAV), and its price per share is quoted in the newspaper. After fund NAVs are calculated, fund companies use this price to buy shares from investors who are redeeming and sell shares to investors who are buying. If there are more buyers than sellers, fund companies have the authority to create new shares at the NAV. If there are more sellers than buyers, funds can retire shares. The important point to remember about an open-end mutual fund is that all share creation and redemption is done at the closing NAV priced by the fund company itself.

On the other end of the spectrum are closed-end mutual funds. This fund structure was fairly popular in the 1980s, but pricing inconsistencies held closed-end funds back from achieving mass investor appeal. Unlike open-end funds, buyers and sellers trading on stock exchanges determine the price of a closed-end mutual fund. That means market forces set the price of a closed-end fund rather than the mutual fund company. As a result, the market price of a fund is rarely the same as the NAV. Ordinarily, a mispriced stock will not stay mispriced for very long because its shares would get scooped up by professional traders looking for easy profits. But don't start getting any ideas. The difference between the trading price and NAV of a closed-end fund can last a very long time.

Unlike open-end funds, closed-end funds cannot issue more shares to new investors or easily redeem shares from selling investors. Nor can the fund company trade shares on the stock exchange if the market price for the fund is less than or greater than the NAV of the fund (thus creating a risk-free profit). In fact, closed-end fund companies are prohibited from participating in the daily buying and selling of their own closed-end fund shares without specific approval from the SEC, and that is a rare event. This means the number of shares of a closed-end fund is fixed, and the only way you can buy shares is from a selling shareholder, and vice versa.

Many times the market price of a closed-end fund will trade at a large premium or discount price to its actual underlying NAV. These discounts and premiums are not secret. They are widely reported in the financial press. However, discounts and premiums may persist for several years because there is no "arbitrage" mechanism to bring the market price in line with the underlying NAV. Discounts and premiums would immediately go away if fund companies were allowed to be a market participant in their own shares. The arbitrage mechanism in ETFs is explained in more detail later in this chapter.

THE FIRST EXCHANGE-TRADED FUNDS

In 1990 the SEC issued the Investment Company Act Release No. 17809. This act granted the law firm of Leland, O'Brien, Rubinstein Associates, Incorporated (LOR) the right to create a new hybrid security called a *SuperTrust*. The SuperTrust had the share creation and redemption characteristics of an open-end fund and traded on the stock exchange like a closed-end fund. On November 5, 1992, after additional tweaking and a few regulatory delays, LOR introduced the revolutionary new product called the *Index Trust SuperUnit*. The SuperUnit was an index fund of sorts designed to give institutional investors the ability to buy or sell an entire basket of stocks in one trade on the stock exchange. The 1992 SuperTrust had a "maturity" of 3 years, at which time a new SuperTrust was to be introduced in 1995 to replace maturing units.

The SuperUnit was a unique idea because institutional investors could trade the units for the actual shares of stock in the underlying investment. SuperUnits sold on an exchange, just like closed-end funds. Unlike closed-end funds, if SuperUnits started selling at a discount to their NAV, investors could profit risk-free by purchasing the underpriced units while simultaneously selling the underlying shares in the unit. They would then turn in the unit and would be issued stocks. These stocks would replace the stocks that they sold. This entire transaction created a risk-free profit for the institutional investor. If the SuperUnits were selling at a premium, there was a reverse trade that allowed investors to profit risk-free. Although the arbitrage of SuperUnits sounds like a lot of work, institutional investors could accomplish the task with a few keystrokes. The redemption feature built into SuperUnits neatly eliminated the discount and premium problem that plagued closed-end funds.

The SuperTrust was launched in 1992 with $1 billion in assets. It was a 3-year trust that terminated in 1995. The idea was to issue replacement units in 1995, but that never happened. The SuperTrust idea began as a response to the 1987 crash, but by the time LOR received regulatory approval (5 years in the making), the over-the-counter (OTC) market was developing a simpler product. The cost, complexity, and adverse rulings by the IRS precluded any trading from developing or occurring in the retail marketplace, which meant no demand from individual investors.

The American Stock Exchange took advantage of the Super-Trust Act of 1992 and petitioned the SEC to allow the creation of the first Standard & Poor's Depository Receipts (SPDRs), better known as *Spiders*. The first "exchange-traded fund" began trading on the American Stock Exchange in January 1993. Spiders are benchmarked to the S&P 500 Index and had the same redemption feature as SuperUnits. Spiders have become so popular over the years that over $30 billion worth of SPDRs trade on the AMEX today, the largest of any AMEX listed security.

One reason Spiders succeeded whereas the SuperUnit failed was because individual investors could afford to buy them. Each SPDR unit trades at approximately one-tenth the index value of the S&P 500 Index. For example, if the S&P 500 were quoted at 1200, the price of one SPDR unit would be within pennies of $120. The low price per unit of Spiders gave it broad investor appeal. Individuals could buy as few as one unit if they preferred. The low cost of Spiders also allowed them to compete head to head with the open-end index funds, such as the Vanguard 500 Index Fund. Stockbrokers now had an attractive alternative for clients considering transferring to Vanguard. The fees and expenses of SPDR units were only slightly higher than Vanguard 500 Index Fund shares.

The market value of Spiders is kept very close to the underlying index through an arbitrage mechanism similar to SuperUnits.

Institutional investors have the opportunity to profit from a small mismatch in price between the market value of Spiders and the stocks in the underlying S&P 500 Index. If one value is greater than the other, the expensive one is sold and the cheap one is bought. This "risk-free" arbitrage trade is repeated until there is a near equilibrium in price. The two prices will get very close but are rarely the same because arbitrage will stop when the transaction costs become greater than the profit. According to the AMEX, actively traded ETFs trade within 0.25 percent of their underlying index value nearly 80 percent of the time.

ADVANCES IN ETF DEVELOPMENT

Riding high on the success of Spiders, the Bank of New York introduced the MidCap SPDR in 1995. This security is nicknamed *Middies* and was the first ETF created to track the performance of the S&P MidCap 400 Index. The MidCap 400 Index is a composite of stocks that have market values between $2 billion and $10 billion. The structure of the MidCap SPDR is similar to the S&P 500 SPDR.

In 1996 Morgan Stanley joined forces with Barclays Global Investors and the American Stock Exchange to create World Equity Benchmark Shares (WEBS). This series of ETFs was benchmarked to 13 different world equity markets from Australia to Belgium. The structure of WEBS was different from SPDRs. The older SPDRs were organized as a unit investment trust (UITs), which by SEC standards meant they must replicate an index exactly. There can be no variation of holdings between SPDRs and the market benchmark. WEBS are organized as an investment company, which means they are not required to match the indexes exactly. This gives fund managers some discretion to modify the funds as needed to work around difficult operational and trading demands inherent in foreign indexes. Instead of buying all the stocks in an index, managers could "sample" the index and create optimized portfolios. This is important because in some countries, the stocks of one or two companies dominate the index, and the SEC mandates that no one issue may be larger than 25 percent of the portfolio. In addition, issues greater than 5 percent may not be greater than 50 percent of the portfolio in aggregate.

The second difference between SPDRs and WEBS was the way

dividends were handled. Under the unit investment trust structure of SPDRs, cash dividends paid by the underlying stocks are retained in a noninterest bearing account until the end of the quarter, and then they are paid out to shareholders as one lump sum. WEBS have more flexibility in dividend payments. The investment company structure allowed WEBS to reinvest dividends immediately after they are received by the fund. The WEBS still pays out dividends like any traditional mutual fund; however, the reinvestment feature allows for a closer tracking to the indexes.

WEBS are responsible for other important innovations in ETFs. They made a specific advance in a method of arbitrage that acts to reduce the tax liability of individual investors holding WEB shares. SPDRs initially did not petition the SEC to use this tax-reducing trading strategy, but they have since changed. We will discuss this tax benefit in more detail later in this chapter. In a final innovation, WEBS were allowed to use the terms *index fund* and *ETF* together in their marketing literature, a combination the SEC had not allowed previously.

Diamonds, Sector SPDRs, and Cubes

In 1997 the SEC issued an order covering *Diamonds,* which are an ETF based on the Dow Jones Industrial Average (DJIA) and are managed by State Street Global Advisors. Diamonds incorporate the tax benefits of WEBS although they were created in a unit investment trust structure. I personally believe the 30-stock DJIA is too narrow of a benchmark to invest in, but the cachet of the name makes it attractive to many self-directed retail clients. As a result, Diamonds have become the fifth largest ETF on the market with $2.8 billion in assets and 2 million shares traded daily.

State Street changed ETF structures in 1998 when they filed for *Sector SPDRs.* The firm opted to organize Sector SPDRs as an investment company. This change allowed the new funds to have all the tax benefits and dividend reinvestment benefits of WEBS. The nine ETFs were benchmarked to nine S&P 500 sectors, and only stocks included in the S&P 500 are included. The sectors are materials, health care, consumer stables, consumer discretionary, energy, financial, industrial, technology, and utilities (see Chapter 7 for more information). In 1998 the SEC also issued an order allowing the older SPDRs to incorporate the same favorable tax treatment as the new funds.

In 1999 the Bank of New York introduced the NASDAQ-100 Trust under the unit investment trust structure. The NASDAQ-100 Index is made up of the largest 100 stocks that trade over the counter in the NASDAQ marketplace. The trust was nicknamed *Cubes* because the exchange symbol it trades under is QQQ. In 1999 technology stocks were bubbling hot, and Cubes gained a massive following by institutional and individual investors. As of September 28, 2001, technology made up 68.91 percent of the QQQ. The largest holdings were technology stocks Microsoft, Intel, and Cisco Systems.

iShares Swamp the Market

Barclays Global Investors (BGI), as the creator of the first index strategy in 1971, recognized the appeal of ETFs and decided to expand its ETF product offering. In 1999 BGI petitioned the SEC for an order covering 50 ETF products. iShares launched into the marketplace beginning in May 2000. As of October 31, 2001, there were 72 iShares listed in the United States, and 17 of those are the original WEBS that were renamed iShares. BGI uses an investment company structure similar to WEBS, which gave the funds advantages over the unit trust structure of SPDRs used by State Street.

iShares cover a wide variety of U.S., international, and global stock benchmarks including S&P, Russell, Morgan Stanley Capital International (MSCI), and Dow Jones indexes, among others. The funds cover market capitalization, style (value and growth), sectors or industries, and single countries or regions. With the extensive selection within the iShares fund family, BGI became the ETF leader as measured by the number and depth of funds (although State Street still leads in assets under management).

The New, New Thing

In 2001 Vanguard introduced the first *VIPER*. The Vanguard Total Stock Market VIPER is the first ETF to be offered as a share class of an existing open-end mutual fund. The only difference between Vanguard's open-end Total Stock Market Index Fund and the new

FIGURE 4-1

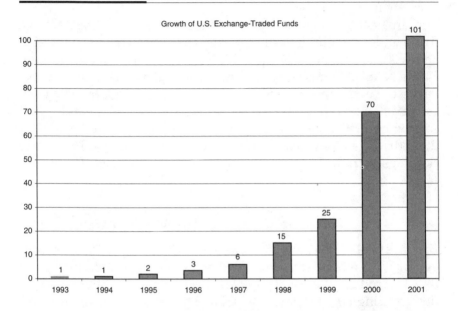

Growth of U.S. Exchange-Traded Funds

VIPER share is that the ETF trades when the stock market is open and the open-end fund shares trade after the market is closed. In January 2002 Vanguard launched its second ETF offering, the Vanguard Extend Market VIPER. This fund tracks the performance of the Wilshire 4500 Index, which includes all stocks except those in the S&P 500. VIPERs are a unique twist to the ETF marketplace and may prompt other open-end mutual funds to issue exchange-traded shares.

Over 100 ETFs have been issued on the U.S. exchanges (Figure 4-1), and more than 100 have been issued on foreign exchanges. The value of all ETFs combined total over $100 billion. Almost all of these securities are benchmarked to U.S. and international stock indexes, but the marketplace is growing rapidly. BGI has recently introduced ETFs benchmarked to the U.S. bond market, and several more unique funds are in the pipeline. The AMEX is not sitting still. It beefed up development of ETFs in the summer of 2001 by creating a new business unit dedicated to servicing sponsors and shareholders. This group will assist institutional investors to develop and launch new ETF products in the United States and abroad.

In the near future we are likely to see more ETFs benchmarked to several bond indexes and possibly new ETFs expanding to commodity indexes and economic indicators. In addition, several foreign markets trade their own unique brand of ETFs. Some of those securities have found their way to the U.S. markets, and in exchange Europe and Asian markets are cross-selling U.S. funds.

Someday there may even be actively managed ETFs. The Securities and Exchange Commission recently requested public comment in recognition of the industry's keen interest and likely investor demand. The most obvious stumbling block for an actively managed ETF is how it would disclose the contents of its portfolio because active managers are loath to reveal their trades for fear of being front run by the market. This is only the beginning.

HOW EXCHANGE-TRADED FUNDS WORK

The underlying structure of an ETF is very different from the structure of an open-end index fund. Open-end funds offer shares directly to the public for cash and redeem shares directly from the public for cash. Open-end funds are distributed either through a direct sale, as in the case of most no-load funds, or through a brokerage firm, which implies a commission of some sort.

Unlike open-end mutual funds, new exchange-traded fund shares are not sold directly to the public for cash. Instead, a fund company exchanges large blocks of ETF shares called *creation units* for actual shares of stock turned in by "authorized participants" such as Goldman Sachs, Smith Barney, and Merrill Lynch. These are not small exchanges of common stock for ETF shares. Most transactions are at least 50,000 ETF shares or multiples thereof. Participants must turn in the exact names and quantity of the underlying stock that make up an ETF block, plus a cash component which represents the accumulated stock dividends that have yet to be paid. After an ETF creation unit is issued, the institutions either hold the unit in their own portfolio or break it up and sell individual ETF shares to the general public via the stock exchange. When institutions redeem ETF creation units, everything happens in reverse. An authorized institution turns in a creation unit, and in return they receive individual securities plus a cash portion from unpaid dividends.

If you were interested in buying a single ETF share, it would require going through a brokerage firm to purchase the share on the stock exchange. That share would be from a creation unit that was broken up by an institutional investor and is selling individual ETF shares on the open market. It does not matter which creation unit your share comes from because they are all exactly the same.

The market price of a single ETF share usually trades close to its NAV. The NAV price could be targeted at one-tenth of the index value, one-twentieth of the index value, or some other set fraction depending on the fund. For example, the NAV of S&P 500 SPDRs should trade a level close to one-tenth of the index value of the S&P 500. The value of ETF shares should closely track their NAV price but may not match that index ratio exactly because of dividend accruals and market spreads. If an ETF is not trading at its NAV, it is either trading at a market premium or discount. This is a mismatch of price, and the NAV is similar to that which occurs in closed-end mutual funds, but the mismatch will not last long. Arbitrage of ETF shares eliminates the premium and discounts that persist in closed-end mutual funds.

If the ETF shares are trading at a large enough discount or premium to their NAV, this is where institutions can make a risk-free return. If market forces have caused the price of an ETF to be less than the price of the underlying stocks and cash in a fund, institutional investors will trade in common stocks and buy creation units. Conversely, if the price of an ETF is trading at a price higher than the underlying stocks and cash, institutions can trade back ETF blocks and receive higher priced individual stocks. Institutional investors continuously monitor ETF prices and underlying securities looking for a risk-free return.

ETF ARBITRAGE CREATES A TAX BREAK

Chapter 5 covers the tax benefits of index funds in more detail. This section explains a specific tax benefit that is unique to ETFs. Investors who buy ETF shares in taxable accounts, such as a joint account or trust account, will find their tax bill is slightly lower at the end of the year than if they had purchased the same amount in a comparable open-end index fund. This tax break is a benefit created from the arbitrage mechanism.

When a new creation unit is created and issued by a fund company, institutional investors turn in the individual stocks underlying the creation unit. The fund assigns each stock a cost basis based on the market price of the stocks when they were turned in. For example, whatever the market price of Microsoft (MSFT) was at the time it was turned in is the cost of MSFT shares in that particular creation unit. These new MSFT shares are added to the already existing shares of MSFT stock in the fund. Every time a new creation unit is formed, more MSFT stock is turned in, and those shares are given a cost basis.

When institutions redeem creation units, they receive common stock back, *but not necessarily the same shares they turned in.* The ETF fund manager can issue out different, lower cost basis MSFT stock than what the institution originally turned. Since there are many different tax lots of each stock in the fund, the manager of an ETF can choose which lot of MSFT shares to send back to the redeeming institution. If the manager issues the lowest-cost MSFT shares back to the redeeming institutions, they reduce the unrealized capital gains that remain in the fund. As long as there is an active market for creation units, most of the unrealized capital gains of an ETF can be erased.

This tax-loss concept is no different than an individual investor

TABLE 4-1

Capital Gain Distributions as a Percentage of NAV

	SPDR	Vanguard 500 Index
1993	0.07%	0.07%
1994	0.00%	0.47%
1995	0.02%	0.23%
1996	0.16%	0.36%
1997	0.00%	0.66%
1998	0.00%	0.37%
1999	0.00%	0.74%
2000	0.00%	0.00%
2001	0.00%	0.00%

Source: Bloomberg, Morningstar Principia

making a gift from a stock portfolio. If a taxable investor bought 100 shares of MSFT at two different times and at two different prices, and both "tax lots" are at a profit, one of the 100-share lots will have a different unrealized profit than the other 100 shares. If the investor chooses to gift 100 shares of MSFT to a charity, they should gift the lowest-cost shares first because that offers the best tax advantage.

Table 4-1 illustrates the tax advantage of ETF shares over an open-end mutual fund. SPDRs have issued minimal realized capital gains to investors only a few times, whereas the Vanguard 500 Index Fund issued capital gains to investors each year the stock market was positive for the year.

Open-End Funds Can Use ETFs as a Structure to Lower Taxes

More mature open-end stock index funds have no way to rid themselves of unrealized capital gains that built up during the bull market of the 1990s. However, an interesting development occurred in 2001. The Vanguard Group issued Total Stock Market VIPERs, which are ETF shares based on an existing open-end fund, the Vanguard Total Stock Market Fund. VIPERs will allow Vanguard to take advantage of the arbitrage mechanism in ETFs to reduce the capital gains imbedded in the existing open-end shares. As arbitrage of VIPER shares occurs, the fund manager can distribute some of the low-cost basis stock built up over the years in the open-end fund. This will lower the unrealized gains in the fund, which will ultimately benefit all classes of shareholders.

Vanguard will likely extend VIPER offerings to their other open-end index funds and perhaps to their actively managed funds. It would not be a surprise if other large mutual fund companies follow Vanguard's lead and offered ETF shares in addition to open-end shares. This strategy would help lower the capital gain tax liability that has built up in existing open-end shares.

THE COST OF INVESTING IN ETFs

There are four potential costs individual investors face when investing in exchange-traded funds. First, there is a management charge in all mutual funds. Second, there is a brokerage commission to buy and sell ETFs. Third is the spread between the true underlying value of the fund and the market value of ETF shares. Fourth is the dividend drag of holding cash in a stock fund.

Internal Expenses

The ETF management fee is an internal expense that is paid to the fund sponsor. The *expense ratio* is the percentage of a fund that is deducted each year to pay for portfolio management, accounting, legal expenses, advertising, and other miscellaneous charges. In addition all index funds must pay a licensing fee to the firm whose index it uses. For example, all S&P 500 Index funds pay Standard & Poor's a negotiated royalty each year. The total internal fees of ETFs are similar to low-cost, open-end index funds. However, some ETFs are very expensive in comparison to open-end funds, and individual investors should avoid these higher cost ETFs. Table 4-2 presents a sample cost comparison. A complete list of current ETF fees is available at www.Indexfunds.com.

Commission Costs and Market Spreads

The expense ratios of the most popular ETFs are about the same as open-end index funds, but there are other costs to buy and sell

TABLE 4–2

Select ETF Expenses Compared to Vanguard Funds

ETF Name	Ticker Symbol	ETF Expense Ratio	Vanguard Index Fund Expense
iShare S&P 500	IVV	0.09%	0.18%
SPDR Mid-Cap	MDY	0.25%	0.25%
iShare S&P Small-Cap 600	IJR	0.20%	0.25%
iShare DJ US Real Estate	IYR	0.60%	0.33%
iShares MSCI EMU (European Monetary Union)	EZU	0.84%	0.29%
iShares 5 Single Country Emerging Market Funds	Various	0.84%–0.99%	0.58%

Source: Barclays Global Research, Morningstar, June 30, 2001

shares. ETFs trade on stock exchanges, with the American Stock Exchange (AMEX) listing the greatest number of funds. All ETF trading is conducted through brokerage firms. This means you must pay a brokerage commission. The commission can be expensive depending on where you trade. Besides the commission, there is a second cost to trading that is inherent in all stock transactions. The *spread* is the difference between a stock's *ask* price (what you can buy it for) and its *bid* price (what you can sell it for). Spread costs can vary. The less volume of trading activity that occurs in a security, the larger the spread between the bid and ask.

Let's look at an example of an ETF trade using Spiders to show the impact of commissions and the bid-ask spread. Suppose it is midday and you heard the S&P 500 was down 5 percent. Your hunch is that the market will recover some of its loss by the end of the day, so you call your broker and place an order to buy 100 Spiders at the current market price. Your broker immediately executes the trade at $110.05 per share, which is approximately one-tenth the value of the S&P 500 at the time. The total cost to trade 100 Spiders is $11,055 including a $50 commission. The extra $5 represents the spread between the bid of $110 and the ask price of $110.05. If you are right about the market and the S&P 500 recovers the 5 percent loss by the end of the day, the value of your 100 Spiders increases to $11,500, and you earned an extra $445. If you sell at $115, you will pay another $50 commission, and your total gain will be $395. That is quite a bit less than the theoretical no-commission, no-spread gain of $500. The $105 given up to Wall Street is over 20 percent of the investment's profit potential. Obviously, the more you trade, the more you lose to commissions and spreads, which is one reason I advocate a buy and hold strategy.

Premiums and Discounts

As we have discussed, ETF shares trade independently of the stocks that they are composed of. This means the market value of an ETF share can differ from the underlying net asset value of the stocks and cash that make up that share. Premiums and discounts create an arbitrage opportunity for institutional investors, but they also add an element of risk for individuals. If an ETF is trading at a premium

TABLE 4-3

Examples of ETF Trading Symbols and Trading Values*

ETF Name	Trading Symbol	Underlying Trading Value
SPDR (S&P 500)	SPY	SXV
Vanguard 5000 VIPERs	VTI	TSJ
NASDAQ 100	QQQ	QXV
iShare Russell 1000	IWB	NJB
iShare S&P Mid-Cap 400 Value	IJJ	NJJ
*For a complete list visit the Indexfunds.com Web site		

when you buy shares, you paid more than it was worth. If you sell at a discount, you sold at less than the shares were worth.

Since individual investors have no idea what the true underlying value of an ETF should be at the time of a trade, the listing exchange disseminates that information every 15 seconds. The underlying trading value of an ETF is available by typing a symbol into a quote machine (see Figure 4–3), which your broker can do for you before trading. Remember to use real-time quotes when checking the underlying trading value. Most of the quotes you get on a home computer have a 20-minute delay. Unfortunately, the underlying trading value of many international ETFs is not readily available.

Dividend Drag

A second hidden cost of UITs is called *dividend drag*. Many underlying stocks in an ETF pay dividends, and these dividends accumulate in the fund over a period of time. After the fund deducts management fees and other expenses from the dividend, the remaining cash is passed through to shareholders on a quarterly basis. Once a dividend is distributed, investors can automatically reinvest the cash in more shares through their broker. Due to different dividend payment dates by companies, there is always a small "cash component" of the ETF that is not invested in stocks. Since cash generates less return than stocks (most of the time), it creates a slight drag on the performance of the fund.

Dividend payments are also treated differently by index providers who calculate an index return. S&P assumes that stock dividends are automatically reinvested in the stock of the companies on the index on the ex-dividend date. Unfortunately, the ex-date can be a month or so before the dividend payment date. The payment date is the day shareholders are actually paid the cash dividend. Since the index date for dividend reinvestment is different from the actual pay date of the dividend, it is technically impossible for any index fund, including all ETFs, to attain the same performance of the benchmark index.

The iShare structure allows BGI to reinvest dividends back into the market while waiting for the next dividend payment date; however, SPDRs cannot reinvest dividends. The unit trust structure of SPDRs means they must hold dividends paid by companies for up to 3 months before the quarterly payment to shareholders. This cash buildup affects the performance of SPDRs. When the markets go up, SPDRs lag the market, but when the market goes down, the cash can help performance. During the bull market in the 1990s, the dividend drag of S&P 500 SPDRs was about 0.25 percent per year.

CHAPTER SUMMARY

There are benefits and disadvantages of using ETFs in a portfolio. The benefits include the flexibility to trade anytime the markets are open and the inherent tax advantage that institutional arbitrage creates. The disadvantage is the added cost of commissions, market spreads, and potential dividend drag. Depending on your objective, ETFs may be the best way for you to invest in index funds.

Exchange-traded funds are a new and exciting area of the index fund marketplace. Each year the structure and depth of this marketplace expands exponentially. Today more than 200 ETFs trade worldwide with a market value worth over $1 billion U.S. It is my belief that there will be thousands of ETFs on the market in the next 10 years. Perhaps in a few years half of all mutual fund trades will be exchange traded. This is just the beginning.

CHAPTER 5

The Tax Advantage of Index Funds

Key Concepts

- ◆ Understand mutual fund taxation.
- ◆ Compare the tax efficiency of index funds to active funds.
- ◆ Mutual fund managers can reduce your taxes.
- ◆ Index fund tax swapping can increase your total return.

All mutual fund investors pay several different expenses. These costs include management fees, legal fees, and administrative charges. In addition, some mutual funds charge a sales commission and an ongoing 12b-1 (marketing) fee. Investors who buy mutual funds in a taxable account incur another fee that can dwarf all others. This is the cost of taxation. If you are considering investing taxable money in a mutual fund, pay close attention to this chapter. It highlights one of the great advantages that index funds have over actively managed mutual funds. Index funds are very tax-efficient, which can save you a bundle of money.

THE MECHANICS OF MUTUAL FUND TAXATION

There are four different events that can trigger a tax to mutual fund shareholders. Three of these events are direct cash distributions by the mutual fund, and selling shares triggers the fourth event.

Each year all mutual funds distribute ordinary income dividends and realized capital gains. Capital gains are further divided into long-term and short-term gains. These distributions are subject to personal income tax, even if the shareholder automatically reinvests the cash in more shares. Most mutual fund managers do not hesitate to distribute all income and capital gain earnings to shareholders because the fund itself would have to pay a 35 percent tax if they were not passed along.

All income and capital gain distributions are reported to shareholders annually on Form 1099-DIV. The form is sent in late January for the previous tax year. Form 1099 is compiled and sent by the brokerage firm or the mutual fund company that holds your fund shares, otherwise known as the custodian. The form will list all taxable distributions by type so there is no misunderstanding between ordinary income, short-term capital gains, and long-term capital gains. Not all cash distributions are taxable. Municipal bond funds distribute mostly tax-free interest income, and some mutual funds will return a portion of your original investment. All of these distributions will be listed on Form 1099.

A fourth event that may trigger a tax liability is the personal sale or exchange of mutual fund shares. You are required to track the purchase and sales price of your mutual fund shares and report any gains or losses to the IRS. Even if you exchange one mutual fund for a different mutual fund of the same fund family, you are still liable to pay capital gains tax. The IRS has stated that it is your responsibility to track gains and losses on the sale of mutual fund shares, not the mutual fund company or brokerage firm. So, keep good records. At a minimum you should keep a separate folder for each mutual fund and at the end of each year match up any share sales with a purchase price. Any gain or loss should be reported on Schedule D of your tax return.

The Taxation of Ordinary Income Dividends

Whether you buy a stock mutual fund or bond mutual fund, the securities in the fund will likely pay income. *Ordinary dividend income* represents the distribution of all dividend and interest income earned from stocks, bonds, and cash equivalents in a mutual fund. Shareholders must report all ordinary income the tax year for which they are generated. Unless otherwise designated by the fund, this income is reported as "dividend income" on Form 1040 of an individual tax return.

Dividend income is taxed as ordinary income, which is taxed at the same rate as your earned income from employment. Ordinary income tax is based on a progressive, tiered system. That means the more you make, the higher your tax rate. According to the Tax Act of 2001, the top ordinary income tax rate will gradually be reduced to 35 percent by 2006. There is little a mutual fund company can do to reduce the effect of taxes on ordinary dividend income. Most mutual funds draw their management fees and expenses from dividend and interest income earned, which reduce the amount of the distribution (as well as your wealth). Index fund expenses are typically low, so the dividend and interest income are typically much greater than the cost of running the fund.

The Taxation of Capital Gain Distributions

The underlying holdings of all mutual funds change each year as assets are bought and sold. This is true for index funds as well as actively managed accounts. Some of these trades result in a capital gain, and others result in a capital loss. The losses are offset against the gains, and the net trading profit for the year is distributed to shareholders. Mutual funds distribute capital gains once or twice per year, normally in June and December. Shareholders who hold mutual funds in a taxable account must pay capital gains tax on these distributions.

There are two types of capital gains distributed by mutual funds and two tax rates. The first type of capital gain is a *short-term gain*. These are the net gains on securities held less than 1 year. The short-term capital gains tax is the same as your ordinary income tax rate. For example, if you are paying 35 percent in income tax on ordinary income, you will also pay 35 percent on short-term capital gain distributions. The second type of capital gain distribution is a *long-term gain*. This is reported to you in a different block on Form 1099-DIV. Long-term capital gains are taxed at a lower rate than short-term gains. For example, you may have to pay 35 percent on short-term gains but only 20 percent on long-term gains. Depending on an investor's ordinary income tax rate, 20 percent is the highest tax rate the individual would pay on long-term capital gain distributions.

Reducing Capital Gain Distributions

Since mutual fund managers must pay net capital gains each year and taxable shareholders must pay taxes on these gains, it seems logical that the fund manager would try to reduce the amount of realized gains by holding the winning stocks in the mutual fund rather than selling them. But sometimes logic does not prevail in the investment industry. On average, mutual fund managers do not manage portfolios in the most tax-efficient way. There is too much turnover of securities, which creates a heavy tax burden for some investors.

Table 5-1 illustrates the average effect of taxes on mutual fund returns. The after-tax performance of nearly all categories of U.S. equity funds has been approximately 3 percent less than the pretax return. Much of this loss has been the result of an annual capital gains tax, which is caused by heavy portfolio turnover. Since December 2001 the SEC has mandated that mutual fund companies report the after-tax performance of all funds. This ruling has made the tax effect of turnover more transparent. Table 5-1 assumes the funds are sold at the end of the period; therefore, it shows the actual after-tax return an investor subject to the highest tax rates would have achieved.

TABLE 5–1

Median Annual Mutual Fund Returns for Ten Years Ending December, 2001

Type of Fund	Pretax Return	After-Tax Return*	Amount Lost to Taxes
Large-Cap U.S. Equity	11.3%	8.5%	2.9%
Mid-Cap U.S. Equity	12.3%	9.3%	3.0%
Small-Cap U.S. Equity	12.4%	9.4%	3.0%

Source: Morningstar
*Assumes funds were held for 10 years and sold on December 31, 2001

Paying 3 percent of your portfolio to Uncle Sam in the form of taxes is a significant amount. If mutual fund managers were able to eliminate or defer realized capital gains by reducing the amount of trading, investors would pay less tax and have more money to spend or invest. A few mutual fund companies have introduced "tax-managed" funds, which are also referred to as "tax-sensitive" or "tax-efficient" funds. These mutual funds employ an investment strategy designed to minimize the effects of capital gains on a fund. The strategies include reducing portfolio turnover, mitigating the effect of realized capital gains by taking offsetting losses in other securities, and weighing the portfolio toward growth stocks that have a lower dividend payout.

The amount of buying and selling that occurs in a mutual fund is called *portfolio turnover.* Most active fund managers buy and sell stocks often, sometimes holding onto a position for only a few days. High turnover tends to generate a lot of realized capital gains in a portfolio. Part of the gain from heavy turnover is short term, which means taxable shareholders are subject to ordinary income tax rates on that amount. Low turnover is typically better for taxable fund investors. The less a fund manager trades, the less realized capital gains are generated, and less tax is paid by shareholders. Unrealized gains can stay in the fund indefinitely, and those gains will not be taxable to shareholders until the fund manager sells the position.

In addition to low turnover, mutual fund managers can reduce capital gains distributions by selectively choosing which shares of a stock position to sell. As new contributions come into a fund, the manager adds to the current stock positions. The periodic buying of shares creates different "tax layers" of cost basis for each stock position. As investors begin to redeem shares, the manager can choose which layer to sell first. The manager should sell the highest cost shares of a stock first, leaving the low-cost stock in the fund. This technique reduces realized capital gains and saves taxes. Fund managers who employ good tax-management techniques can avoid capital gains distributions for a long time.

If a large number of shareholders decide to redeem all at once, a fund must sell large amounts of securities to meet the redemption. Some tax-managed mutual funds charge a fee to shareholders for redemption if they do not hold a fund for at least 1 year. This is done in an effort to slow shareholder redemption during adverse market conditions. Sometimes the redemption fee goes back into the mutual fund to compensate remaining shareholders who are adversely affected by taxes and internal fund costs.

Index Funds Are Very Tax Efficient

By their nature index funds have lower portfolio turnover, which makes them an excellent choice for tax-conscious investors. As a result most index funds distribute only a small amount of realized capital gains to shareholders, which is beneficial to shareholders. This is especially true for index funds that are benchmarked to large indexes, such as the S&P 500. The S&P 500 has had a turnover of about 6 percent per year over the last 10 years, according to the *S&P 500 Directory*. Most of those changes occurred as a result of company mergers and acquisitions.

Table 5-2 compares the 10-year performance of the Vanguard 500 Index Fund to the median (middle of the road) actively managed large-cap U.S. stock fund through December 2001. The table shows the after-tax performance if the funds were held after the 10-year period and if the fund were sold after 10 years.

On the pretax basis the Vanguard 500 Index Fund outperformed the average large-cap fund by 1.4 percent. On an after-tax basis the Vanguard fund beat the median active fund by 3.4 percent, assuming neither fund was sold at the end of the period. The Vanguard 500 Index Fund beat the median fund by 2.1 percent, assuming both the funds were sold at the end of the period. The drop in return between the presale and postsale numbers is the result of the

TABLE 5-2

Comparing the Vanguard 500 to the Median Large-Cap Active Fund

Fund	Pretax Return Before Sale	After-Tax Before Sale	After-Tax After Sale	Lost to Taxes
Vanguard 500 Index Fund	12.8%	12.0%	10.6%	2.2%
Median Large-Cap Fund	11.4%	8.6%	8.5%	2.9%

Source: Morningstar, *2001 S&P Directory*

funds per share price increase in net asset value over the period. Since index funds have lower stock turnover than active funds, there is less tax liability during the holding period and more in the end. Nevertheless, the net result is a gain to shareholders. The higher after-tax return is not so much a sign that Vanguard does a great job of tax management; rather it is proof that active fund managers do a poor job. The Vanguard 500 Index Fund is just one example of tax efficiency. On average, all index fund shareholders pay far less in tax than those of comparable actively managed funds.

Exchange-Traded Fund Advantage

Exchange-traded funds (ETFs) are index funds that trade during the day on one of the major stock exchanges. Individual investors can buy and sell ETF shares just like they buy and sell individual shares of common stock. There are a number of different ETFs on the market covering different indexes. See Chapter 4 for a complete explanation of ETFs.

One advantage of the ETF structure over an open-end fund format is that its structure creates an extra tax benefit for taxable investors. Capital gains that build up in an ETF can be "pushed off" onto institution investors rather than distributed to individual shareholders. In fact, many actively traded ETFs have never paid a capital gain distribution. This is possible through the share redemption mechanism built into ETF structure.

ETFs are created when a large institution exchanges individual stocks of companies for a creation unit composed of 50,000 ETF shares. Those ETF shares are either held for investment or broken apart and resold on the stock exchange. Frequently, creation units are turned back in by institutions and reissued as individual stocks, and during this redemption process an ETF fund manager can purge the fund of low-cost stock. By assigning lower cost stock to redeeming institutions, the fund permanently reduces the tax liability in the ETF. Figure 5-1 illustrates the tax advantage that an S&P 500 ETF format may have had over actively managed funds and an open-end S&P 500 index fund for 10 years ending in 2001. The return of the S&P 500 ETF is simulated. Figure 5-1 assumes the fund is sold at the end of 10 years. Although the extra tax advantage of ETF shares is not huge, every little bit helps.

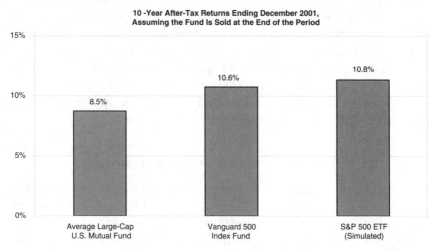

10 -Year After-Tax Returns Ending December 2001,
Assuming the Fund Is Sold at the End of the Period

Source: Median fund and index fund data from Morningstar

Tax on a Sale or Exchange of Fund Shares

When you sell shares of any mutual fund in a taxable account, you will incur either a taxable gain or tax loss. Very rarely are shares sold at the exact price they were purchased. To measure the gain or loss accurately, you need to keep good records of the cost basis. Three accounting methods are acceptable when tracking the cost basis of an open-end mutual fund: the average cost method, the FIFO method, and the actual cost method. If you sell a partial position in an open-end mutual fund and report the gain or loss to the IRS, you cannot switch from one method to another. ETFs are handled somewhat differently. Since they trade like stock, you need to account for them like stock, which means tracking every new purchase and assigning a cost to those shares individually.

Average cost accounting means using the average price of all open-end mutual fund shares to compute a gain or loss, including the reinvestment of dividends. This method may seem simple, but it can be a tax nightmare. You must keep track of when you purchased individual shares to determine if you are selling long-term shares or short-term shares. There are two steps involved in the process. First, you add all the money you invested to purchase shares held for more than a year, including the cash from dividend reinvestment, and divide that amount by the number of shares you owned for more than 1 year. This gives you the average cost per share on long-term investments. The second part of the equation is to add all the shares you owned for 1 year or less, including the reinvestment of dividends, and divide that amount by the number of shares held for less than 1 year.

When selling shares under the *first in, first out,* or *FIFO,* inventory accounting method, your oldest shares are sold first, and the newest shares are sold last. The profits from shares you held for more than 1 year are taxed at a long-term capital gain rate, and the profit for shares held 1 year or less generate short-term capital gains, which are taxed at your higher ordinary income rate. If you do not know when you purchased your shares, contact the mutual fund company or your broker. They are required to keep records of share purchase dates and trade amounts.

The last accounting method is *actual cost.* This is similar to FIFO, only you can designate which shares are being sold. For example, assume you bought 100 shares of a mutual fund in 1995, another 100 shares in 1998, and a third 100 shares in 2001. Then in 2002 you decided to sell 100 shares. For tax and accounting purposes, you can designate the 1995 shares, the 1998 shares, the 2001 shares, or any combination thereof. Under most circumstances you would choose the tax lot with the highest cost basis, so you can reduce your taxable gain. This method of tax management will save you money on April 15.

The actual cost method of share accounting gives you the most tax flexibility, but it is also the most time consuming. When you call your broker or mutual fund company to sell shares, make sure you tell them which shares you are selling. Some firms will print that information in the trade ticket, which makes your accounting easier.

Overall, I do not recommend the average cost method of mutual fund accounting in a taxable account. It is too restrictive, and you may end up paying more in taxes than you should. FIFO accounting is better, and the actual cost method is best.

Whichever method you choose, I do not recommend the automatic reinvesting of mutual fund distributions in a taxable account. The bookkeeping that is required to track dividend reinvestment data is not worth the aggravation or the expense. Instead, accumulate cash from all mutual fund distributions and reinvest the total amount in one mutual fund and in one lump sum. This makes accounting much simpler, which saves your CPA time and you money. See Chapter 15 for more details on these and other portfolio strategies for taxable accounts.

TAX SWAP TO REDUCE CAPITAL GAINS TAX

Your goal as an investor is to keep as much as possible of what you earn. Therefore, tax efficiency is an important concept. To add another dimension to tax management, I have included a section on tax swapping index funds. Most of the advanced portfolio management techniques are found in Part III of this book; however, the strategy of tax swapping fits best in this chapter.

The Concept of Tax Swapping

Tax management is as important to a financial plan as choosing the right investments. A dollar saved in taxes is a dollar increase in your wealth. One way to increase your total return is to use tax swapping in a portfolio of index funds. The idea is buy stock index funds on different dates throughout the year and establish multiple tax lots. As the stock market moves up and down during the year, these tax lots can be selectively sold and simultaneously replaced by a similar index fund. This creates a realized capital loss but never puts you out of the stock market. Using this tax-swap strategy, you will increase your overall net worth due to a tax deduction from the realized loss. It is important to understand that the money invested in stocks will always stay in stocks. This strategy is designed to lower your tax bill, not your allocation to the stock market.

The best way to explain the concept of tax swapping is by reviewing how it is done in a bond portfolio. Bond swapping is an established tradition among taxable fixed-income investors. Tax swapping bonds involves selling one issue for the tax loss and simultaneously buying another issue that is very similar but not "substantially identical." For instance, you would sell a 5-year, 6 percent yield General Motors bond and buy a 5-year, 6 percent yield Ford

Motors bond. Those bonds are very similar but are issued by different companies, so they are not substantially identical.

A bond swap creates a tax loss while not affecting the total return of the bond portfolio. In the GM for Ford bond swap, let's assume we have realized a $3000 loss on the trade but are still earning the same 6 percent yield on the new bond, so your total return has not changed. However, the $3000 loss can be used to offset a $3000 realized capital gain that may be in your portfolio. That gain may have come from another bond trade, a stock trade, a mutual fund trade, the sale of real estate, or the sale of a business. If there are no realized gains, the loss can be used to reduce your adjusted gross income up to a maximum of $3000 per year. However you use the loss, it will reduce the amount of tax you owe. Swapping is a very useful strategy for reducing taxes.

It is important not to swap into a security that is substantially identical to the one sold. If the new security is substantially identical, the transaction will be considered a "tax wash" by the IRS, and the loss would not be allowed. For example, if you sold General Motors stock at a loss and bought the same General Motors stock back the next day, the loss would not be allowed. Tax wash rules state that you need to wait 30 days before buying back a substantially identical security to take a tax loss. The definition of substantially identical is in the gray area in the tax code. Tax courts have ruled that if you swap the stock of one company for the stock of an unrelated company, then there is no tax wash. For example, it is not a tax wash to sell General Motors stock and buy Ford Motors stock.

Let's apply the tax-swapping strategy to index funds. If you had a loss in a broad-based U.S. stock index fund issued by one mutual fund company and simultaneously bought a broad-based U.S. stock index fund issued by a different mutual fund company, a legitimate tax loss has been created. This also means you never missed a day in the market. As long as two unrelated mutual fund companies manage the two funds, no tax wash has occurred. There are several broad-based U.S. stock index funds to choose from, so creating this transaction is easy. Now, I must warn you, to date the IRS has not contested tax swapping of index funds, but that does not mean it will not be contested in the future. Consult your tax adviser before proceeding.

Setting Up for Tax Swapping

Most people put money into the markets over time. They invest a little here and a little there. Rather than simply investing when you have the money on hand, I recommend saving your taxable dollars and making regularly scheduled quarterly investments. For example, instead of investing $1000 one month, $500 the next, and $1500 the next, I recommend investing $3000 once per quarter. This strategy is commonly known as dollar cost averaging. One reason dollar cost averaging makes sense is because it establishes different tax lots for your shares. Each quarter you will buy index fund shares at different prices, thereby establishing different tax positions.

To see how tax swapping works, let's look at an example. Assume you are buying $3000 per quarter in Vanguard Total Stock Market VIPERs (VTI) on the first day of each quarter (for an explanation on VIPERs, see Chapter 4). From January through July the purchases would be as follows:

Purchase Date	Index fund NAV	Number of Shares	Cost	Value on July 1
Jan. 1	$100	30	$3000	$3600
Apr. 1	$100	30	$3000	$3600
Jul. 1	$120	25	$3000	$3000
Total account value on July 1		85		$10,200

Assume that during the third quarter the stock market suffers a 10 percent correction, and on August 1 the price of the Total Market VIPERs is trading at $108 per share. Your account value and tax lot values are now as follows:

Purchase Date	Cost	Number of shares	Value on October 1	Gain /loss
Jan. 1	$3000	30	$3240	+240
Apr. 1	$3000	30	$3240	+240
Jul. 1	$3000	25	$2700	(300)
Total account value		85	$9026	+180

The overall account has a gain of $180. However, the 25-share tax lot bought on July 1 has a loss of $300. If you decide to take the tax loss and sell 25 shares, you will need to designate the shares to be sold. If you do not, your broker will assume the shares being sold were the ones bought on January 1. Remember, tax selling goes first in, first out unless you designate otherwise. By designating for sale the tax lot bought on July 1, the portfolio would realize a loss of $300. This tax loss would reduce your tax liability for the year by about $105, assuming a 35 percent tax bracket.

Immediately following the sale of the 25 VIPERs share tax lot, you buy $2700 of the iShare Russell 3000 ETF (IWV). The Russell 3000 is very similar to the Vanguard Total Stock Market Fund but is not substantially identical because it is based on a different market index and issued by a different fund company. The net result of this transaction is a tax loss that you can write off against income taxes while remaining 100 percent invested in a broad market index. This transaction is easily accomplished through any discount brokerage firm at a nominal commission rate.

Lets look a little closer at the total economic impact of this index fund swap. On August 1 you had an overall unrealized profit of $180 in the account. That is a gain of 2 percent on the original $9000 invested. Assuming you are in the 35 percent tax bracket and take a $300 tax loss, your federal income tax saving amounts to $105. This increases your overall return on the portfolio from $180 to $285, which is an extra gain of 1.1 percent. Your portfolio did not increase in value by an extra $105, but your net worth did because of a $105 tax savings. A dollar saved on taxes is a dollar added to your wealth. That is the advantage of tax-swapping index funds.

There are a few warnings about tax swapping. Depending on where you trade, commissions and other fees may reduce the effectiveness of a tax swap. Seek low-commission rates on ETF trades and stick with no-load mutual funds. Finally, this is not a book about income taxes. Always consult your tax adviser before using tax swaps in your portfolio. There is no clear definition of what is considered a substantially identical index fund. Your accountant's interpretation of the tax code may differ from my own.

CHAPTER SUMMARY

The avoidance of taxes is the only intellectual pursuit that carries any reward.

John Maynard Keynes

Mutual fund investors pay a variety of expenses, but none are as expensive as the tax that Uncle Sam can levy on your portfolio. As you invest your taxable money in a taxable account, pay close attention to the tax efficiency of those investments. Stick with low-cost, low-turnover index funds and practice good tax-management techniques such as tax swapping. You have worked hard for the money. Don't let Uncle Sam take more than he deserves.

PART TWO

Different Types of Stock and Bond Index Funds

CHAPTER 6

Broad U.S. Equity Index Funds

Key Concepts

- There are four major U.S. index providers.
- Compare and contrast broad U.S. index funds.
- Divide the market into size and value categories.
- The S&P indexes are considered managed indexes.

The index fund revolution had it roots in the U.S. stock market. In 1976 John Bogle of the Vanguard Group introduced the Vanguard 500 Index Fund, which was the first index fund available to the general public. Unfortunately, the fund was not an instant success. Many people had their doubts whether the concept of a low-fee, market-based mutual fund could survive in an industry that was completely dominated by active fund companies with large advertising budgets. However, through perseverance and a solid investment performance, the Vanguard 500 Index Fund has become one of the biggest success stories in mutual fund history.

Success breeds imitation, and as of this writing there are well over 400 open-end and exchange-traded index funds offered through various mutual funds companies, brokerage firms, and banks. In total more than $500 billion is invested in index funds by individual investors. About 100 of these funds are benchmarked to the S&P 500, and the amount in those funds exceeds $250 billion. These figures do not include index funds sold through insurance company products like variable annuities. Nor do the figures include institutional investors who have enough assets to create a private index fund. When all the money is added, the total amount of money indexed in the S&P 500 Index is over $1 trillion.

The S&P 500 may have the largest number of index funds tracking it, but it is only one of several broad U.S. stock indexes available to individual investors. S&P has created dozens of U.S. benchmarks based on various market segments, and mutual fund companies have rushed to form open-end index funds or exchange-traded funds that track many of those benchmarks. Other research companies offer competing U.S. equity indexes. Major index providers include Frank Russell & Company, Wilshire Associates, and Dow Jones & Company. There is tremendous competition for index recognition on Wall Street because of pride and the cash royalty indexes can create. To limit the length of this chapter, only U.S. stock indexes that have at least one low-cost index fund benchmark are listed.

The newest member of the index provider group is Morningstar.® Widely known as a mutual fund research firm, Morningstar is set to enter the industry as an active participant in the role of index licensor. UBS Global Asset Management has announced that they will be the first fund company to license at least some of Morningstar's 16 proprietary equity indexes as the basis for exchange-traded funds (ETFs). Information on the new Morningstar indexes and UBS ETFs benchmarked to them are not included in this chapter due to the limited information at the time of publication, and because the funds were not yet available. Current information about Morningstar indexes and UBS ETFs is available online at *www.Morningstar.com.*

This chapter and the next compare and contrast the U.S. equity indexes of S&P, Russell, Wilshire, and Dow Jones. This chapter explores each broad index by size, style, and structure, allowing you to visualize the underlying strengths and weaknesses. Chapter 7 continues an analysis of U.S. equity benchmarks by breaking down broad indexes by industry sector and reviewing low-cost index funds based on those sectors.

SIZE AND STYLE

Style boxes popularized by Morningstar can help investors visualize the difference between different U.S. equity indexes. The equity

FIGURE 6-1

Morningstar Style Boxes

Value	Blend	Growth	
LV	LB	LG	Large-Cap
MV	MB	MG	Mid-Cap
SV	SB	SG	Small-Cap

style box is a nine-box matrix that displays a fund's investment methodology based on the size of the companies in which it invests and the style. Combining these two variables offers a broad view of a fund's holdings and risk. The equity style box compares market capitalization on the vertical axis and valuation on the horizontal axis (Figure 6–1).

Market Capitalization

U.S. equity index funds can be categorized by the average size of the companies they hold. Index funds that invest in predominantly large company stocks are classified as large-cap funds. Those that invest in smaller companies are labeled mid-cap funds. Those that invest in the smallest companies are small-cap funds.

The market value of each stock in a large-cap index fund is generally over $10 billion in value, although there is not a hard rule on size. Only about 5 percent of all U.S. stocks can be classified as large-cap, yet they make up over 75 percent of the dollar value of the entire U.S. stock market. These stocks include GE, MSFT, and IBM. The next level of size is mid-cap. The market value of mid-cap stocks generally falls between $2 billion to $10 billion. About 15 percent of all U.S. stocks are classified as mid-cap. Index funds that hold companies that have a market value of less that $2 billion each are generally classified as small-cap. More than 80 percent of public U.S. companies are small-cap, yet their aggregate market value equals less than 10 percent of the value of the broad U.S. market. All the major index providers use roughly the same criteria to divide large-, mid-, and small-cap stocks.

In addition to large-, mid-, and small-cap, a fourth size category needs to be mentioned to complete the rankings. Micro-cap stocks have a market capitalization below $200 million and represent less than 2 percent of the total market capitalization. Although there are thousands of micro-cap stocks, there are very few micro-cap mutual funds and only one index fund. Many micro-cap stocks do not trade with enough volume to make them a suitable investment for mutual funds. The Dimensional Fund Advisors 9-10 Micro-Cap Portfolio is an index fund available to investors who use a qualified investment adviser.

If you put all sizes of stocks together in a market-weighted portfolio, you have an *all-cap index* or *total market index.* For example, iShares Russell 3000 Index Fund holds 3000 large-, mid-, and small-cap stocks. Depending on the total market index provider, it may or may not include micro-cap stocks. The Russell 3000 holds very few micro-cap stocks.

Growth or Value Decision

The division of stocks between growth and value companies is more difficult to comprehend than size differences, and value methodology varies between index providers. As a result, the composition and performance of growth and value index funds will vary depending on the index that they are benchmarked against. Examples of growth stocks typically include Microsoft and Cisco Systems, and examples of value stocks include General Motors and U.S. Steel. The categories of these stocks are not cut in stone. Valuations change daily, and what was a value stock one day may be categorized as a growth stock the next. To add more confusion, not all stocks are classified as growth or value. One index provider may classify a stock as both value and growth, and another index provider may classify the same stock as neither value or growth but rather in a third category called core.

To give you an idea of the growth and value differences between index providers, here is a quick snapshot. The S&P style indexes uses only price-to-book value (p/b) ratios to classify growth and value stocks. Wilshire and Russell use p/b and also incorporate a forecasted earnings growth rate. Finally, Dow Jones utilizes six factors to classify style: projected price-to-earnings (p/e), projected earnings growth, trailing p/e, trailing earnings growth, p/b, and dividend yield.

S&P simply takes all of its stocks ranked by p/b and classifies the top 50 percent of market cap as growth and the bottom 50 percent of market cap as value. This gives equal value to the growth and value indexes. Russell uses a nonlinear probability algorithm to determine style membership weights. Under this system 35 percent of stocks are classified as all value, 35 percent are classified as all growth, and 30 percent are weighted proportionately to both value and growth. This means some stocks are in both indexes. For example, the market value of General Electric may be allocated to 60 percent growth and 40 percent value. Dow Jones uses cluster analysis to identify growth and value stocks. In the Dow Jones methodology, stocks that do not fit clearly into growth or value are placed in the core category.

This can be confusing, but don't become frustrated. Most professionals have trouble getting it straight, especially because stocks can flip back and forth between growth and value indexes each year.

THE INDEX PROVIDERS

The major index providers for the U.S. equity market are Wilshire Associates, Frank Russell & Company, Standard & Poor's, and Dow Jones & Company. In this chapter each provider is analyzed for portfolio structure, ongoing management, and completeness of their indexes. No performance data are provided because it is counterproductive to the discussion. One company's method is not better or worse than another, just different.

We will look at the Wilshire indexes first because they offer the most "complete" indexes, meaning the indexes hold the most securities. Then we will look at the Russell, Dow Jones, and finally Standard & Poor's indexes, which hold the least securities. In addition to broad market indexes, each provider has created a number of size, style, and sector indexes. Keep in mind that one index is not better or worse than another. The purpose of Part II of this book is to provide you with meaningful information about indexes so you can make an informed decision as to which benchmarks are right for you.

Wilshire U.S. Equity Indexes

Wilshire Associates is a privately owned investment firm headquartered in Santa Monica, California. Since its founding in 1972, Wilshire Associates has evolved from an investment technology firm into a global investment advisory company specializing in mutual funds, consulting services, and financial data.

Wilshire has developed a wide variety of U.S. indexes, of which the Wilshire 5000 is the most popular. The Wilshire 5000 was the first U.S. equity index to capture the return of the entire U.S. stock market. When originally introduced in 1974, the index held 5000 stocks, thus the name. However, the number of stocks in the Wilshire 5000 is now closer to 6500. The index name confuses many people who think there are still 5000.

In addition to the broad 5000 index, Wilshire has created a number of size, style, and sector indexes. For the sake of space and relevance, the indexes listed here must have at least one low-cost index fund benchmarked to it.

Wilshire 5000

<u>Size and Style: Total Market/Blend</u>   The Wilshire 5000 Total Market Index represents the broadest index for the U.S. equity market, measuring the performance of all U.S. headquartered equity securities with readily available price data. No other index offers its comprehensiveness. When the index was created in 1974, Wilshire's founder took advantage of then-new technologies that made it possible to collect stock prices and calculate returns for a volume of issues never before brought together. According to the Wilshire Associates' Web site at www.Wilshire.com, this is the construction methodology of the 5000 index.

Membership
- The company must be headquartered in the United States.
- The issue must trade in the United States.

- The issue must be the primary equity issue for the company.
- Equity issues include common stocks, real-estate investment trusts (REITs), and limited partnerships.
- Primary equity issue selection criteria include volume, institutional holdings, and conversion criteria.
- Shares outstanding for multiple classes of stock are combined into the primary issue's shares outstanding to reflect the total market capitalization of the firm.

Exclusions

- Very small "bulletin board" issues are excluded from the monthly addition process by the assumption that they do not have consistent, readily available prices.
- Nondomiciled U.S. stocks, foreign issues, and American Depository Receipts (ADRs) are excluded.

Adjustments and Maintenance

- Additions to the index are made once a month after the month-end close.
- Initial public offerings will generally be added at the end of the month.
- Issues spun off from index members will be added to the index as soon as prudently possible.
- A security will be removed from the index on the day it fails index inclusion guidelines.
- A security will be removed from the index on the day it stops trading but may reenter the index when it resumes trading.
- Shares outstanding may be adjusted to reflect corporate events during the month; otherwise, shares outstanding are updated once a month.

Investors who want the broadest possible breadth of stocks in the U.S. market will find that an index fund benchmarked to the Wilshire 5000 provides it. However, you will not be able to invest in an index funds that holds all 6500 stocks because some of the smallest stocks in the index do not have enough liquidity. This means some stocks

TABLE 6-1

Low-Cost Index Funds Benchmarked to the Wilshire 5000

Fund	Structure	Fee	Minimum	Symbol
Vanguard Total Stock Mkt.	Open-end	0.20	$3,000	VTSMX
Fidelity Spartan Total Mkt.	Open-end	0.24	$15,000	FSTMX
T. Rowe Price Total Equity Mkt.	Open-end	0.40	$2,500	POMIX
Schwab Total Stock Mkt.	Open-end	0.40	$2,500	SWTIX
Vanguard Total Stock VIPERs	ETF	0.15	None	VTI
Source: Morningstar Principia, Indexfunds.com				

in the index rarely trade in enough volume to be bought by an
index fund. In all fairness the Wilshire 5000 was not designed to be
an "investable" index. Rather its original goal was to measure the
wealth of the U.S. market in aggregate. Since the Wilshire 5000 cannot be fully replicated in an actual portfolio, an index fund manager will work around the problem by sampling the smaller stock universe. The logic behind sampling is to buy an assortment of liquid
small stocks representing different industries, trying to develop a
portfolio that replicates the movement of the small-cap portion of
the index without owning all stocks in the group. The typical index
fund benchmarked to the Wilshire 5000 is composed of about 3100
stocks. Table 6–1 lists low-cost index funds benchmarked to the
Wilshire 5000 index.

Wilshire 4500

Size and Style: Mid- and Small-Cap/Blend   The Wil-
shire 4500 measures the performance of only the small- and mid-cap
stocks in the Wilshire 5000. Basically, it is the Wilshire 5000 Index
with all the companies in the Standard & Poor's 500 Index removed.
The approximately 6000 stocks left over provide an excellent benchmark for "extended" index funds. The Wilshire 4500 was created on
December 31, 1983.

TABLE 6-2

Low-Cost Index Funds Benchmarked to the Wilshire 4500

Fund	Structure	Fee	Minimum	Symbol
Vanguard Extended Mkt.	Open-end	0.25	$3,000	VEXMX
Fidelity Spartan Ext. Mkt.	Open-end	0.24	$15,000	FSEMX
T. Rowe Price Ext. Eq. Mkt.	Open-end	0.40	$2,500	PEXMX
Vanguard Extended Mkt. VIPER	ETF	0.15	None	VXF
Source: Morningstar Principia				

Membership and Exclusions

◆ All stocks in the Wilshire 5000 excluding stocks in the S&P 500.

Adjustments and Maintenance

◆ Issues spun off from the S&P 500 Index members will be added to the Wilshire 4500 as soon as prudently possible if they are not staying in the S&P 500.

◆ All else is the same as the Wilshire 5000 (Table 6–2).

Wilshire Style Indexes

<u>Size and Style: Large- and Small-Cap/Value and Growth</u>
The Wilshire Style Indexes were created in 1996 by separating the Wilshire 5000 into four capitalization groups (large, mid-cap, small, and micro-cap) and then dividing the large, mid, and small issues by capitalization into equally weighted growth and value indexes. Wilshire divides stocks between growth and value based on an analysis of price-to-book ratio and projected price-to-earnings ratio. A stock is either in the growth or value category, but not both.

There are only a few index funds benchmarked to the Wilshire Style Indexes, and Wilshire Associates manages most of them. Ordinarily, I would not have listed these Wilshire funds in this section because the fees are relatively high compared to most broad U.S.

TABLE 6-3

Index Funds Benchmarked to the Wilshire Style Indexes

Fund	Structure	Fee	Minimum	Symbol
Wilshire Target Large Growth	Open-end	0.85	$2500	DTLGX
Wilshire Target Large Value	Open-end	1.01	$2500	DTLVX
Wilshire Target Small Growth	Open-end	1.56	$2500	DTSGX
Wilshire Target Small Value	Open-end	1.17	$2500	DTSVX
Source: Morningstar Principia				

stock index funds. However, since these are the only funds benchmarked to the Wilshire Style Indexes, Table 6–3 presents the list.

Russell U.S. Equity Indexes

In 1984 Frank Russell & Company of Tacoma, Washington, created the Russell family of stock indexes. Russell calculates the value of 21 indexes daily, from the largest 200 growth companies to the smallest capitalization value companies. Today, more than $180 billion is invested in funds modeling Russell's 21 U.S. stock indexes. Monthly return data are available starting from January 1979.

Each year Russell constructs its indexes by ranking the 3000 largest U.S. stocks using their market values on May 31. These 3000 stocks are selected and ranked strictly by size, and the list does not reflect any subjectivity. Although companies that started in the index at the beginning of a year may leave the index during the year due to mergers or bankruptcies, replacements for these securities do not occur until the annual rebalancing.

The Russell U.S. indexes are market cap-weighted and include only common stocks domiciled in the United States and its territories. The indexes represent the free-float value of U.S. stocks rather than all shares outstanding. Free-float means including only shares of stock available for purchase by the public and does not include shares that are closely held by insiders. Closely held stock can account for up to 80 percent of a small publicly traded company.

All Russell indexes are subsets of the Russell 3000 Index, which represents approximately 98 percent of the investable free-float U.S.

equity market. This is a summary of how these indexes are constructed. A more in-depth description of the index methodology is available at the Frank Russell & Company Web site at www. Russell.com.

Membership

- Rank the U.S. common stocks from largest to smallest market capitalization at each annual reconstitution period (May 31).
- The top 3000 stocks are included in the Russell 3000 Index.
- The largest 1000 stocks are included in the Russell 1000 Index.
- The next 2000 stocks are included in the Russell 2000 Index.

Exclusions

- Stocks trading below $1 on May 31 of each year.
- Pink sheet and bulletin board stocks.
- Closed-end mutual funds, limited partnerships, royalty trusts.
- Berkshire Hathaway, Inc. (considered an investment company).
- Non-U.S. domiciled stocks, foreign stocks, ADRs.

Adjustments and Maintenance

- Adjust shares outstanding for cross-ownership and privately held shares to reflect shares available for trading.
- Adjust book value due to FAS 106 & 109 writeoffs when determining price-to-book ratio for style classification.
- Stocks deleted between reconstitution dates are not replaced.
- Spin-offs are the only additions between reconstitution dates.
- Dividends are reinvested on the ex-date.

Determining Style Index Membership

- Rank each stock in the Russell 1000 and Russell 2000 by price-to-book ratio and forecast long-term earnings growth averages.

◆ Combine variables to create a composite value score (CVS) for each stock.

◆ Rank the stocks by their CVS and apply a mathematical formula to the distribution to determine style membership weights. Of the stocks, 70 percent are classified as all value or all growth, and 30 percent are weighted proportionately to both value and growth and are listed in both indexes.

Russell 3000 Index

<u>Size and Style: Total Market/Blend</u>   The Russell 3000 Index measures the performance of the 3000 largest U.S. companies based on total market capitalization, which represents approximately 98 percent of the investable U.S. equity market. As of May 31, 2001, the average market capitalization of companies included in the index was approximately $4.6 billion, and the median market capitalization was approximately $732 million. The companies had a total market capitalization range of approximately $487 billion (largest) to $147 million (smallest).

The TIAA-CREF Equity Index Fund is an open-end mutual fund that tracks the Russell 3000 Index. Barclays Global Investors offers an ETF that is also benchmarked to the index. Both funds began trading in the spring of 2000. I anticipate there will be more funds tracking the Russell 3000 as the benchmark gains popularity.

Barclays Global Investors is the only mutual fund company that has an index fund benchmarked to the Russell 3000 Index (Table 6–4). However, I anticipate there will be more in the future as the Russell 3000 Index gains popularity.

TABLE 6-4

Low-Cost Index Funds Benchmarked to the Russell 3000

Fund	Structure	Fee	Minimum	Symbol
TIAA-CREF Equity Index Fund	Open-end	0.26	$1,500	TCEIX
iShares Russell 3000	ETF	0.20	None	IWV
Source: Barclays Global Investors, TIAA-CREF				

TABLE 6-5

Low-Cost Index Russell 3000 Value and Growth Funds

Fund	Structure	Fee	Minimum	Symbol
iShares Russell 3000 Value	ETF	0.25	None	IWW
iShares Russell 3000 Growth	ETF	0.25	None	IWZ
Source: Barclays Global Investors				

Russell 3000 Value and Growth Indexes

Size and Style: Total Market/Value and Growth   The Russell 3000 Value Index measures the performance of those Russell 3000 Index companies with lower price-to-book ratios and lower forecasted growth values. The index represents 50 percent of the total market value of the Russell 3000. The stocks in this index are also members of either the Russell 1000 Value or the Russell 2000 Value indexes.

The Russell 3000 Growth Index measures the performance of those Russell 3000 Index companies with higher price-to-book ratios and higher forecasted growth values. The index represents 50 percent of the total market value of the Russell 3000. The stocks in this index are also members of either the Russell 1000 Growth or the Russell 2000 Growth indexes (Table 6–5).

Russell 1000 Index

Size and Style: Large- and Mid-Cap/Blend   The Russell 1000® Index measures the performance of the 1000 largest companies in the Russell 3000 Index, which represents approximately 92 percent of the total market capitalization of the Russell 3000 Index. As of the latest reconstitution, the average market capitalization was approximately $13 billion; the median market capitalization was approximately $3.8 billion. The smallest company in the index had an approximate market capitalization of $1.4 billion. The index represents approximately 89 percent of the total market value of the Russell 3000 (Table 6–6).

TABLE 6-6

Low-Cost Index Funds Benchmarked to the Russell 1000

Fund	Structure	Fee	Minimum	Symbol
Schwab 1000*	Open-end	0.47	$2500	SNXFX
iShares Russell 1000	ETF	0.15	None	IWB

Source: Barclays Global Investors, Morningstar
*The Schwab 1000 Fund is benchmarked to the Schwab 1000 Index®, which measures the performance of the 1000 largest publicly traded companies in the United States, with size determined by market capitalization. The fund differs slightly from the Russell 1000 in that it holds all the largest 1000 publicly traded U.S. stocks regardless of the types of security. In other words, the Schwab 1000 will hold investment companies such as Berkshire Hathaway, Inc. For all practical purposes the Russell 1000 Index and the Schwab 1000 are the same index. There has been a 99 percent correlation of returns between the two since 1995.

Russell 1000 Value Index and Growth Indexes

Size and Style: Large- and Mid-Cap/Value and Growth

The Russell 1000 Value Index measures the performance of those Russell 1000 companies with lower price-to-book ratios and lower forecasted growth values. The index represents 50 percent of the total market value of the Russell 1000.

The Russell 1000 Growth Index measures the performance of those Russell 1000 companies with higher price-to-book ratios and higher forecasted growth values. The index represents 50 percent of the total market value of the Russell 1000 (Table 6–7).

Of the stocks in the Russell 1000, 30 percent have a percentage weighting in both indexes, so these indexes do not make a pure large-cap growth or large-cap value index fund.

TABLE 6-7

Low-Cost Index Funds Benchmarked to the Russell 1000 Value and Growth

Fund	Structure	Fee	Minimum	Symbol
iShares Russell 1000 Value	ETF	0.20	None	IWD
iShares Russell 1000 Growth	ETF	0.20	None	IWV

Source: Barclays Global Investors

TABLE 6-8

Low-Cost Index Funds Benchmarked to the Russell 2000 Index

Fund	Structure	Fee	Minimum	Symbol
Vanguard Small Co. Index	Open-end	0.25	$3000	NAESX
Summit Apex Russell SmCp	Open-end	0.35	$5000	SARSX
Schwab Small Cap Index*	Open-end	0.49	$2500	SWSMX
iShares Russell 2000	ETF	0.20	None	IWM

Source: Barclays Global Investors, Morningstar
*The Schwab Small Cap Index Fund is benchmarked to the second largest 1000 publicly traded companies in the United States, with size determined by market capitalization. The benchmark fund differs from the Russell 2000 in that it basically tracks only the 1000 largest stocks in the Russell 2000 Index. Although not a perfect fit, the Schwab Small Cap Index Fund has had a 90 percent correlation with the Russell 2000 since 1995 with nearly identical risk.

Russell 2000 Index

Size and Style: Small-Cap/Blend   The Russell 2000 Index measures the performance of the 2000 smallest companies in the Russell 3000 Index, which represent approximately 8 percent of the total market capitalization of the Russell 3000 Index. As of the latest reconstitution, the average market capitalization was approximately $530 million; the median market capitalization was approximately $410 million. The largest company in the index had an approximate market capitalization of $1.4 billion. The index represents approximately 11 percent of the total market value of the Russell 3000 (Table 6–8).

Russell 2000 Value and Growth Indexes

Size and Style: Small-Cap/Value and Growth   The Russell 2000 Value Index measures the performance of those Russell 2000 companies with lower price-to-book ratios and lower forecasted growth values. The index represents 50 percent of the total market value of the Russell 2000.

The Russell 2000 Growth Index measures the performance of those Russell 2000 companies with higher price-to-book ratios and higher forecasted growth values. The index represents 50 percent of the total market value of the Russell 2000 (Table 6–9).

TABLE 6—9

Low-Cost Index Funds Benchmarked to the Russell 2000
Value and Growth

Fund	Structure	Fee	Minimum	Symbol
iShares Russell 2000 Value	ETF	0.25	None	IWN
iShares Russell 2000 Growth	ETF	0.25	None	IWO
Source: Barclays Global Investors				

Of the stocks in the Russell 2000, 30 percent have a percentage
weighting in both indexes, so these indexes do not make a pure
small-cap growth or small-cap value index fund.

Russell Top 200 Index

Size and Style: Very Large/Blend   The Russell Top 200®
Index measures the performance of the 200 largest companies in the
Russell 1000 Index, which represent approximately 75 percent of the
total market capitalization of the Russell 1000 Index. As of the latest
reconstitution, the average market capitalization was approximately $48 billion; the median market capitalization was approximately
$26 billion. The smallest company in the index had an approximate
market capitalization of $12 billion. There are currently no index
funds benchmarked to the Russell Top 200 Index; however, it bears
mentioning for future reference.

Russell Midcap Indexes

Size and Style: Midcap/Blend, Value, and Growth   The
Russell Midcap Indexes® measure the performance of the 800 smallest companies in the Russell 1000 Index, which represent approximately 25 percent of the total market capitalization of the Russell
1000 Index. As of the latest reconstitution, the average market capitalization was approximately $4 billion; the median market capi-
talization was approximately $2.9 billion. The largest company in
the index had an approximate market capitalization of $12 billion.

TABLE 6-10

Low-Cost Index Funds Benchmarked to the Russell Midcap Indexes

Fund	Structure	Fee	Minimum	Symbol
iShares Russell Midcap	ETF	0.20	None	IWR
iShares Russell Midcap Value	ETF	0.25	None	IWS
iShares Russell Midcap Growth	ETF	0.25	None	IWP
Source: Barclays Global Investors				

The Russell Midcap Index is evenly divided by capitalization into value and growth indexes. The Russell Midcap Value Index measures the performance of those Russell mid-cap companies with lower price-to-book ratios and lower forecasted growth values. The stocks are also members of the Russell 1000 Value Index. The Russell Midcap Growth Index measures the performance of those Russell mid-cap companies with higher price-to-book ratios and higher forecasted growth values. The stocks are also members of the Russell 1000 Growth Index.

The Russell Midcap Indexes are not widely followed, and I do not expect them to be embraced by individual investors. However, like the Wilshire Style Indexes, there are a few index mutual funds benchmarked to the Russell Midcap Indexes, so Table 6–10 is warranted.

Dow Jones U.S. Equity Indexes

Dow Jones launched its first stock indicator in 1884 with an index composed of 12 railroad stocks. This indicator would later become known as the Dow Jones Transportation Average®. In 1896 the company introduced the Dow Jones Industrial Average (the Dow), the world's most widely followed stock market indicator. The Dow is comprised of 30 blue-chip U.S. stocks and is quoted in thousands of newspapers, magazines, and television and radio shows. It flashes on millions of computer screens everyday.

The Dow is not the only index tracked by the Dow Jones Company. The firm has created more than 3000 U.S. and international indexes, including industry indexes. Several of those indexes are replicated in niche index funds. This chapter looks at only the broad U.S. Dow Jones Total Market Index, the DJ Large and Small Growth and Value Indexes, and the not very broad Dow Jones Industrial Average.

Dow Jones U.S. Total Market Index

Size and Style: Total Market/Blend   Until 2000 the oldest and best known name in market indexes had no broad market index fund. Therefore, that year Dow Jones launched the U.S. Total Market Index. The U.S. Total Market Index represents the top 95 percent of the free-float value of the U.S. stock market. By free-float Dow Jones means counting only those stocks available for purchase by the public, rather than closely held shares and other illiquid positions.

The Dow Jones U.S. Total Market Index holds about 1850 stocks, making it a smaller list than either the Wilshire 5000 or the Russell 3000. Nevertheless, Dow Jones subdivided the index by size and style, similar to the Wilshire and Russell. Dow Jones labeled the top 70 percent of stocks in the U.S. Total Market as large-cap, the next 20 percent as mid-cap, and the remaining 5 percent as small-cap. The Total Market Index is also divided into growth, value, and "neutral" slices based on book value and price-to-earnings ratios. The Dow Jones Company is the only index provider that recognizes a neutral style, also referred to as core. Prices of the indexes have been backdated to January 1, 1987 (Table 6–11).

TABLE   6–11

Low-Cost Index Funds Benchmarked to the DJ Total U.S. Market Index

Fund	Structure	Fee	Minimum	Symbol
iShares DJ U.S. Total Market	ETF	0.20	None	IYY
Source: Barclays Global Investors				

Membership

- The company must be headquartered in the United States.
- The issue must trade in the United States.
- The issue must be the primary equity issue for the company.
- Equity issues include common stocks and REITs.
- Shares outstanding for multiple classes of stock are combined into the primary issue's shares outstanding to reflect the total market capitalization of the firm if both issues are eligible.

Exclusions

- Thinly traded stocks are excluded by the assumption that they do not have liquidity.
- Nondomiciled U.S. stocks, foreign issues, and ADRs are excluded.
- Mutual funds, closed-end funds, ETFs, limited partnerships, and Berkshire Hathaway, Inc. are excluded.

Adjustments and Maintenance

- Additions to the index are made quarterly, effective the Monday after the third Friday in March, June, September, and December.
- Initial public offerings will generally be added at the beginning of the quarter.
- Issues spun off from index members will be added to the index as soon as prudently possible.
- A security will be removed from the index on the day it fails index inclusion guidelines.
- A security will be removed from the index on the day it stops trading but may reenter the index when trading resumes.
- Stocks that are removed will not be replaced until quarterly balancing.
- Shares outstanding may be adjusted to reflect corporate events during the month if they affect 10 percent or more of the stock; otherwise, shares outstanding are updated quarterly.

T A B L E   6–12

Low-Cost Index Funds Benchmarked to the DJ Industrial Average

Fund	Structure	Fee	Minimum	Symbol
Orbitex Focus 30 D Shares	Open-end	1.82	$2,500	OFTDX
Potomac Dow 30 Plus*	Open-end	1.50	$10,000	PDOWX
SPDR Diamonds	ETF	0.18	None	DIA

Source: Indexfunds.com
*The Potomac Dow 30 Plus fund is leveraged to produce a return that is approximately 125 percent the return of the DJIA.

Dow Jones Industrial Average

Size and Style: Large/Blend   No discussion of Dow Jones would be complete without a mention of the Dow Jones Industrial Average (DJIA) and the index funds that are benchmarked to it. The DJIA is a 30-stock index that is followed by more people around the world than any other stock market benchmark. Although the methodology used to construct the index is terribly outdated and the narrowness of the 30-stock portfolio makes it unsuitable for academic study or performance measurement, it nevertheless commands attention. For this reason, mutual fund companies have stepped up to the plate and created index funds that track DJIA performance.

I do not recommend buying index funds benchmarked to the DJIA because there are much better indexes available. That being said, a list of index funds benchmarked to the DJIA is provided in Table 6–12. Notice the expense ratios on a couple of these funds. They are designed for naive investors. Obviously, if you are going to buy a DJIA index fund, the SPDR Diamonds are the best deal.

Dow Jones Style Indexes

Large and Small/Growth and Value   One of the primary objectives of the Dow Jones Style Index® methodology is to create indexes that correctly distinguish among and thus accurately represent, large, mid-cap, small, growth, and value stocks. Starting

TABLE 6–13

Low-Cost Index Funds Benchmarked to the DJ U.S. Style Indexes

Fund	Structure	Fee	Minimum	Symbol
StreetTRACKS DJ Large Value	ETF	0.20	None	ELV
StreetTRACKS DJ Large Growth	ETF	0.20	None	ELG
StreetTRACKS DJ Small Value	ETF	0.20	None	DSG
StreetTRACKS DJ Small Growth	ETF	0.20	None	DSV

Source: Indexfunds.com

with the Dow Jones U.S. Total Stock Market Index, the top 70 percent of the index are divided into the large stocks, the next 20 percent are in the mid-cap index, and the remaining 5 percent are in the small-cap index. Each size index is then divided into growth, value, and core style indexes based on book value and price to earnings.

Dow Jones is trying to do investors a favor with their style methodology. Their decision to include a core style in addition to growth and value attempts to seek a purer growth and value index than Russell, Wilshire, or S&P. For investors who are seeking a more definitive growth or value, the Dow Jones Style Indexes may provide an answer. So far there are four funds that track the Dow Jones Style Indexes (Table 6–13).

Standard & Poor's U.S. Equity Indexes

There is more money benchmarked to the S&P 500 Index than all other index funds combined. So did I save the best for last? Not necessarily. All the index providers have their strengths and weaknesses, and S&P is no exception. Of the four index providers presented, Standard & Poor's has the most subjective stock selection methodology. As a result, the S&P indexes are not "all inclusive," and therefore, they do not represent the entire stock market.

Indexes created by Wilshire, Russell, and Dow Jones include at least 95 percent of the value of all stocks listed on U.S. exchanges, whereas S&P methodology includes less than 85 percent. The S&P indexes differ because of stricter selection criteria. Rather than use a straight computer selection model like the other providers, S&P uses a team of analysts to physically pick the stocks that go in their indexes. Because this is a subjective process, it is often said that S&P indexes are actively managed. The interesting question is: Does a human touch provide a better or worse investment result than an unconscious computer? Many people believe that a committee is a good idea. Others say that human subjectivity degrades the essence of an unbiased index. In my opinion it makes no difference. If you are going to put hundreds of stocks in an index, a monkey could pick them.

There is a second difference between S&P and other providers. S&P starts with subindexes and works up to a market index, whereas the other providers start with a market index and divide it into subindexes. For example, the Russell 3000 divides into the Russell 1000 Large-Cap and Russell 2000 Small-Cap Indexes. The S&P committee starts by selecting stocks for three indexes: the S&P 500 Large-Cap, S&P SmallCap 600, and the S&P MidCap 400. Then they pool the three indexes to create the S&P 1500 SuperComposite. In January 2002 S&P launched the new S&P 1000 Index, which folds together only the S&P MidCap 400 and the S&P SmallCap 600. S&P officials said the new S&P 1000 Index was introduced in response to demand by "investors who want to allocate assets between large capitalization stocks and the rest of the investable market."

General Criteria for S&P U.S. Index Membership   All S&P indexes consist of hand-selected stocks based on the discretion of the Index Investment Committee. This committee examines several criteria when looking for index candidates (i.e., trading analysis, liquidity, ownership, fundamental analysis, market capitalization, and sector representation). Even then the criteria to get in an index are guidelines and not rules. Occasionally, the committee may go outside the guidelines to include a stock.

Membership
   ◆ The company must be headquartered in the United States, although eight companies have been grandfathered into the S&P 500 (Royal Dutch Petroleum, Unilever N.V., Nortel Networks, Alcan Aluminum, Inco, Placer Dome, Seagram, and Barrick Gold).

- REITs were included after October 10, 2001.
- The issue must trade in the United States.
- The common stock must be the primary equity issue for the company.
- Shares outstanding for multiple classes of stock are combined into the primary issue's shares outstanding to reflect the total market capitalization of the firm.
- The company must show at least four quarters of net income, unless there is a loss due to merger or acquisition.

Exclusions

- Exclude stocks that trade less than 0.3 percent of shares on average each month on the New York Stock Exchange and American Exchange and trade less than 0.6 percent of shares outstanding per month on the NASDAQ.
- Nondomiciled U.S. stocks, foreign issues, and ADRs are excluded.
- ETFs, closed-end funds, and tracking stocks are excluded.
- There are no IPOs less than 6 months old in the S&P 400 and 600, and no IPOs less than 12 months old in the S&P 500.
- S&P will analyze a stock's price history in an effort to limit the single-digit stocks in the indexes.
- No single entity can own more than 50 percent of the stock in a company, and multiple entities cannot hold more than 60 percent, excluding mutual funds.

Adjustments and Maintenance

- The S&P indexes are dynamic. Additions to the indexes can occur on an ongoing basis, but most changes are normally made once per month.
- Issues spun off from index members will be added to the index as soon as prudently possible if they qualify.
- A security will be removed from the index on the day it stops trading but may reenter the index when trading resumes.
- Shares outstanding will be adjusted to reflect corporate events during the month.

♦ Although the committee has set certain market capitalization guidelines for each index, change in market capitalization is not an adequate criterion for removing a company
from an index. There are typically over 100 stocks in each
index that are trading above or below the guidelines at any
time.

S&P 500 Index

<u>Size and Style: Large/Blend</u>   The S&P 500 Index is widely
regarded as the professional standard for measuring the performance of the U.S. stock market. The index is used by 97 percent of
money managers and pension plan sponsors as a benchmark in one
form or another. It is included in the government's Index of Leading Economic Indicators and is widely followed by economists as
an early indicator of consumer confidence. The amount of money
indexed to the S&P 500 is enormous. More than $1 trillion is invest-
ed in S&P 500 Index funds by individual investors and institutions
(Table 6–14).

A popular misconception about the S&P 500 is that it contains
only large companies. Actually, there is not a market capitalization
limit for inclusion in the index. The guiding principle is that the
company must be a leader in an important industry, but that does
not mean the company chosen to represent the industry has to be

TABLE   6–14

Low-Cost Index Funds Benchmarked to the S&P 500 Index

Fund	Structure	Fee	Minimum	Symbol
Vanguard 500 Index	Open-end	0.18	$3,000	VFINX
USAA S&P 500	Open-end	0.18	$3,000	USSPX
SSgA S&P 500 Index	Open-end	0.18	$10,000	SVSPX
Fidelity Spartan 500 Index	Open-end	0.19	$10,000	FSMKX
IShares S&P 500 Index	ETF	0.09	None	IVV
SPDR S&P 500	ETF	0.17	None	SPY

Source: Indexfunds.com

highly valued. Visteon (VC), a spin-off from Ford, was added to the S&P 500 when it had a market cap of only $1.6 billion. That barely earns the company a mid-cap status. Nevertheless, Visteon made it into the S&P 500 because sales were similar to other companies in the index and it was considered a leader in the auto parts industry. Since most leading companies are large, the average market value for an S&P 500 stock is about $25 billion compared to $2.5 billion for the S&P 400 MidCap 400 Index and $700 million for the S&P Small-Cap 600 Index.

Companies turnover in the S&P 500 at about 5 percent per year. That is the average from its inception in 1926 until 2001. Companies exit the S&P 500 mostly through mergers and acquisitions, and a few fall out of favor. The Index Investment Committee usually replaces a void in the index within 30 days.

S&P 500/Barra Value Index

Size and Style: Large/Value   In 1992 Standard & Poor's and Barra® began a collaboration to produce growth and value subsets of S&P's equity indexes. Companies in the S&P 500 are split into two groups based on price-to-book ratio to create growth and value indexes. The Value Index contains companies with lower price-to-book ratios, and the Growth Index contains those with higher price-to-book ratios (Tables 6–15 and 6–16). The indexes are equal weight, so each represents approximately 50 percent of the market cap of the S&P 500. Barra rebalances the Growth and Value Indexes every 6 months, on or about January 1 and July 1, using November 30 and May 31 data. The exact rebalance date is selected and announced by Standard & Poor's well in advance.

TABLE 6–15

Low-Cost Index Funds Benchmarked to the S&P 500 Value Index

Fund	Structure	Fee	Minimum	Symbol
Vanguard Value Index	Open-end	0.22	$3000	VIVAX
iShares S&P 500/Barra Value	ETF	0.18	None	IVW

TABLE 6—16

Low-Cost Index Funds Benchmarked to the S&P 500 Growth
Index

Fund	Structure	Fee	Minimum	Symbol
Vanguard Growth Index	Open-end	0.22	$3,000	VIGRX
iShares S&P 500/Barra Growth	ETF	0.18	None	IVE

S&P 500/Barra Growth Index

Size and Style: Large /Growth   The S&P 500 / Barra Growth
Index is constructed using the same methodology as the Value Index and includes all stocks not included in the Value Index. Both indexes are equal weight, so each represents approximately 50 percent
of the market cap of the S&P 500. The Growth Index contains those
with higher price-to-book ratios.

S&P 400 MidCap Indexes

Size and Style: MidCap/Growth and Value   More than
$25 billion is indexed to the S&P MidCap 400. This index is used by
most mutual funds and pension plan sponsors to measure the performance of the mid-size company segment of the U.S. market.
Companies in the S&P 400 are split into two groups based on price-
to-book ratio to create Growth and Value Indexes (Table 6–17). The
Value Index contains companies with lower price-to-book ratios,
and the Growth Index contains those with higher price-to-book ratios. The indexes are equal weight, so each represents approximately 50 percent of the market cap of the S&P 400.

S&P 600 SmallCap Indexes

Size and Style: SmallCap/Growth and Value   The S&P
SmallCap 600 Index is gaining wide acceptance as the preferred
benchmark for both active and passive small-cap managers due to

TABLE 6—17

Low-Cost Index Funds Benchmarked to the S&P 400
MidCap Index

Fund	Structure	Fee	Minimum	Symbol
Vanguard MidCap Index	Open-end	0.25	$3,000	VIMSX
California Invmt S&P MidCap	Open-end	0.40	$5,000	SPMIX
MidCap SPDRs	ETF	0.25	None	MDY
IShares S&P 400 Index	ETF	0.20	None	IJH

Index Funds Benchmarked to the S&P 400/Barra MidCap
Value and Growth Indexes

Fund	Structure	Fee	Minimum	Symbol
iShares S&P 400/ Barra Value	ETF	0.25	None	IJJ
iShares S&P 400/ Barra Growth	ETF	0.25	None	IJK

its low turnover and high liquidity. Approximately $8 billion is indexed to the S&P SmallCap 600. Companies in the S&P SmallCap 600 are split into two groups based on price-to-book ratio to create Growth and Value Indexes (Table 6–18). The Value Index contains companies with lower price-to-book ratios, and the Growth Index contains those with higher price-to-book ratios. The indexes are equal weight, so each represents approximately 50 percent of the market cap of the S&P SmallCap 600.

S&P SuperComposite 1500 Index

Size and Style: Total Market/Blend Combining the S&P 500, MidCap 400, and SmallCap 600 Indexes together makes up the S&P SuperComposite 1500. This index represents 87 percent of the total U.S. equity market capitalization (as measured by the Wilshire 5000). There are currently no index funds offered that are benchmarked to the SuperComposite 1500, but I remain hopeful.

TABLE 6–18

Low-Cost Index Funds Benchmarked to the S&P 600
SmallCap Index

Fund	Structure	Fee	Minimum	Symbol
Vanguard Tax-Mgd. Small Cap	Open-end	0.19	$10,000	VTMSX
Galaxy II Small Co. Index	Open-end	0.41	$2,500	ISCIX
Dreyfus Small Cap Index	Open-end	0.50	$2,500	DISSX
iShares S&P 600 Index	ETF	0.20	None	IJR

Index Funds Benchmarked to the S&P 600/Barra SmallCap
Value Index

Fund	Structure	Fee	Minimum	Symbol
Vanguard Small Co. Value	Open-end	0.25	$3,000	VISVX
iShares S&P 600/Barra Value	ETF	0.25	None	IJS

Index Funds Benchmarked to the S&P 600/Barra SmallCap
Growth

Fund	Structure	Fee	Minimum	Symbol
Vanguard Small Co. Growth	Open-end	0.25	$3,000	VISGX
iShares S&P 600/Barra Growth	ETF	0.25	None	IJT

S&P 100 Index (OEX)

<u>Size and Style: Large/Blend</u>   The S&P 100 Stock Index is
better known by its ticker symbol OEX. It is a measure of the largest
U.S. stocks. This index is a subset of the S&P 500 and is used mainly by institutions that want to hedge a large-cap U.S. stock portfolio. The S&P 100 is a market capitalization-weighted index that is
made up of 100 major blue-chip stocks across diverse industry
groups. The index represents approximately 40 percent of the market value of all listed U.S. equities. The only index fund benchmarked to the S&P 100 Index is the iShares S&P 100 Index Fund,
symbol OEF.

CHAPTER SUMMARY

This chapter gave you a comprehensive overview of the major U.S. equity indexes and examples of low-cost index funds benchmarked to those indexes. There are many similarities and several differences among the Wilshire, Russell, Dow Jones, and Standard & Poor's U.S. stock index methodology. Each index structure has it good points and less desirable points. However, one methodology is not better than another; they are only different. In the end, it is very likely that the performance of all competing U.S. stock averages will be very close. I am fond of saying "All roads lead to Rome" when you are selecting an index provider. I do recommend selecting one index provider and using only their indexes. That will ensure there is no overlap of stock holdings and will help you organize your portfolio according to one system.

This chapter included many examples of index funds that are benchmarked to broad U.S. equity indexes. These samples do not represent a complete list of index funds available to the public. For a complete list of index funds and their benchmarks, visit Index-funds.com or contact the fund providers listed in Appendix A.

CHAPTER 7

U.S. Sector
Index Funds

Key Concepts

- There are differences in industry classification systems.
- Some index funds are benchmarked to industries.
- Real estate investment trust index funds are indirect investments in real properties.
- Socially responsible index funds exclude companies that do not pass certain social criteria screens.

"**D**ivide and conquer" is an ideal strategy in war, but it is a questionable tactic for index fund investors. Nevertheless, this chapter explains how investment firms divide the stock market by industry classification and how mutual fund companies have created a number of index funds benchmarked to those classifications. Industry sector investing has tremendous appeal because of the large potential rewards, but the risk of a loss is also magnified. Proceed with caution.

The stock market is made up of thousands of individual companies. Without a way of classifying stocks, the market would be a quagmire of names and symbols. Classifying stocks by industries makes it easier for researchers to study different parts of the market and to gauge the movement of capital from one industry to another. In addition, new technology often creates new companies, which are financed in part by an issuance of common stock. The listing of new companies often leads to the formation of new industries sectors and subsectors. At the same time new industries are created, established industries can fade away. The idea of sector fund investing is to anticipate which industry sector will get the money next and to benefit from that cash.

INDUSTRY CLASSIFICATION SYSTEMS

There are several ways competing investment firms slice and dice index data to create industry sectors. Although there are some differences in the methodology, in the final analysis the difference in industry classification systems is not drastic. They all hold 10 or 11 basic industry groups, and the names of those industry groups are fairly consistent. The big difference in the competing classification systems lies mainly in the subgroups. In my opinion, there is no need for individual investors to become too concerned with the details of an industry classification. Just pick one group of index funds and stick with it.

There are three industry classification systems used by most index fund providers. These are the Dow Jones classification structure, the "old" S&P U.S. industry classification system (now run by Merrill Lynch), and the "new" S&P global industry classification standard (GICS). Why are there two S&P systems? In early 1998 S&P and Merrill Lynch created the first U.S. industry classification system designed for specific use by index funds. Later that year State Street launched a group of nine Select Sector SPDR Trusts, which were benchmarked to the S&P industry sectors.

Since their introduction, the Select Sector SPDR Trusts have surpassed State Street's most optimistic exceptions. Unfortunately, it quickly became apparent that the original S&P classification system had structural limitations and was not going to meet the needs of a growing global marketplace. In 2000, with the help of Morgan Stanley Capital International (MSCI), S&P reorganized its industry standards to better align with the global economy. In an attempt to reduce the turmoil of reorganization, a guideline was established to ensure that at least 75 percent of the companies fell into the same industry group as they did under the old system. In addition, the new industry sectors had to be at least 85 percent correlated with the old sectors. S&P made these changes and fully implemented GICS in January 2002.

Despite the restructuring guidelines, a move to GICS represented a major problem for the Select Sector SPDR Trusts. It was not practical for the funds to switch because of trading costs and tax implications. The only solution was to continue under the old system, and that meant someone needed to continue the old system. Starting in January 2002, Merrill Lynch took over the responsibilities of providing S&P sector data using the old classification system. That gave the Select Sector SPDR Trusts an index to benchmark. Then, in June 2002, Merrill Lynch announced changes to the classification system, which affected 25 percent of the companies. They are now aligned more closely with the new GICS. It is still okay to use the Select Sector SPDR Trusts as long as you stick with that series of funds. In any event make sure you understand which classification system your funds are following.

In this chapter we compare the three major industry sector providers and review index funds that are benchmarked against their indexes. This discussion of index providers will help you select a sector index fund series that is right for you. In addition, we will look at index funds outside of the basic industry sectors such as real estate investment trust index funds and a few niche markets.

"Old-Style" S&P U.S. Industry Classification

The old Standard & Poor's industry classification system began with the broad S&P 1500 Index (see Chapter 6). The S&P 1500 Index was unbundled into 11 economic sectors and 115 industry groups. Companies were added or removed from sectors as they entered or left the S&P 1500. There were more than 20 sector index funds benchmarked to the S&P sectors and groups. The S&P sectors were as follows, with examples of industry groups:

1. **Materials**—mining/metals, paper, forest products, chemicals
2. **Consumer Cyclical**—retailing, apparel, department stores, leisure
3. **Consumer Services**—publishing, media, hotels, restaurants
4. **Consumer Stables**—food, beverage, tobacco, home products

5. **Energy**—oil and gas exploration, refining, equipment and services

6. **Financials**—banks, financial services, property and life insurance

7. **Health Care**—health insurance, care providers, drugs, medical products

8. **Industrial**—defense, aerospace, machinery, manufacturing

9. **Technology**—chips, hardware, software, communication equipment

10. **Transportation**—automobiles, airlines, railroads, trucking

11. **Utilities**—electric utilities, natural gas utilities, phones, wireless

When Merrill Lynch took over management of the old S&P industry indexes in January 2002, they set out to change them. In June 2002 Merrill Lynch implemented changes to the classification system, which affected 25 percent of the companies. The indexes are now aligned more closely with the new GICS.

There are several low-cost index funds benchmarked to the old S&P industry classification standard, which were converted to the new Merrill system. The most popular are Select Sector SPDR Trusts managed by State Street Global Advisors. These exchange-traded funds can be bought and sold like a stock anytime the American Stock Exchange is open. Following is a list of the nine Select Sector SPDRs that are available. Notice that three of the funds combine other related sectors together: Consumer Discretionary includes autos, while industrials includes airlines, rail, and shipping. Consumer stables includes media, publishing, and other consumer services. Technology includes telecom. The fee quoted in Table 7–1 is based on 12 months ending September 30, 2000.

The value of each industry group floats with the market, so there can be huge swings in industry valuation. Figure 7-1 illustrates the changes that can occur in industry group valuations over time. Using perfect hindsight, investors would have significantly outperformed the S&P 500 if they bought only technology and financial stocks since 1980. Of course hindsight is 20/20, and trying

TABLE 7-1

Select SPDR ETFs

Select Sector SPDR Funds	Symbol	Fee
Materials	XLB	0.43
Health care	XLV	0.42
Consumer stables with services	XLP	0.42
Consumer discretionary with autos	XLY	0.43
Energy	XLE	0.41
Financial	XLF	0.44
Industrial with transportation	XLI	0.44
Technology with telecom	XLK	0.42
Utilities	XLU	0.40

FIGURE 7-1

Changing Industry Sector Weights in the S&P 500

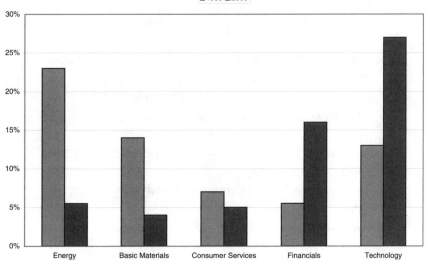

S&P 500 Sector Weights

■1980 ■2000

to guess the next hot industry is difficult, if not impossible. In addition, fortunes can quickly reverse. The S&P 500 weighting in the technology sector collapsed to about 15 percent in 2001. Regardless of the obvious risks, large gains in some sectors entice many investors to try and keep many magazines and investment newsletters in business.

The "New" S&P Global Industry Classification Standard

The new GICS system was developed in 1999 by collaboration between S&P and MSCI. GICS divides the S&P 1500 into 10 industry sectors, 23 industry groups, 59 industries, and 123 subindustries. The S&P/MSCI broad industry sectors are listed next, with examples of groups and industries. At first glance you will not notice much difference from the old system. But a closer look reveals that the consumer cyclical and transportation indexes are gone, and a few new industries, including consumer discretionary and telecommunication services, have been added.

1. **Basic Materials**—chemicals, paper and forest products, metals/mining
2. **Consumer Discretionary**—automobiles, apparel, leisure, media
3. **Consumer Stables**—food and drug retailing, household products
4. **Energy**—energy equipment, oil and gas exploration, refining
5. **Financials**—banks, financial services, all insurance
6. **Health Care**—managed care, medical products, drugs, biotech
7. **Industrials**—capital goods, transportation, building, aerospace, defense
8. **Information Technology**—hardware, software, communication equipment
9. **Telecommunication Services**—telecommunication services, wireless
10. **Utilities**—electric utilities, natural gas utilities

Since the S&P GICS system is new, there are no low-cost index U.S. sector funds benchmarked to the new standards yet. But I am sure we will not have to wait long.

The Dow Jones U.S. Industry Classification Structure

The Dow Jones U.S. sector indexes track the performance of U.S. stocks under the Dow Jones classification structure, which looks like a combination of the old S&P industry sectors and the new S&P GICS structure. Although many industry names are the same, there are important differences between the S&P structures and the Dow Jones system. For example, the old S&P consumer stables index includes pharmaceutical companies, whereas the Dow Jones includes the drug industry under the health care sector. Dow Jones has 10 economic sectors, 18 market sectors, 40 industry groups, and 68 subgroups. The 10 industry sectors are:

1. **Basic Materials**—mining, metals, forest and paper products, chemicals
2. **Consumer Cyclical**—autos, travel, airlines, retailers, leisure, homes
3. **Consumer Non-Cyclical**—food, beverage, cosmetics, home products
4. **Energy**—coal, oil and gas exploration, pipelines, equipment and services
5. **Financials**—banks, financial services, property and life insurance
6. **Health Care**—drugs, biotech, health insurers, health care providers
7. **Industrial**—defense, aerospace, heavy equipment, construction, shipping
8. **Technology**—hardware and software, communication equipment
9. **Telecommunications**—fixed line and wireless
10. **Utilities**—electric, natural gas utilities, water

In mid-2000 Barclays Global Investors introduced a series of 14 sector iShares based on the Dow Jones U.S. classification structure

TABLE 7-2

iShares Industry ETFs

iShares Dow Jones U.S. Sector Index Funds	Symbol	Fee
Basic Materials	IYM	0.60
Consumer Cyclical	IYC	0.60
Consumer Non-Cyclical	IYK	0.60
Energy	IYE	0.60
Financial	IYF	0.60
Health Care	IYH	0.60
Industrial Fund	IYJ	0.60
Technology Fund	IYW	0.60
Telecommunications	IYZ	0.60
Utilities Fund	IDU	0.60
Chemicals (group)	IYD	0.60
Financial Services (group)	IYG	0.60
Internet (subgroup)	IYV	0.60
Real Estate (subgroup)	IYR	0.60

(Table 7–2). Ten of these funds are benchmarked to the Dow Jones economic sectors, and the rest are benchmarked to lower industry groups and subgroups.

REAL ESTATE INVESTMENT TRUST INDEX FUNDS (REITS)

Real estate is a different asset class than common stock. Several years ago the only way you could invest in real estate was through direct ownership or a limited partnership, but not any more. The magic of modern finance now allows us to buy an assortment of real estate on the stock exchange by purchasing a real estate investment trust (REIT).

A REIT represents an indirect investment in a group of real properties. You basically buy common stock in a publicly traded management company whose purpose is to acquire and manage commercial real estate. The structure of a REIT is similar to a closed-end mutual fund. The market value of a REIT goes up and down with the supply and demand of REIT shares, even though the actual underlying value of the properties likely differs from the net asset value of the REIT fund. The difference between the market value of a REIT and the actual cash value of the property is known as a market premium or discount.

There are several unique features about REITs that make them desirable. First, management companies do not pay corporate income tax on any distributions to shareholders as long as 90 percent of the income is passed on to shareholders. At least 75 percent of the income must be from rents, mortgages, and the sale of properties. That makes the dividend income from REIT index funds higher than other equity index funds and also makes REIT funds an ideal choice for investors needing more income. In addition, holding REITs in a taxable account may provide certain tax benefits because the depreciation of properties within the investment is also passed on. This reduces the taxable portion of the dividend. Last, and most important, REITs add an asset class to a portfolio that acts differently than stocks and bonds, which helps reduce portfolio risk (see Chapter 14).

There are five real estate investment trust indexes that are used by index fund companies. The most popular indexes are the Morgan Stanley REIT Index, which covers about 109 companies, and the Wilshire REIT Index, which holds all publicly traded REITs. Next in line is the S&P REIT Index holding 100 companies. Fourth is the Dow Jones REIT Index, which holds 60 companies. Finally, the Cohen Steers Majors REIT Index barely qualifies as an index, with only 30 of the largest U.S. property REITs. All index providers select from U.S. REITs that trade on the NYSE, AMEX, and NASDAQ stock markets.

All of the indexes have different selection methodologies. All indexes include commercial property such as apartments and office buildings. Table 7–3 provides a guide to what is included in each index, and Table 7–4 lists a few low-cost REIT index funds and their benchmarks.

SPECIAL SECTOR FUNDS

Mutual fund companies are always looking for something new and exciting to offer investors. The number of index funds that can be

TABLE 7-3

REIT Indexes and What They Include

REIT Index	Health Care: Long-Term Care, Nursing Homes	Commercial Mortgage Lenders	Large Land Tracts and Farming
Morgan Stanley	No	No	No
Wilshire REIT	No	No	No
S&P REIT	Yes	No	Yes
Dow Jones REIT	Yes	Yes	Yes
Cohen & Steers Maj.	Yes	No	No

TABLE 7-4

Low Cost REIT Index Funds and Their Benchmarks

REIT Fund	REIT Benchmark	Symbol	Fee
Vanguard REIT	Morgan Stanley	VGSIX	0.33
streetTRACKS Wilshire REIT	Wilshire	RWR	0.25
iShares DJ U.S. Real Estate	Dow Jones	IYR	0.60
iShares Cohen & Steers Majors REIT Index	Cohen & Steers Majors Index	ICF	0.35

created is only limited by the number of indexes that are available, and there is no shortage of indexes.

Socially Responsible Index Funds

Some investors have a moral dilemma with index funds because they include companies that profit from the moral vices of tobacco, alcoholic beverages, and pornography. For those people, socially responsible index funds may be the answer. These funds seek to gain broad-based equity exposure while excluding companies that do not pass certain social criteria screens. Following is a list of low-cost index funds that fit the needs of many socially responsible investors. For more information on socially responsible investing, visit www.socialinvest.org.

The Vanguard Calvert Social Index Fund (VCSIX) is benchmarked to the Calvert Social Index. The benchmark starts with 1000 of the largest U.S. companies and screens for alcohol, tobacco, gambling, and nuclear-power businesses. In addition, Calvert's in-house social research department looks for companies that meet its standards on issues such as the environment, workplace issues, product safety, community relations, military weapons contracting, international operations, and human rights. The fund charges a 0.21 percent expense ratio for its retail shares.

The TIAA-CREF Social Choice Equity Fund (TCSCX) seeks a favorable long-term rate of return that tracks the investment performance of the U.S. stock market while giving special consideration to certain social criteria. This fund invests primarily in a diversified set of common stocks and attempts to track the return of the U.S. stock market as represented by its benchmark, the S&P 500 Index. The fund does not currently invest in companies that (a) fail to adhere to sound environmental policies; (b) have significant involvement in weapons manufacturing; (c) have significant interest in gaming or gambling; (d) operate in Northern Ireland without adopting the MacBride principles or complying with the Fair Employment Act of 1989 (Northern Ireland); (e) produce and market alcoholic beverages or tobacco products; or (f) produce nuclear energy. The fund charges a 0.77 percent per year fee, but 0.50 percent of the fee is waived through 2005.

The Domini Social Equity (DSEFX) Fund seeks long-term total return that corresponds with the performance of the Domini 400 Social Index, which consists of approximately 400 companies and is pegged to the DSI 400. The DSI 400 is governed by rules that exclude companies that engage in military weapons, alcohol, tobacco, gambling, and nuclear power. The Domini Social Equity Fund was launched in 1991 and is the granddaddy of socially responsible funds with more than $1 billion in assets. The fund has an expense ratio of 0.96 percent, which is rather steep.

The Bridgeway Ultra-Large 35 Index Portfolio (BRLIX) is a highly tax-efficient index fund investing in 35 of the largest publicly traded U.S. companies. Bridgeway is a no-load family of funds with a stringent code of ethics. All Bridgeway portfolios screen for tobacco. The management fee is only 0.15 percent per year.

Merrill Lynch HOLDRS, a QUASI-INDEX IDEA

In early 2000 Merrill Lynch introduced a new series of unit investment trusts called HOLDRS. These securities are exchange-traded funds that have creation and redemption characteristics similar to other ETFs described in Chapter 5. HOLDRS can come in handy because not all industry sectors and subsectors of S&P GICS are available using a full index fund (Table 7–5). There are several unique features of HOLDRS that investors should be aware of:

- HOLDRS invest in top 20 stocks of industry sectors and subsectors using the S&P Global Industry Classification Standards, but they do not fit the definition of a true index fund because they do not attempt to replicate an industry group.
- HOLDRS invest an equal amount of money in each stock in the industry sector.
- Existing HOLDRS units are not rebalanced to the index after mergers and acquisitions. When a fund expires, a new HOLDRS is created using new industry data. Old units can be rolled into new units without a tax consequence.
- Individual investors can turn in HOLDRS in round lots in 100 units and receive the underlying stock in return. This allows an investor to sell specific stocks in the fund rather than the entire fund.
- The owners of HOLDRS retain voting rights on the stocks in a fund. This means an investor in one HOLDRS unit will get 20 annual reports and voting proxies stuffed in their mailbox each year.

There are costs to buying and holding HOLDRS. First, these are exchange-traded funds; therefore, a brokerage commission is charged when you buy or sell HOLDRS units. Second, an annual $2 per 100-unit trustee and custody fee must be paid to the Bank of New York. This fee is typically paid out of stock dividends, but it does cut down your total return. Since the market price of HOLDRS units varies

TABLE 7-5

U.S. Industry Sector HOLDRS

HOLDRS Sector Funds	Symbol
Biotech	BBH
Broadband	BDH
Business to Business	BHH
Infrastructure	IIH
Internet	HHH
Internet Architecture	IAH
Oil Service	OIH
Pharmaceutical	PPH
Regional Bank	RKH
Retail	RTH
Semiconductor	SMH
Software	SWH
Telecom	TTH
Utilities	UTH
Wireless	WMH

from fund to fund, the $2 per 100 units fee can represent a varying cost. For example, the $2 charge is only 0.02 percent of a $100 per unit fund, but it is 0.4 percent of a $5 per unit fund. Third, if you redeem units for stock, there is a $10 per 100 unit round lot redemption fee.

CHAPTER SUMMARY

The allure of sector funds is tantalizing. All you have to do is figure out which industry investors will embrace next and get in front of an avalanche of cash. Unfortunately, the public is usually too late getting into a sector and too late getting out. My advice is to avoid most sector funds. This is a dangerous sandbox to play in.

From 1998 through early 2000, the investment world was bubbling in tech stocks, and Wall Street gladly fueled the fire. At the very peak of the craze, more growth and technology mutual funds came to the market than ever before. Investors who bit deep into these funds were nearly wiped out. Many hopeful early retirees will have to work many more years just to break even. The recent tech wreck was not the first time the public got hurt by "chasing the hot dot." In the mid-1990s a meltdown in emerging country funds claimed a number of greedy souls. Prior to that it was a boom/bust in small-cap stocks.

U.S. sector index funds may have a place in your investment portfolio, but a very small one. Part III of this book will help you discover how a moderate investment in industry sector funds may enhance your long-term returns. If you do invest in sector funds, it is better to pick funds that use one methodology (i.e., either the Dow Jones industry classification standard or one of the S&P industry classification standards). Selecting one sector index fund provider ensures that there is no overlap of stocks in the fund you own.

CHAPTER 8

Global and International Index Funds

Key Concepts

- ◆ Global index funds offer the broadest diversification.
- ◆ International index funds invest outside the United States.
- ◆ Regional index funds are confined to one part of the globe.
- ◆ Country funds are available but not recommended.

The global equity markets have grown dramatically over the last 25 years. In the early 1970s, the U.S. stock market accounted for over 70 percent of the global equity market. Today, U.S. companies account for only about 50 percent of the global marketplace despite compounding at double-digit returns during the period. International equity markets have grown in size, scope, and operational efficiency. As a result, several new and comprehensive global and international indexes have been formed to track the growth. In the last few years, the number of index funds benchmarked to the international markets has rapidly expanded.

There are several reasons to consider international exposure in a portfolio of stock index funds. Adding international index funds to an all-U.S. index fund portfolio historically lowered portfolio risk and increased potential return. Another reason for adding international stocks is that these investments carry currency exposure, which hedges an investor against devaluation in the U.S. dollar. Although some foreign markets have had long periods of poor performance, the reasons to invest in international markets have not changed.

Before presenting the specifics of the international index funds, it is important to clarify some terminology. *International* funds are composed of stocks whose corporate main headquarters are located outside the United States. International funds are often referred to as *foreign* funds and *overseas* funds, but they all mean the same thing. *Global* mutual funds invest in both international stocks and U.S. stocks.

There are two basic types of foreign markets. *Developed markets* are countries whose economy has advanced to the point where the per capita gross domestic product (GDP) is at least $10,000 per year. Examples of developed markets include Australia, Germany, Japan, and the United Kingdom. *Emerging markets* are countries that do not meet the GDP requirement yet still have a free-market system and an active stock exchange. Emerging markets can be divided into early stage and late stage depending on their stage in the evolution to a free-market system. Examples of early-stage emerging markets include Russia, Turkey, Poland, and Indonesia. Late-stage emerging markets are more developed and include Mexico, South Korea, and India.

This chapter presents global and international index fund investing starting from the broadest global indexes down to the individual countries. The presentation of index funds is in the following order:

1. Global market funds
2. International funds (multiregional, including emerging markets)
3. Regional funds (Pacific Rim, Europe, Latin America)
4. Individual country funds

GLOBAL MARKET INDEX FUNDS

If you are going to buy only one stock index fund, you might consider a global developed markets fund. Global index funds invest in the largest companies from around the world, including the United States. The three main providers of global index funds are Morgan Stanley Capital Investments (MSCI), Standard & Poor's (S&P),

and Dow Jones (DJ). S&P and MSCI often work together to compile international data. All of the index providers have at least one global index fund benchmarked to them.

The S&P Global 1200 Index

The S&P Global 1200 Index combines the features of a broad global portfolio with sufficient liquidity in the underlying equities, making the index ideally suited for index-related investment products. Unfortunately, there are no index funds benchmarked to this index yet. Nevertheless, this index needs to be explained before moving on.

The S&P Global 1200 Index covers approximately 70 percent of the global market capitalization. The index is comprised of six regional indexes: S&P 500, S&P/TSE 60 (Canada), S&P Latin America 40, S&P/TOPIX 150 (Japan), S&P Asia Pacific 100, and S&P Europe 350. An index committee made up of Standard & Poor's staff worldwide selects companies for inclusion in each index and maintains those indexes on a regular basis. The S&P Global 1200 is a free-float weighted index constructed in a joint effort with Morgan Stanley. Free-float means that large blocks of stock held by insiders do not count when valuing the company for inclusion in the index. For example, Bill Gates is a large private holder of Microsoft (MSFT) stock. The value of his personal stock does not count toward the valuation of MSFT shares for the Global 1200. Free-float also removes corporate cross-holdings, government ownership, strategic holders, and foreign investment restrictions.

An S&P Global 1200 Index Fund is expected to start trading by mid-2002. Barclays Global Investors will manage the new ETF. Exchange-traded funds are available covering the S&P 500, S&P/TSE 60, S&P Europe 350, S&P Latin America, and S&P/TOPIX 150. Thus, you can adjust your portfolio's regional weighting by combining, adding, or subtracting amounts of these funds.

The S&P Global 100 Index

The S&P Global 100 Index consists of 100 leading companies listed in the S&P Global 1200. The Global 100 does not represent the largest 100 companies, although it comes very close. Rather, S&P selects individual companies for the index based on strong fundamentals, industry leadership, market liquidity, and size. The companies themselves play no role in the selection process and are not consulted regarding their inclusion in an index.

The largest holding in the Global 100 Index is General Electric (GE), representing about 6 percent of the index at the end of 2001. The largest foreign holding is BP Amoco PLC, representing less than 3 percent. Currently, U.S. companies make up about 60 percent of the Global 100 Index. Much of the recent gain in U.S. exposure has been a result of the strength of the dollar. Currencies are not hedged in the S&P Global indexes. General information on the S&P 100 Index follows. For complete data visit the S&P Global Web site at www.spglobal.com.

- The S&P Global 100 Index measures the performance of 100 stocks in global markets.
- The S&P Global 100 Index provides diversification across countries, regions, and sectors.
- The market capitalization of the index is adjusted to reflect only those shares available to foreign investors.
- The S&P Global 100 Index provides both a price and total return series.
- Index values are provided real time every 15 seconds in U.S. dollars.
- All exchange rates are calculated live throughout the day. The index calculation begins with the opening of the first stock exchange and closes when the last stock exchange closes.
- A complete list of the S&P Global 100 members is available from Standard & Poor's and the iShares Web site (www.iShares.com).

One index fund is benchmarked to the Global 100 Index (Table 8–1).

TABLE 8–1

S&P Global 100 Index Funds	Type	Symbol	Fee
iShares S&P Global 100 Index	ETF	IOO	0.40

The Dow Jones Global Titans

The Dow Jones Global Titans is a global stock index consisting of 50 of the world's largest companies. To be included in the index, a stock must meet four criteria:

1. It must be a well-established company with a solid financial situation and a broad client base.
2. It must be well known to global investors for its long history of success or widely used products and services.
3. It must be a market leader in its industry with either a dominant position or a competitive advantage.
4. It must be among the largest of the blue-chip companies in the global arena.

Dow Jones uses a multifaceted process for selecting stocks. First, 5000 global stocks are screened for size and liquidity, creating a pool of 100 companies. Every company in the pool must derive some revenue from foreign operations. Next, the stocks are ranked by four fundamental factors that include asset size, book value, sales, and net profit. The stocks are then divided into industry groups and sorted by market value. The largest stocks in each industry group are determined based on a composite score of their market size and the four fundamental values. Fifty of the largest stocks are included in the Dow Jones Global Titans Index (Table 8–2).

Unlike S&P methodology, inclusion in the Global Titans in no way implies that Dow Jones believes the company is an attractive investment. Aside from the four basic valuation screens listed earlier, Dow Jones does not conduct an in-depth fundamental evaluation. Dow Jones methodology is more "size" oriented, whereas the S&P method is "value" oriented. Regardless of that fact, nearly all 50 stocks in the Dow Jones Global Titans are included in the S&P Global 100 Index.

TABLE 8–2

Dow Jones Global Titans Funds	Type	Symbol	Fee
StreetTRACKS DJ Global Titans	ETF	DGT	0.50

INTERNATIONAL INDEX FUNDS (MULTIREGIONAL)

International index funds invest in companies whose main head-quarters are outside the United States. These companies may do a substantial amount of business in the United States, or they may do none at all. Most Americans would be shocked to discover that a number of their favorite brand names are not owned by a U.S. company. For example, Skippy® peanut butter is owned by Unilever N.V., a Netherlands firm.

Many times a foreign company will buy a U.S. company to gain global market share and increase distribution. One of the best examples is Daimler-Chrysler. Even though a large volume of Daimler-Chrysler sales is to U.S. customers, Chrysler stock was delisted from the New York Stock Exchange, and Daimler-Chrysler stock is now listed on the German stock exchange.

Developed Market Index Funds

There are several indexes that track developed international markets. The most widely quoted index is the Morgan Stanley Capital International Europe, Australasia, and the Far East Index, better know as the MSCI EAFE® Index. This index is comprised of approximately 1000 large company stocks from 21 developed markets located in Europe and the Pacific Rim. The EAFE includes at least 85 percent of the market value of each industry group within each country. The best way to think of the EAFE index is as a big international S&P 500 Index that covers all developed countries, except the United States and Canada.

The EAFE is a float-adjusted index and includes only tradable securities (Table 8–3). Closely held blocks of stock and industry cross-holdings are not counted. Morgan Stanley does not attempt to control sector weights, country weights, or regional weights in the EAFE index. As a result, the value of the index can swing dramatically between industry sectors, countries, and regions. In 1990 Japan dominated the EAFE with a weight of 70 percent. However, due to a long bear market in Japan and a bull market in Europe, as of January 2002, Japan represents less than 22 percent of the index.

If you take the S&P Global 1200 discussed earlier, and minus the S&P 500, you get the S&P International 700. In the spring of 2002,

TABLE 8-3

Low-Cost EAFE Index Funds

EAFE Index Fund Name	Type	Symbol	Fee	Min
Fidelity Spartan Int'l. Index	Open-end	FSIIX	0.25	$15,000
Vanguard Developed Markets	Open-end	VDMIX	0.31	$3,000
Vanguard Tax-Managed Int'l.	Open-end	VTMGX	0.31	$10,000
Summit Apex EAFE Int'l. Index	Open-end	SAEIX	0.56	$5,000
Dreyfus Int'l. Stock Index	Open-end	DIISX	0.60	$2.500
Schwab International Index*	Open-end	SWINX	0.58	$2.500
iShares MSCI EAFE	ETF	EFA	0.35	None

*Charles Schwab developed its own developed markets index and called it the Schwab Total International Index. The index includes common stock of 15 developed countries outside the United States. Within these countries Schwab identified the 350 largest companies according to their market capitalization, which became the basis for the index. The Schwab Total International Index does not maintain any particular country weighting, although no country can make up more than 35 percent.

Barclays Global Investors will start trading an ETF based on the S&P International 700. The symbol and management fee were not available as of this writing. An update on the fund can be found on the iShares Web site at www.iShares.com.

Emerging Market Index Funds

The phrase *Third World countries* may conjure up images of famine and poverty in your mind. The title did not sit well with the marketing wizards on Wall Street who were trying to sell Third World securities, and they decided to change the name to something that sounded more sophisticated. Thus, the term *emerging markets* was created. Broadly defined, an emerging market is a less fortunate country that is making an effort to change and improve its economy. These countries are going to considerable lengths to make their economies strong, more open to international investors, and more competitive in global markets.

There are two major providers of emerging market index data: S&P and MSCI. S&P's Emerging Markets Data Base (EMDB) is one of the world's leading sources for information and indexes on stock

T A B L E   8 – 4

Diversified Emerging Market Index Funds	Type	Symbol	Fee	Min
Vanguard Emerging Market Stock Index Fund	Open-end	VDMIX	0.31	$3000

markets in developing countries. The International Finance Corporation (IFC) launched EMDB in 1981 to collect data on emerging markets for in-house use. Over time, demand from the financial community for these data increased, and in 1987 IFC began offering its indexes and underlying data as a commercial product. S&P acquired the EMDB database in 2000. As of March 2001 the S&P Emerging Market Index covered 54 countries. The index is float-adjusted to reflect restrictions on foreign investment.

The MSCI Emerging Market Index covers 27 emerging market country indexes. Designation as an emerging market is determined by a number of factors. MSCI evaluates gross domestic product per capita, local government regulations, perceived investment risk, foreign ownership limits, and capital controls.

The only index fund available to the general public that invests exclusively in emerging markets is the Vanguard Emerging Market Stock Index Fund (Table 8–4). This fund tracks a subset of the MSCI index called the MSCI Select Emerging Markets Free Index. Vanguard invests in more than 600 stocks that are spread across Africa, Asia, Europe, and Latin America. The major holdings are in Brazil, Mexico, Hong Kong, and South Africa.

Total Market Funds

If you add the MSCI Select Emerging Market Index to the MSCI EAFE Index, you have a "total" international index that covers developed countries and emerging markets. This is precisely what Vanguard did with their Total International Portfolio (Table 8–5). The fund is actually a fund of funds. It holds a market weighting in the Vanguard Pacific Stock Index Fund, the Vanguard European Stock Index Fund, and the Vanguard Emerging Market Stock Index Fund.

TABLE 8—5

Total International Funds	Type	Symbol	Fee	Min
Vanguard Total International Portfolio	Open-end	VGTSX	0.40	$3000

The fee for the Vanguard Total International Portfolio is the weighted average charged to the Vanguard Pacific Stock Index Fund, the Vanguard European Stock Index Fund, and the Vanguard Emerging Market Stock Index Fund. Since the composition of the portfolio changes with global market conditions, the fee also varies. On average the fund cost is about 0.40 percent.

One disadvantage of VGTSX is that it does not qualify for the foreign dividend tax exclusion. When a foreign company pays a cash dividend, its home country often taxes that dividend before the cash is sent overseas. According to the U.S. tax code, investors are entitled to a tax credit for the amount of foreign tax withheld. This is not true for the Vanguard Total International Portfolio. U.S. tax rules do not permit the pass-through of foreign dividend tax credits in a fund-of-funds investment.

REGIONAL INDEX FUNDS

The MSCI EAFE Index is divided into two large geographic regions: Europe and the Pacific Rim. This creates the opportunity for the formation of regional index funds. Vanguard has created two index funds benchmarked to the MSCI Europe Index and the MSCI Pacific Index (Table 8–6). The Vanguard European Stock Index Fund in-

TABLE 8—6

MSCI Regional Index Funds	Type	Symbol	Fee	Min
Vanguard Pacific Stock Index	Open-end	VPACX	0.37	$3000
Vanguard European Stock Index	Open-end	VEURX	0.29	$3000

vests in 550 stocks in 15 developed European countries, and the Vanguard Pacific Stock Index Fund replicates the performance of the MSCI Pacific Free Index of 400 stocks. Both of these funds are included in the Vanguard Total International Portfolio discussed earlier.

There are two types of European index funds available in the exchange-traded fund format. One includes the United Kingdom and one does not. The iShares S&P Europe 350 Index Fund is based on a Pan Euro index that seeks investment results that correspond to the performance of a broad range of stocks in continental Europe, including the United Kingdom. The iShares MSCI EMU Index Fund seeks to provide investment results that correspond generally to the price and yield performance of the aggregate publicly traded securities in the European Monetary Union (EMU) markets, as measured by the MSCI EMU Index. The EMU Index does not include stocks from the United Kingdom.

In October 2001 Barclays Global Investors introduced two new regional funds (see Table 8–7). The funds are based on separate regions in the S&P family of global indexes and are both included in the S&P Global 1200 Index. The Pacific ex-Japan Fund has no Japanese stocks. This fund allows investors to control their exposure to Japan through a separate purchase of an ETF benchmarked to the TOPIX 150 (see country funds). The second fund is benchmarked to the largest 40 stocks in Latin America, which has exposure to telecommunication stocks in Mexico and Brazil. One good sign for investors is that the fee on the new funds dropped to 0.50 percent.

TABLE 8–7

Regional ETF Index Funds	Type	Symbol	Fee	Min
iShares MSCI EMU Index	ETF	EZU	0.84	None
iShares S&P Europe 350 Index	ETF	IEV	0.60	None
iShares MSCI Pacific ex-Japan	ETF	EPP	0.50	None
iShares Latin America 40	ETF	ILF	0.50	None

COUNTRY INDEX FUNDS

MSCI constructs a country index by listing every security on the market, and collects price data, outstanding shares, significant ownership, free float, and monthly trading volume. The stocks are categorized according to industry group, and individual companies are selected from each industry. MSCI methodology requires at least 85 percent representation of each industry group. Therefore, a country index captures at least 85 percent of the market capitalization of that country. Industry replication, more than any other single factor, is a key characteristic of a single country market index.

Once stocks are selected for a country index, companies with

TABLE 8-8

iShares Country Funds	Symbol	Fee
Australia	EWA	0.84
Austria	EWO	0.84
Belgium	EWK	0.84
Brazil	EWZ	0.99
Canada	EQC	0.84
Canada—S&P TSE 60	IKC	0.50
France	EWQ	0.84
Germany	EWG	0.84
Hong Kong	EWH	0.84
Italy	EWI	0.84
Japan	EWJ	0.84
Japan—S&P TOPIX 150	ITF	0.50
Malaysia (Free)	EWM	0.84
Mexico	EWW	0.84
Netherlands	EWN	0.84
Singapore (Free)	EWS	0.84
South Korea	EWY	0.99
Spain	EWP	0.84
Sweden	EWD	0.84
Switzerland	EWL	0.84
Taiwan	EWT	0.99
United Kingdom	EWU	0.84

greater than a 40 percent float are included at their full market cap-italization weight. Companies that are added to an index with less than a 40 percent float are included at a fraction of their market cap-italization in accordance with the MSCI partial inclusion schedule. This partial inclusion policy facilitates the inclusion of companies with a modest float, while taking into consideration potential limit-ed supply. Currently, there are 22 separate iShares country funds (Table 8–8). Most are based on MSCI indexes (two are based on S&P Global Indexes). Some of the funds were originally issued as WEBS shares in 1996 (see Chapter 4).

GLOBAL INDUSTRY SECTORS: THE NEXT NEW THING

In 2000 MSCI, in collaboration with Standard & Poor's, introduced the Global Industry Classification Standard (GICS). MSCI and S&P categorize the stocks in each of its indexes according to the GICS structure of 10 sectors, 23 industry groups, 59 industries, and 123 subindustries. MSCI offers industry indexes based on GICS cover-ing all global, regional, and country indexes.

The next step for index fund providers is to create a broad range of global industry sector funds. Global industry funds allow investors the ability to build exposure to the global marketplace in-dustry classification rather than by geographical regions. Barclays Global Investors got off to a good start in late 2001 with the intro-duction of five iShares S&P global industry funds (Table 8–9). You can expect to see a full range of global industry sector funds offered

TABLE 8–9

iShares S&P Global Sector Funds	Symbol	Fee
Technology sector	IXN	0.65
Telecommunications sector	IXP	0.65
Energy sector	IXC	0.65
Financial sector	IXG	0.65
Health Care sector	IXJ	0.65

by BGI and other fund companies in the marketplace in the coming years.

CHAPTER SUMMARY

The global stock market is becoming more diverse and easier to access. A little international stock exposure makes a lot of sense for today's investors because of its diversification benefits. While there are no hard and fast rules for the amount of international equity exposure placed in a portfolio, historically, a 30 percent exposure has helped reduced the risk of an all-U.S. stock portfolio and adds slightly to the return.

One of the best ways to gain exposure to the global markets is through a diversified global or international index fund. Make sure you check the fees in a fund before you buy. They can vary widely in the international index fund marketplace. Also ensure that you know which index the fund follows, so you will not have redundant country exposure in your portfolio. Finally, I do not recommend buying individual country funds due to the high risk involved. It is a much better idea to stick with regional funds and multiregional funds.

CHAPTER 9

Bond Index Funds

Key Concepts

- Bond index funds add diversification to a portfolio.
- Bond funds can be categorized by maturity and credit risk.
- Most bond index funds sample a fixed-income index.
- In markets without index funds, choose a low-cost active fund.

A well-diversified investment portfolio almost always contains a fixed-income component. Adding bond index funds to a portfolio of stock index funds lowers investment risk without significantly lowering returns. Although bond funds play a crucial role in portfolio management, a majority of investors do not pay nearly as much attention to selecting their bond investments as they do to their stock investments. By understanding the dynamics and structure of the bond market, you can select the appropriate bond funds for your needs. The best way to build a bond portfolio is through index funds that charge minimal fees. In the absence of index funds, low-cost actively managed bond funds also work well.

If this book were to recommend only bond index funds, it would be a very short book. Unfortunately, there are not many bond index funds available. There are dozens of mutual fund companies offering hundreds of stock index funds, but only a handful offer bond index funds. The Vanguard Group currently manages four

open-end bond index funds, and Barclays Global Investors has recently filed for four exchange-traded funds benchmarked to the
Lehman Brothers U.S. Treasury Indexes and one benchmarked to
the Lehman Brothers Government/Credit market. Despite the efforts of Vanguard and Barclays, a lack of funds leaves many holes
in the fixed-income market where no index funds exist. To fill the
gaps, this chapter also includes a section on "almost" index funds.
These funds are low-cost, actively managed bond funds that are the
next best thing to indexing.

One reason for the lack of bond index funds is that it is actually more difficult for mutual fund companies to manage a bond index fund than a stock index fund. Most of the popular bond indexes are not designed with the underlying objective of being used as
a benchmark for index funds. Rather, the indexes have historically
been used as a theoretical guide to measure the movement of the
broad bond market. This is evidenced by the fact that most of the indexes hold thousands of bonds, many of which are illiquid. For example, the Lehman Aggregate Bond Index tracks over 6000 bonds,
most of which do not trade on a regular basis. Index funds need access to all bonds in the index to fully replicate an index. Since full
replication is not possible, index fund managers resort to using a
technique called *sampling.*

Sampling Strategies

Sampling is the portfolio management method used by most bond
index funds to make up for a lack of liquidity in a bond index. Basically, fund managers try to combine the liquid, "investable" bonds
in the index to form a portfolio that has the same characteristics and
return as the index. This strategy is similar to a total stock market
index fund approach that samples the smaller stocks in the Wilshire
5000 rather than trying to buy all 6500 issues.

Sampling is a complex mathematical procedure that requires
index fund managers to categorize each bond in an index by different quadrants based on factors such as industry, issue size, credit
rating, maturity, and bond coupon. The manager then selects a few
of the larger bonds from each quadrant to represent all bonds in that
quadrant. The new model portfolio is then run through a mathe-

matical test called an *optimizer* to see if there is a difference in past returns between the model and the index. If there is a difference, it is called *tracking error.* If the tracking error of a model is too high, the model does not reflect the characteristics of the index, and different bonds are selected for the model. This procedure continues until the tracking error of the model is within acceptable limits.

Sampling may appear to take a lot of time; however, once the data are entered and the programming is complete, computers do most of the heavy number crunching. Portfolio managers spend a lot of time testing models and tweaking the program before actual trading takes place. A successful model will require only a few hundred bonds in the index fund, and the tracking error between the fund and the index will be very low. One of the most successful bond index funds is the Vanguard Total Bond Index Fund. It invests in about 600 bonds and tracks the 6000-bond Lehman Aggregate Bond Index.

BOND MARKET STRUCTURE

The fixed-income market is divided into two general types of bond funds: taxable and tax-free. We will cover tax-free municipal bonds later in the chapter. Taxable bond funds can be categorized on two axes. On the horizontal axis is the average maturity of the bonds in a fund, and on the vertical axis is the average creditworthiness of the portfolio.

The average maturity of a bond fund is illustrated on the horizontal axis in Figure 9-1. Maturity can be divided into three ranges. Short-term funds hold bonds that have an average maturity of 3 years or less, intermediate bond funds have an average maturity of 4 to 9 years, and long-term funds have an average maturity of 10 years or more. If a fund has an average maturity of 5 years, it does not mean all bonds in the fund mature in 5 years. The bonds could mature from 1 year through 10 years or any combination thereof. It does not matter as long as the average maturity of the portfolio is 5 years.

Under normal economic conditions, you should expect a higher return in a long-term bond fund because there is more *interest rate risk.* This means the value of a long-term bond fund will fluctuate a

FIGURE 9–1

Bond Maturity and Credit Worthiness

Short-Term	Intermediate	Long-Term	
SH	IH	LH	High-Yield Corporate
SI	II	LI	Investment Grade U.S. Corporate & Foreign
SG	IG	LG	U.S. Government

lot with changes in general interest rates. Since a long-term bond portfolio moves around more than a short-term fund, you should get paid a higher return.

The credit risk on the vertical axis in Figure 9–1 is more complex. On the bottom of the chart are the least risky government bonds. These bond funds hold direct obligations of the U.S. government or indirect obligations of quasi-government agencies such as the Federal National Mortgage Association (FNMA). The middle credit level includes investment grade U.S. corporate bonds and foreign "Yankee" bonds that trade in U.S. dollars on a U.S. exchange. U.S. corporations with sound fundamental characteristics receive an investment grade rating from credit rating agencies such as Standard & Poor's. At the top of the risk level are high-yield bond funds. These funds invest in below-investment grade corporate bonds. Companies with below-investment grade debt ratings have a questionable ability to repay their obligations. Below-investment grade bonds are also referred to as "junk" bonds. Historically, over 90 percent of these bonds are paid off with no problem. However, the risk of default certainly justifies a higher return.

By putting the two factors in Figure 9–2 together, you can see the expected return of a bond fund is a function of its average ma-

F I G U R E   9–2

Bond Fund Interest Rate Risk and Credit Risk

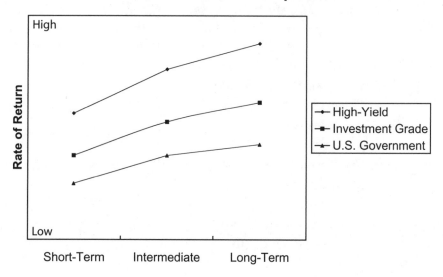

Fixed-Income Return Comparison

turity and average credit rating. The greater the risk, the higher the expected long-term return. Figure 9–2 illustrates the spread that occurs between the various types of bond funds based on these two factors. Short-term government funds have the lowest interest rate risk and the lowest credit risk; therefore, they are expected to produce the lowest long-term return. On the other hand long-term, high-yield bond funds have the highest interest rate risk and highest credit risk; therefore, they are expected to generate the highest long-term return.

FIXED-INCOME INDEXES

The three most widely recognized providers of fixed-income indexes are Lehman Brothers, Merrill Lynch, and Salomon Smith Barney (formerly Salomon Brothers). All three companies construct hundreds of fixed-income indexes covering all the global bond markets. Since all of the indexes are constructed from the same universe of bonds, they look very much alike. A short-term corporate bond index of one provider holds nearly the same bonds as the short-term corporate bond index of another provider. The liquidity of bonds in an index is not a problem for the provider of the index because the indexes are theoretical. The liquidity problem is only an issue for the index fund managers who attempt to buy the bonds in the index.

The standard aggregate bond market index for all three providers is structured as follows:

1. **Government/Credit Markets**
   a. Government
      i. Treasury
      ii. Agency
   b. Corporate (investment grade, BBB, or better)
      i. Industrial
      ii. Finance
      iii. Utility
      iv. Yankee bonds (foreign bonds trading in U.S. dollars)
2. **Mortgage Market**
   a. Government National Mortgage Assoc. (GNMA)
   b. Federal Home Loan Mortgage Corp. (FHLMC)
   c. Federal National Mortgage Assoc. (FNMA)
3. **Asset Backed Securities**
   a. Credit card receivables
   b. Auto loans
   c. Home equity loans

Although the structure used by all three providers is the same, there are a few subtle differences among the indexes. The first difference is how interest payments are reinvested. The Lehman indexes assume that interest paid during the month is not reinvested until the end of the month. Salomon Smith Barney assumes interest paid during the month is reinvested in Treasury bills for the remainder of the month. Finally, the Merrill Lynch index assumes interest is automatically reinvested at the market rate of return. This difference in accounting for interest does not affect the makeup of bonds in an index, only the performance results. Naturally, the Merrill Lynch method should generate slightly higher returns due to the assumed automatic reinvestment of interest payments at the bond market rate during the month. It is an unrealistic assumption for index fund managers to follow the Merrill Lynch reinvestment method in their "live" portfolios, which is probably one reason no index funds are benchmarked to the Merrill Lynch indexes.

The minimum size of a bond issue also differs among providers. Lehman requires a bond to have an issue size of at least $100 million, whereas Merrill Lynch only requires a float of $25 million, and Salomon Smith Barney's minimum depends on the type of bond. The size issue is a moot point for index fund managers because they are not able to buy most of the smaller issues. Managers typically sample the largest and most liquid bonds from the indexes.

Of the three main fixed-income index providers, Lehman Brothers is clearly the most popular with index fund managers. Currently, all index funds except one are benchmarked to Lehman indexes. Only one index fund is benchmarked to a Salomon Smith Barney index, and no index funds are benchmarked to the Merrill Lynch index, not even the Merrill Lynch Aggregate Bond Index Fund.

Lehman Brothers Indexes

The broadest and most popular index in the Lehman Brothers (LB) fixed-income series is the Lehman Aggregate Bond Index. This LB index tracks over 6600 U.S. Treasuries, government agency, corporate, and foreign bond issues. The bonds in the index have an average maturity of less than 9 years, which places the index in the intermediate-term category. It is also a highly rated index, with more than 60 percent of its holdings in U.S. Treasuries, agency, and government-backed securities. The rest are investment grade corporate and Yankee bonds. There may be a handful of noninvestment grade bonds in the index due to credit downgrades by the rating agencies during the middle of a month. Those bonds will eventually be deleted from the index. As of July 2001, the assets held in the LB Aggregate Bond Index were as shown in Table 9–1.

Several index funds track the Lehman Aggregate Bond Index (Table 9–2). All the fund managers use a sampling technique to

TABLE 9–1

The Lehman Brothers Aggregate Bond Index as of 12/01

Distribution by Issuer		Distribution by Quality	
Govt. mortgage backed	36%	AAA	62%
Treasury/agency	24%	AA	5%
Corporate—Finance	15%	A	14%
Corporate—Industrial	17%	BBB	18%
Corporate—Utility	6%	BB (noninvest. grade)	1%
Foreign—Corp. and govt.	2%	B (noninvest. grade)	0%

TABLE 9–2

LB Aggregate Bond Market Index Funds	Type	Symbol	Fee
Vanguard Total Bond Market Index	Open-end	VBMFX	0.20
Summit Apex Lehman Bond Index	Open-end	SALAX	0.30
Schwab Total Bond Market Index	Open-end	SWLBX	0.35
Dreyfus Bond Market Index	Open-end	DBMIX	0.40
Vantagepoint Core Bond Index 1	Open-end	VPCIX	0.47
iShares Government/Credit Index	ETF		
Source: Indexfunds.com, Morningstar Principia			

replicate the index. The difference in performance between one fund and another is based on the manager's ability to sample the index effectively and the fee charged to the fund. I recommend buying the fund with the lowest fee.

LB Government/Credit Index Funds

The Lehman Aggregate Bond Index is the starting point for the creation of smaller subsets. The bonds in the aggregate index are sorted by maturity into various categories. These categories become subindexes. The category with the shortest average maturity is the

TABLE 9-3

Index Funds	LB G/C Index	Type	Symbol	Fee
Firstar Short-Term Bond	1–3 Year	Open-end	FISTX	0.50
Vanguard Short-Term Bond Index	1–5 Year	Open-end	VBISX	0.20
Schwab Short-Term Bond Mkt.*	1–5 Year	Open-end	SWBDX	0.35
Vanguard Intermediate-Term Index	5–10 Year	Open-end	VBIIX	0.20
Vanguard Long-Term Bond Index	Long-Term	Open-end	VBLTX	0.20

Source: Indexfunds.com, Morningstar Principia
*The Schwab Short-Term Bond Market Index Fund is benchmarked to the LB Mutual Fund Short (1–5 Year) U.S. Government/Credit Index. The makeup of this index is similar to the original LB 1–5 Year Government/Credit Index less some illiquid securities.

LB 1–3 Year Short-Term Government/Credit Index. Other categories include the LB Intermediate-Term Government/Credit Index and the LB Long-Term Government/Credit Index.

The Vanguard Group and other index fund providers have created index funds that benchmark LB subindexes (Table 9–3). The funds allow you to control the amount of interest rate risk in a portfolio. As you may recall, the longer the average maturity of a fund, the more the fund fluctuates with general interest rate movements. If you invest in a long-term fund, the reward for taking greater risk is a higher return.

Treasury Bond Funds

In May 2002 Barclays Global Investors received approval to introduce the first exchange-traded funds benchmarked to the U.S. Treasury bond market. The Treasury bond portion of the Lehman Aggregate Bond Index was chosen as the benchmark for four of the funds, and a fifth fund will track the aggregate index (Table 9–4). As of this writing, the fund symbols and fees had not been made available.

LOW-COST ACTIVE BOND FUNDS

Fixed-income index funds are still in their infancy, and managers are learning to work around issues such as tracking error problems and

TABLE 9-4

Exchange-Traded Fund	LB Treasury Index	Type	Symbol & Fee*
iShares 1–3 Year Treasury Index	1–3 Year	ETF	SHY 0.15%
iShares 7–10 Year Treasury Index	7–10 Year	ETF	IEF 0.15%
iShares 20+ Treasury Index	Long-Term	ETF	TLT 0.15%
iShares All Treasury Index	Total Treasury	ETF	(TBD)
iShares Government/Credit Index	Aggregate	ETF	(TBD)

Source: Barclays Global Investors
*Barclays Global Investors. Visit www.iShares.com Web site or contact Barclays Global Investors for an update.

sampling techniques. As a result not many bond indexes are covered by index funds. That may change in the future, but for now there are two ways around this dilemma. First, you can buy individual bonds and create your own fixed-income portfolio. Second, you can invest in a low-cost actively managed mutual fund that is close to an index but may not track one directly. It is relatively easy to buy individual Treasury bonds and build your own bond portfolio. However, I strongly recommend using mutual funds for a higher risk market such as the junk bond market. It is much safer to buy a mutual fund than to invest in individual issues in particularly risky parts of the market.

The following section is about "almost" bond index funds. The funds in this section do not follow a published benchmark exactly, but they come close. The benchmark column in the fund list represents the index most similar to the fund. These funds are an acceptable alternative to index funds because they are low-cost, no commission funds, and the fund manager does not drift from the stated investment style.

Treasury and Government Bond Funds

Government bonds are a major part of every aggregate bond index. This group includes U.S. Treasury bond funds and those that hold government agency bonds, including government-insured home mortgages (Table 9–5). Agencies are quasi-government entities

TABLE 9-5

Almost Treasury Bond Index Funds

Mutual Fund	Benchmark	Symbol	Fee
Vanguard Short-term Treasury	LB 1–5 Year Treasury	VFISX	0.27
Vanguard Intermediate Treasury	LB 5–10 Year Treasury	VFITX	0.27
Vanguard Long-term Treasury	LB Long Treasury Index	VUSTX	0.28
Galaxy U.S. Treasury Index*	Aggregate Treasury Index	IUTIX	0.41
Vanguard Inflation-Protected	LB Treas. Inflation Notes	VIPSX	0.22

*Seeks to replicate a proprietary U.S. Treasury index.

Almost Government Index Funds

Mutual Fund	Benchmark	Symbol	Fee
Vanguard Short-Term Federal	LB 1–5 Year Government	VSGBX	0.27
Vanguard GNMA Fund	LB GNMA Index	VFIIX	0.27
USAA GNMA Fund	LB GNMA Index	USGNX	0.32
Payden GNMA Fund	LB GNMA Index	PYGNX	0.35

Source: Indexfunds.com, Morningstar Principia

such as the Guarantee National Mortgage Association (GNMA), Federal National Mortgage Association (FNMA), and the Federal Home Loan Mortgage Corporation (FHLMC).

Only U.S. Treasury securities have a direct government guarantee. FNMA, FHLMC, and other government agencies carry an implied government guarantee on their direct issue bonds and the mortgages that they insure. As a result, agency bonds yield slightly higher interest than Treasury bonds. The credit rating of almost all agency bonds and insured mortgages is AAA, the best grade you can buy.

The Vanguard Inflation-Protected Securities Fund (VIPSX) is a unique government bond fund. The portfolio invests in inflation-indexed securities (TIPS) that can offer protection against a rising inflation rate. Although the interest payment you receive on the fund is low, the value of TIPS increases if there is inflation in the economy, thereby keeping up with inflation. One caution on TIPS: If you own these securities in a taxable account, you are subject to ordinary income tax on the interest distribution and the increase in the annual inflation adjustment.

Investment Grade Corporate Bond Funds

The yield on investment grade corporate bonds is about 1 percent higher than government bonds. But that does not mean you will always earn a 1 percent higher rate of return. The extra yield is your payment for taking credit risk. Even the best bonds can quickly be downgraded from investment quality to junk bond status in a matter of months. In 2001 Lucent Technologies (LU) plunged from a solid growth company with a strong balance sheet to a cash-strapped company on the verge of bankruptcy. As a result, the bonds fell to junk status and went down in value. That is credit risk.

Investment grade corporate bonds are generally divided into four industry sectors: finance, utility, industrial, and Yankee bonds. Yankee bonds are foreign debt that trades on the U.S. markets in U.S. dollars. Foreign companies frequently issue Yankee bonds when interest rates in the United States are more favorable than in their home country. Many bond mutual funds exclude Yankee bonds.

There are no index funds that track the Lehman corporate bond indexes directly; however, Vanguard manages a series of investment grade corporate bond funds that come close. There are between 130 and 250 bonds in each fund, so they are well diversified. Vanguard also includes Yankee bonds in their funds for added diversification. Table 9–6 lists funds that are close to the Lehman corporate bond indexes.

TABLE 9–6

Almost Corporate Bond Index Funds

Mutual Fund	Lehman Benchmark	Symbol	Fee
Vanguard Short-Term Corporate	1–5 U.S. Credit Index	VFSTX	0.25
Vanguard Intermediate Corporate	5–10 U.S. Credit Index	VFICX	0.25
Vanguard Long-Term Corporate	Long Credit A or Better	VBLTX	0.20

TABLE 9-7

Almost High-Yield Bond Index Funds

Mutual Fund	Lehman Benchmark	Symbol	Fee
Vanguard High-Yield Corporate	High-Yield Index	VWEHX	0.28
TIAA-CREF High-Yield Bond	High-Yield Index	TCHYX	0.34

High-Yield Bond Funds

Below-investment grade, high-yield "junk" bonds are speculative. Most of the companies who issue junk bonds, or whose rating has been degraded to junk status, have only a good chance of paying off their debts, although there is a higher risk of default than with investment grade. Since there is a higher risk, there is a potentially high return. As a group, junk bonds achieve almost the same return as the broad stock market. I do not recommend investing in individual junk bond issues. If you venture into this area, buy a well-diversified mutual fund that invests in higher quality high-yield bonds.

Currently, there are no index funds that track the high-yield bond market. Some high-yield bonds in the high-yield indexes are extremely illiquid and rarely trade. Therefore, it makes no sense for a fund manager to attempt to replicate an index. There are a couple of index funds that invest in the higher quality issues and have delivered long-term results consistent with the indexes (Table 9-7). Vanguard's High-Yield Corporate Fund is a good fund to look at. It has very low fees and invests in B or better quality bonds. The TIAA-CREF High-Yield Bond fund also invests in B or better bonds and tracks the LB High-Yield index fairly closely.

Municipal Bond Funds

Investors in a high income tax bracket may be wise to invest in tax-free municipal bond funds in place of taxable bond funds. Generally, the interest from a municipal bond issued in the state you live in is free from all federal, state, and city income taxes. Since the interest is free of tax, municipal bonds have lower returns than taxable

TABLE 9-8

Almost Municipal Bond Index Funds

Mutual Fund	Lehman Benchmark	Symbol	Fee
Vanguard Short-Term Tax-Free	1-Year Municipal Index	VWSTX	0.18
Vanguard Limited-Term Tax-Free	1–5 Year Municipal Blend	VMLTX	0.18
USAA Tax-Exempt Short-Term	3-Year Municipal Index	USSTX	0.38
Vanguard Intermediate Tax-Free	7-Year Municipal Index	VWITX	0.18
Vanguard Long-Term Tax-Free	20-Year Municipal Index	VWLTX	0.18
Vanguard High-Yield Tax-Free	15-Year Municipal Index	VWAHX	0.18

government bonds or corporate bonds. There is a rough rule of thumb you can use to determine if you should own tax-free bonds. Generally, if your combined state and federal income tax rate is 30 percent or more, then municipal bonds may be an appropriate choice for taxable accounts.

All of the low-cost, tax-free bond funds listed in Table 9–8 are national series funds. That means the bonds in the funds are a composite from anywhere in the 50 states, Guam, Puerto Rico, or U.S. Virgin Islands. Most states tax the interest on bonds issued from other states, so if you are in a state that has an income tax, a national bond fund will be subject to the state tax. In addition, the funds in Table 9–8 frequently invest a small portion in Alternative Minimum Tax (AMT) bonds. That means if you are subject to AMT tax, the federal government taxes a portion of the interest on the bond fund.

CHAPTER SUMMARY

The fixed-income index fund market is small, and investors may have to be creative when building a portfolio of mutual funds. The easiest way to capture the broad taxable bond market is to invest in a total bond market index fund that samples the Lehman Brothers Aggregate Bond Index. A total bond market fund has exposure to the government markets, the mortgage market, and the investment grade corporate markets, including some foreign debt. The average maturity of a total bond fund is about 9 years.

If you choose to piece together a bond fund portfolio, many of the indexes are available in an index fund. In such circumstances, investors should buy the closest low-cost mutual fund they can find. Vanguard has the largest selection of "almost" index funds, and there are other providers. As in past chapters, the funds mentioned in this chapter are not meant to be a complete list. They are a sample of the market. For a more complete list of bond funds, go to www.Morningstar.com. For a list of bond index funds, visit www.Indexfunds.com.

CHAPTER 10

Enhanced, Leveraged, and Inverse Index Funds

Key Concepts

+ Enhanced funds attempt to beat the market by making small adjustments.
+ Leveraged funds try to beat the market by using borrowed money.
+ Inverse index funds profit when the market moves down.
+ Most of these strategies are speculative and costly.

There are ways to earn a high return using special index fund strategies, but not without taking more risk. *Speculation* is the best way to describe most of the strategies. The goal of this special group of quasi-index funds is to beat the markets. Some of the strategies are subtle and will not harm your portfolio too much. Others push the limit and can blow up your account in a hurry. Before investing in one of the funds listed in this chapter, know what the risks are. Caveat emptor: Let the buyer beware.

There are several types of special funds discussed in this chapter. Enhanced index funds are one type of special fund that is relatively benign. Enhanced funds attempt to beat the market by making slight adjustments to an index and potentially harvesting an extra one-half percent. Other funds are much more aggressive. They use "leverage" to try and beat the markets. Generally, leveraged funds move up more than the market when the market goes up but get crushed when the market goes down. On the other hand, inverse funds are unique in that they go the opposite direction of the market. So if you think the market is going down, buy an inverse index fund. Regardless of the strategy used in a special index fund, you can guarantee that one thing will be constant: The expenses will be higher than most other index funds discussed in this book.

TYPES OF SPECIAL INDEX FUNDS

There are three basic types of special index funds: enhanced, leveraged, and inverse. Enhanced strategies use various methods to try to beat the market by a small amount each year. These are the safest of the three strategies. Leveraged funds borrow up to 50 percent of the money to buy more shares of stock. Leveraging a fund makes it extremely volatile. Inverse index strategies "short" the market. This means an inverse fund will make money when the markets go down and lose money when the markets go up. Some high-risk funds use a combination of strategies. For example, one company developed an index fund that uses a "leveraged inverse" strategy. This means if the stock market loses 10 percent, the fund should gain 20 percent, and vice versa.

Enhanced Index Funds

The basic idea of indexing is to eliminate the risk of underperforming a market by tracking the returns of a market. Nevertheless, enhanced index fund managers believe they can make a few adjustments to the index and beat that benchmark by a small amount. Enhanced index funds use the most conservative strategies mentioned in this chapter, meaning in the event the portfolio manager fails to beat the market, at least the fund should not underperform by a great amount. There are two basic methods of index enhancement: security-based strategies and synthetic strategies.

Security-Based Enhancements
Security-based enhancements start from the assumption that an index portfolio is okay, but it can be improved upon. With a little tinkering by the fund manager, he or she can achieve a better return than the index without changing the nature of the index fund or taking on extra risk.

Fund managers may underweight or eliminate stocks they think are overvalued and increase the weight of stocks they think are undervalued. For example, between 1997 and 1999 technology stocks went to historically high valuations. An enhanced index fund manager could have reduced technology holdings or capped the weighting of technology stocks in the fund. The gap would be filled with stocks from industry groups that were considered below their historically normal valuations. The rest of the stocks in the index would remain the same, with their appropriate weighting in the fund. If such a fund existed, it would have beaten the market in 2000 and 2001.

Other security-based methods include equally-weighted portfolios. Equally weighted index funds place the same amount of money in each stock in the fund rather than allocating by its value in the index. For example, an equally weighted S&P 500 Index fund would place 0.2 percent of the portfolio in each of the 500 companies rather than placing larger amounts of money in the large stocks and much smaller amounts in the small stocks. Another approach to equal weighting is to invest equal amounts in the 10 industry groups rather than following market weights.

Security-based methods of enhancement involve more trading than a straight index fund, which also means higher transaction charges. In addition, the funds in general have higher management fees. As a result, the fund manager must make up a lot of ground before beating the index. This is not easy to do.

If you are interested in enhanced equity strategies, the funds in Table 10–1 are a good representative of security-based enhancements.

The Vanguard Growth & Income (VQNPX) Fund holds about 175 stocks according to Morningstar. The investment characteristics

TABLE 10–1

Fund	Symbol	Min	Fee
Vanguard Growth & Income	VQNPX	$3000	0.37
Brinson Enhanced S&P 500 C	PESCX	$1000	1.38
TIAA-CREF Bond Plus	TIPBX	$250	0.30

of the fund are similar to the S&P 500 Index in terms of dividend yield, price-to-earnings ratio, return on equity, and price-to-book ratio. The fund also holds a market weighting in industry sectors. The difference is the fund manager selects individual stocks in each industry sector that they believe have the best chance for outperforming that sector. For the last 10 years, the Vanguard Growth & Income Fund actually beat the index by about 0.4 percent, although most of that gain occurred in 1999 when the fund outperformed the S&P 500 Index by 5.0 percent (one good year does not make a great fund). The drawback to VQNPX is the turnover of stocks. There is an average 54 percent turnover rate, which means the fund generates a lot of realized capital gains and is not appropriate for a taxable account.

The Brinson Enhanced S&P 500 C shares (PESCX) was established in April 2000. The fund attempts to beat the market by shifting industry weights within the index. The investment strategy in the fund is to reduce exposure to overvalued industry sectors without radically altering the structure of the fund in relation to the S&P 500 Index. According to Morningstar, as of June 2001 there were 419 stocks in the fund, which means it should track the S&P 500 Index closely. One big disadvantage of the Brinson Enhanced S&P 500 C shares is the cost. The fund expenses are high because this is a loaded fund sold only through brokerage firms. In addition, the fund has two annual expenses: the 0.73 percent management fee and a 0.65 percent 12b-1 fee that is paid as a "trailing commission" to the selling brokers. I do not recommend PESCX because of the high cost. It is on the list only as an example, not as a recommendation.

Enhancements can occur in bond funds as well as in stock funds. About 75 percent of TIAA-CREF Bond Plus Fund is composed of large bond issues in the Lehman Aggregate Bond Index (see Chapter 9). The remaining bonds in the fund are illiquid bonds and below-investment grade securities that offer high yields. The illiquid bonds and high-yield bonds are supposed to enhance the return over the LB index. The TIAA-CREF Bond Plus Fund date of inception was September 1997. For the 3 years ending June 2001, the fund has underperformed the Lehman index slightly.

Synthetic Enhancements

Can you imagine a stock index fund that owns no stocks? That is exactly what synthetic index funds are. These interesting funds create an index fund using eccentric investments called derivatives. Derivatives are manufactured investments such as futures, options, and equity swaps. The price of a derivative fluctuates based on the price of something else. If the price of the S&P 500 Index went up, the price of S&P 500 futures contracts and S&P 500 call options would also go up.

Although derivatives may sound exotic and risky, if a portfolio is managed correctly, it will look and act much like an index. This is called a synthetic index fund. A variety of complex derivative strategies can be used in an attempt to capture small anomalies in stock or bond market pricing; thus, the synthetic fund should beat the market by a small margin. A caution on these funds is that they are not designed for taxable accounts. Derivative strategies generate a lot of interest income, which is taxable at ordinary income tax rates.

Enhanced fund managers attempt to beat the markets in a variety of complex ways. A few of those strategies follow. Don't be concerned if you do not understand these ideas right away. This is not a book on derivatives trading, and these strategies are complicated even for professionals.

1. *Arbitrage*—Slight price discrepancies can occur between the actual value of an index, such as the S&P 500, and values of futures contracts tied to that index. Managers will switch between individual stocks and futures depending on whether futures are undervalued or overvalued relative to the stocks. If they switch at the right time, the manager should earn a risk-free return.

2. *Cash Plus*—In this strategy, an index fund is created using futures contracts. Since buying futures contracts only requires a small down payment called *margin*, the rest of the cash in an account can be invested in other securities. One basic assumption about stock future pricing is that the return on the cash portion of an index fund not used for margin is expected to earn the fed funds rate (the overnight lending rate banks charge each other). If the cash portion earns more than the fed funds rate, there is an extra return for shareholders of the fund.

3. *Option Overwrite Strategies*—Managers can create and sell (write) options against the actual securities in the fund. Writing options generates extra cashflow to the fund but

TABLE 10–2

Fund	Symbol	Min	Fee
Payden Market Return R	PYMRX	$5000	0.45
Managers U.S. Stock Mkt. Plus	MGSPX	$1000	0.88

can also limit the upside profit potential if the market moves up. Managers typically try to write options against underlying stock or futures positions when they perceive the options are overpriced.

These strategies expose the synthetic index funds to many risks above and beyond the risks of the market, but we will not go into the risks because they are beyond the scope of this book. You will have to take my word for the fact that funny things happen in synthetic index fund accounts, and most are not good for you.

There are several mutual funds that use synthetic strategies, but none have consistently beaten the market average. Nevertheless, if a synthetic index fund intrigues you, Table 10–2 lists two no low funds that use one or more of the strategies listed above. Neither one has accomplished its objective.

Leveraged Index Funds

After explaining enhanced index funds, the concept behind leveraged index funds is easy. A leveraged index fund simply borrows extra money from a bank and invests that cash in more stocks or bonds. If the return of the fund is higher than the cost to borrow the money, the fund makes an extra return above the market. On the other hand, if the fund does not make up the borrowing costs, it will underperform the market significantly. The worst case scenario for a leveraged fund is that the stock market goes down. In a bad market the fund is on the hook for the borrowed money as well as the excessive losses in the portfolio. As you can see, leveraged funds are very risky. You can make or lose a lot of money very quickly.

The premier provider of leveraged index funds is Rydex Funds of Rockville, Maryland. The company's trademark is "The Index Al-

TABLE 10–3

Rydex Fund	Index	Leverage	Symbol	Fee
Nova	S&P 500	150%	RYNVX	1.34
Titan 500	S&P 500	200%	RYTNX	1.75
Velocity 100	NASDAQ 100	200%	RYVYX	1.75
Medius	S&P MidCap 400	150%	TBD	1.75
Mekros	Russell 2000	150%	RYMKX	1.74
Large Cap Europe	Stoxx 50 Index	125%	RYEUX	2.06
Large Cap Japan	Topix 100 SM Index	125%	RYJPX	1.77
U.S. Govt. Bond	30 year Treasury bond	120%	RTGBX	0.97
Source: Rydex Funds, Morningstar				

ternative" and rightly so. If you are seeking a lot of action in your index funds, Rydex is the place to shop. Table 10–3 presents Rydex Funds that leverage the stock and bond positions. Most leveraged Rydex Funds impose a $25,000 minimum initial investment.

To get an idea how these funds should be performing, simply look in the newspaper for the return of the index and multiply it times the fund leverage. For example, the Nova Fund invests in 150 percent of the market average. Thus, if the S&P 500 Index is up 10 percent during a certain period, the Nova Fund should be up by 15 percent during the same period. That is the theory at least. In reality, fees chop away at most of the excess gain. For example, over a 5-year period ending June 2001, the S&P 500 Index was up 12.8 percent but the Nova Fund was up only 13.7 percent. You would have expected the performance of the Nova Fund to be up near 18 percent; however, trading costs and high expenses took away most of the advantage. If you look at this another way, investors took 150 percent of stock market risk and only got 107 percent of the return. That does not sound like a good deal to me.

Inverse Index Funds

Want to know a good way to make money if the stock market goes down? The answer is to short the market. This means selling index funds that you do not own and buying them back at a lower price

TABLE 10—4

Rydex Funds	Index	Symbol	Fee
Ursa	Inverse S&P 500	RYVNX	1.75
Arktos	Inverse NASDAQ 100	RYAIX	1.34
Juno	Inverse 30 Year Treasury	RYJUX	1.33
Source: Rydex Funds, Morningstar			

some time in the future. The difference between your initial sell price and buy-back price is a profit, less commissions.

There are other ways to make money in a bad market using derivatives. For instance, you could sell futures on the S&P 500 Index, buy put options on the index, or do an equity swap. This is not a book on derivatives, but you can be certain that inverse index funds use all the methods listed in this book and more to try making money in a falling market.

Inverse index funds are designed to go in the opposite direction of a market. So, if you are bearish on stocks or bearish on bonds, one of the Rydex Funds in Table 10–4 may be for you. There are inverse funds on the S&P 500 Index, the NASDAQ Index, and the long-term Treasury Bond Index.

Leveraged Inverse Index Funds

Leveraged inverse index funds have to be some of the most esoteric funds on the market, and the riskiest. Leveraged inverse index funds basically act the same as a leveraged stock fund but in reverse. If the S&P 500 Index goes down by 10 percent, then an inverse S&P 500 Index fund with 200 percent leverage should go up 20 percent. Of course there are fees and commissions to pay, so the actual result will be less than the theoretical estimate. Two inverse leveraged Rydex Funds began operation in May 2000 (Table 10–5). Notice the very high fees in these risky funds.

CHAPTER SUMMARY

"There is no such thing as a free lunch."

One of the fundamental axioms of economics

TABLE 10-5

Rydex Funds	Index	Leverage	Symbol	Fee
Tempest 500	Inverse S&P 500	200%	RYTPX	1.75
Venture 100	Inverse NASDAQ 100	200%	RYVNX	1.75
Source: Rydex Funds, Morningstar				

In this chapter we reviewed various special index funds whose aim is to beat the stock and bond markets. The funds are divided into three categories: enhanced, leveraged, and inverse (including leveraged inverse). Enhanced funds are further divided into security selection funds and synthetic index funds. The enhanced strategies are only slightly riskier than the market. The others have significantly more risk.

Are these special index funds worthy of your money? That depends on who you are. An index purist would say that these funds are actively managed funds and do not belong in any index fund portfolio. Mutual fund firms who manufacture and sell the funds claim that these funds are index funds that can be used to enhance your portfolio. Academics say none of those arguments matter because the costs of the funds would wipe out the gains, so there is no good reason anyone would want to own one of these funds. I think Federal Reserve Chairman Alan Greenspan said it best in 1998:

> This decade is strewn with examples of bright people who thought they built a better mousetrap that could consistently extract abnormal returns from the financial markets. Some succeed for a time. But while there may occasionally be misconfigurations among market prices that allow abnormal returns, they do not persist.

If you are interested in any of the funds mentioned in this chapter, please order a prospectus and read it carefully before you invest. This chapter only touches on the complexities of the special funds marketplace.

Create Your Own Index Fund

Key Concepts

- ◆ Create your own index fund using an Internet service.
- ◆ Customize a model portfolio or make one from scratch.
- ◆ Web-based services are low cost and easy to use.
- ◆ They work well for U.S. stocks but are limited on fixed income.

Can't find an index fund that suits your needs? Try building one from scratch. Open an on-line investment account with Foliofn.com or E-Trade.com and you can create a customized basket, or *folio*, of stocks in a matter of seconds. Folios are a specific group of individual stocks that can be purchased in a single transaction. They resemble personal index funds, although most folios do not fully replicate a widely followed index.

You can select a folio from over 100 prepackaged stock baskets listed on the sites, or you can create your own basket of stocks from scratch using the analytic tools provided. These tools allow you to screen thousands of stocks using a seemingly unlimited combination of fundamental data. The maximum number of securities in a folio is 50, although most prepackaged folios have between 20 and 40 securities. Some folio baskets focus on a particular market sector, industry, or fundamental factor, and others are broadly based. The prepackaged baskets can be customized to fit your needs.

Folios are useful in a variety of ways. One way is to create maximum diversification from an illiquid stock. For example, a Microsoft (MSFT) employee wants to diversify a large position of MSFT stock. Due to trading restrictions or tax consequences, it is not feasible for that person to sell the MSFT shares. If the person bought an S&P 500 Index Fund, they would be adding more MSFT to their portfolio because it is one of the largest companies in the index. Using a folio, the person can create a basket of large U.S. stocks and exclude MSFT stock from the list. This will create an index type of portfolio that works around the existing MSFT position. If the MSFT employee investor wants to exclude all technology stocks, they can restrict the technology industry from the folio with a few mouse clicks.

There are a few disadvantages to the folio services. First, these services are on-line investment vehicles that require an investor to have Web access. Second, you are required to maintain the portfolio on your own. The services do not include automatically rebalancing of the portfolio in the event of a change in the index. Third, the portfolios are limited to 50 stocks, which may restrict diversification. Fourth, fixed-income management is very limited. You cannot buy individual bonds. The only fixed-income investments available are relatively expensive closed-end bond funds that trade on the stock exchange.

Finally, the Internet brokerage companies that offer folios are still in their infancy, and somewhat unstable. That means the firms may not be around for long. In fact, as this book was being written, Foliofn.com was laying off employees, and a third company, Netfolio.com, went out of business! Nevertheless, if you invest in a folio through an online brokerage firm, there is no reason to fear losing your investments if a firm does fold. Your stocks are actually held at an industrywide clearing and holding firm called the Depositary Trust Corporation (DTC). By law, regardless of the status of a brokerage firm, your stocks are safe. In addition, all brokerage accounts are insured for $400,000 in securities and $100,000 in cash through a federal insurance program.

Despite their limitations, folios offer a unique index fund alternative in special cases or just for fun. The number of personal index portfolios you can create is only limited by your imagination and ingenuity.

Foliofn.com

Foliofn.com offers an alternative to individual stock picking and mutual fund selection. It allows you to easily select and invest in a folio of stocks without the complexities and costs of building it one stock at a time. A folio is a group of securities that you can purchase in a single transaction rather than buying them one at a time. You can select a "ready-to-go" folio or build your own from scratch. A folio can hold anywhere from 1 to 50 stocks, although most ready-to-go folios generally have between 20 and 40 securities. Some folios focus on a particular sector or industry, and others are more broadly based. You can customize any ready-to-go folio to meet your preferences.

Folios have advantages and disadvantages. Individual stock ownership also gives you corporate voting rights, which is a double-edged sword. With voting rights comes a slew of annual reports, proxies, and other required SEC documents that are supposed to be read. Your mailbox will be clogged each spring with tons of paper, and there is no way to turn off the flow.

For taxable accounts, individual ownership gives you the ability to tax manage each stock in the folio. That means you can harvest tax losses on select issues if they are trading below your cost. On the other hand, annual tax reporting to the IRS on a 50-stock portfolio is not as simple as a mutual fund that issues an annual Form 1099. Since there is more tax work involved with folios, it may mean a higher tax preparation bill.

The cost to investing in folios is very reasonable. A low flat fee of $29.95 per month or $295 a year gets you three separate folios and covers all trading costs as long as the stocks are traded during the twice-daily "window" trading period. If you want more than three folios, each additional folio costs $9.95 a month or $95.00 a year.

In an effort to keep trading costs low, Foliofn.com attempts to match buyers and sellers internally. Transactions are matched twice a day during the window period. One window period is conducted in the morning, and the second is in the afternoon. In the event a trade cannot be offset, Foliofn.com executes the order on the open market. Some small stocks are not in Foliofn.com's window universe and are always traded on an exchange. There is an extra transaction charge for nonwindow stocks.

There are over 100 ready-to-go folios listed on the www. foliofn.com Web site. Any folio in this list can be modified to fit your needs. No obligation is necessary to view the list, and you can sign up for a free 60-day cashless trial with no obligation.

Here is a sample of Foliofn.com ready-to-go folios:

Index Folios

Folio 30:	The 30 stocks in the Dow Jones Industrial Average. The Dow is one of the oldest and most widely quoted of all market indicators.
Folio 50:	A folio of the largest 50 stocks from the S&P 500 by market capitalization.
Folio Transport:	The 20 stocks in the Dow Jones Transportation Average. This folio includes stocks from the airline, trucking, railroad, and shipping industries.
Global:	A folio of U.S. and foreign companies from various regions of the world. The folio contains stocks and American depository receipts (ADRs) selected in proportions that reflect a region's market size in relation to all markets.
International:	A folio representing regions of the world, excluding North America. The folio contains American depository receipts selected in proportions that reflect a region's relative market size.
Large Growth:	A folio of stocks with a market capitalization greater than $11 billion and with high price-to-book ratios.
Large Value:	A folio of stocks with a market capitalization greater than $11 billion and with low price-to-book ratios.

Industry Folios

Aerospace:	A folio of stocks related to the aerospace sector, including aerospace de-

fense, aerospace defense equipment, and electronics for military systems.

Automotive: A folio of stocks related to the automotive sector, including autos, tires, and trucks.

Banks: A folio of bank stocks.

Multi Sector 10: A folio of the largest stocks from 10 major sectors of the economy according to the sector classification of Zack's Investment Research.

Select Folios

Socially Responsible: A folio of large companies that do not derive any revenue from the manufacturing of tobacco, firearms, military weapons, alcohol, or from the operation of gambling establishments.

Minority Leaders: A folio of companies with the highest percentages of minority board members according to the EEOC's definition of minority: Native American, Alaskan Native, Asian or Pacific Islander, Black, and Hispanic individuals.

Analyst Growth: A folio of stocks in the Standard & Poor's 500 Index that Wall Street analysts predict will have the highest earnings growth rates.

Analyst Upgrades: A folio of stocks in the Standard & Poor's 500 whose recommendations by Wall Street stock analysts have improved the most.

Folios also offer a unique way to invest in exchange-traded funds. If you buy ETFs on a regular basis or rebalance your holdings regularly, folios are an inexpensive way to manage your account. Trading under the folio design is inexpensive, and if your ETF shares trade during one of the window periods, the spread between the bid and ask will be eliminated. That could add up to big cost savings.

E*TRADE STOCK BASKETS

E*TRADE's stock basket service is very similar to Foliofn. Stock baskets combine certain benefits of mutual funds (diversification, convenience, regular investing) with some of the prominent features of individual stock ownership (customization, tax control). You can build a stock basket from scratch or choose an off-the-shelf basket created exclusively for E*TRADE by Standard & Poor's.

You pay an annual asset-based fee on your E*TRADE stock basket rather than commissions or transaction charges per trade. The fee percentage declines as the amount of money in your stock basket's account increases beyond certain levels. The fee schedule for stock baskets is as follows:

E*TRADE Stock Basket Annual Fees

Size of account:
$0-$49,999	1.25% per year
$50,000–$99,999	1.00% per year
$100,000+	0.75% per year

There is a minimum annual fee of $50
Minimum account size $5000 ($2000 for IRAs)

S&P has created a series of baskets for E*TRADE investors that have the look and feel of S&P indexes. These off-the-shelf baskets can be customized to fit your individual needs. In addition, you can create a custom basket from scratch using the stock analytic tools on the E*TRADE Web site. Here are the types of S&P off-the-shelf baskets that are available:

Index Baskets
+ Dow Jones Industrial Average (30 stocks)
+ S&P 20 (large stocks)
+ S&P Mid 25 (mid-cap stocks)
+ OTC 25 (large over-the-counter stocks)

Style Baskets

- Large Value or Growth
- Mid-Cap Value or Growth
- Small-Cap Value or Growth

Industry Sector Baskets

- Consumer Discretionary
- Consumer Stables
- Energy, Financials
- Information Technology
- Materials
- Utilities
- Health Care
- Industrials
- Telecommunication Services

Stock trading in E*TRADE baskets is similar to trading stocks in Foliofn. All trading occurs twice per day, and E*TRADE attempts to match buyers with sellers during those periods. Stocks that cannot be matched are executed on the exchange. For more information on stock baskets, visit www.etrade.com.

CHAPTER SUMMARY

Special circumstances require special products. When no stock index fund meets your needs, Foliofn and E*TRADE offer investors the ability to create their own personal index fund. Stock baskets and folios combine the diversification, convenience, and the regular investing benefits of mutual funds with the customization and tax control features of individual stock ownership. The number of portfolios you can create is only limited by your imagination. Using folios and stock baskets as an index fund alternative is unique, and it may be helpful in special circumstances or just for fun.

PART THREE

Managing Your Portfolio of Index Funds

CHAPTER 12

Realistic Market Expectations

Key Concepts

- Successful investors understand the potential risks and returns of the market.
- Past history offers some clues to future returns.
- Economic forecasts also aid when developing market expectations.
- No forecast is perfect, and it is better to be conservative.

Effective portfolio management requires an awareness of market history and a framework for fashioning realistic long-term market forecasts. This process will help you establish a method for allocating your portfolio among alternative asset classes. Since the returns of your portfolio will be based 100 percent on the returns of the stock and bond markets, it is logical to spend some time looking at past market data. However, simply reviewing past results and projecting those returns into the future are not a good way to forecast returns. The past will fool you into a false sense of security, especially over the last 20 years. Market returns can differ significantly from their historic norms, and no one can tell you exactly what the market will return going forward. All we can do is make reasonable estimates and hope the returns fall within a close range of those estimates. This chapter reviews the returns of the markets in the past and offers a framework to forecasting expected returns into the future.

THE LIMITATIONS OF FORECASTING

There are various methods for predicting market returns, and none of them are accurate. But in the absence of a crystal ball, this is all we have to work with. One method of forecasting returns projects past performance into the future using simple mathematical models. For many reasons beyond the scope of this book, using only past performance to predict the future can lead to horrendously high market forecasts, especially if the last 20 years are weighted more heavily in the data than very long-term results. A second method of market prediction includes the use of economic forecasts. These methods can be more effective than simple projection, but unpredictable events such as natural disasters, wars, and political instability can derail the best market predictions. It seems that a reasonable way to forecast a market outcome is by combining past market data (technical) with a conservative long-term economic growth forecast (fundamental).

Combining technical and fundamental inputs may yield clues to the future. In any event the market forecasts put forth in this chapter are intended to be a guide, not an absolute. That being said, it is always better to err on the side of conservatism rather than being aggressive. If you use a conservative estimate and the markets perform better than expected, you will end up with more money, which is always better than the other way around.

STOCK PRICE HISTORY

Market forecasts should be very long-term. How long is very long-term? A lifetime would be appropriate, although by the time most people get around to investing, half of their life is over. Therefore, let's call long-term 30 years. The reason 30 years seems about right is that stock prices seem to move in long waves. Each wave includes a multiyear bear market and a multiyear bull market. There have been four major stock market waves since 1880 (see Figure 12–1). Each wave lasted roughly 30 years, which, coincidentally, is the equivalent of one generation. If this secular wave sequence continues, the average person will see two waves during his or her lifetime.

When people experience the first bull market in their lives, they are usually young and do not have a lot of money invested. By the

FIGURE 12–1

Secular Waves of Historic Stock Returns

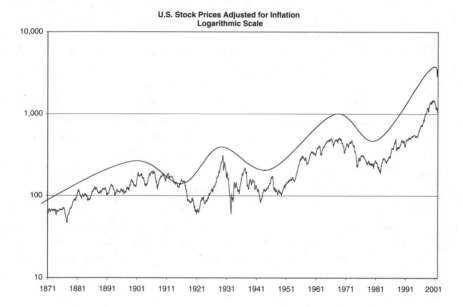

time they experience the second wave, a person is generally well established in a career and has more assets set aside for retirement. It
is during the second wave that people make their gains in the stock
market, not the first. In my opinion, the wave that began in 1982 was
not a direct benefit to baby boomers because most did not have a lot
of money in the market at the beginning. On the other hand, the bull
market of the 1980s and 1990s was a huge benefit to the baby
boomers' parents. It may be several years before the baby boomers
get to participate in a bull market that helps them directly.

Although my market forecast calls for a bull market sometime
over the next 30 years, there have been times when the market did
not go up in value over a 30-year period. Notice in Figure 12–1 that
during the period from 1881 to 1950, the inflation-adjusted price of
stocks did not go up. This does not mean that investors during that
period did not make money. In those years the average dividend
yield on common stock was over 6 percent. Basically, companies
paid shareholders about 70 percent of the earnings they made in the

form of cash dividends. Today companies pay a cash dividend of 1.5 percent, which equals only about 30 percent of corporate earnings. The other 70 percent of earnings is retained internally for corporate growth or used to buy back stock. There are lots of reasons for this change, one being different tax treatment of capital gains and dividends. We do not know how investors will be paid in the future, and it does not really matter. In the long run, dividends and capital gains are all part of the market "total return."

The purpose of discussing waves is to point out that it may take 30 years or more for an investor to be justly rewarded for taking risks in the stock market. Now you may be thinking, "I don't have 30 years!" and that may be true. But according to new annuity tables released by the IRS in 2001, the life expectancy for a 70 year old is another 16 years, and if both a husband and wife make it to age 70, then one of the two is expected to live another 26 years.

Some people in the popular press talk about "getting into" a bull market and "getting out of" a bear mark, but it is all marketing hype. No one knows when the next bull market will begin, how long it will last, and when it will end. The best way to take advantage of the fruits of the stock market is through a consistent, long-term investment strategy.

NOMINAL RETURNS AND REAL RETURNS

We know that over long periods of time, stocks are expected to perform better than bonds, and bonds are expected to perform better than money market funds. Even though all markets go up in value over time, do investors really make any money? That question cannot be answered by looking at unadjusted market returns (the returns everyone uses). You must strip out the inflation rate and look at the inflation-adjusted return to see if you made money. Inflation is a hidden income tax that a government places on its people through faulty fiscal and monetary policy (we will save that discussion for another book). Inflation distorts investment results. Nominal returns may look great on paper, but real returns are what count. For example, if an investment earned 5 percent at the same time inflation was 5 percent, then the "real" rate of return was 0 percent. Actually, it is less than 0 percent. Since the IRS does not take inflation into account, taxes are due on the full 5 percent nominal gain, which makes the real after-tax return negative. Although taxes are a big issue in investing, going forward we do not discuss taxes in this chapter.

THE HISTORY OF MARKET RETURNS

Benjamin Graham once said, "In the short run the market is a voting machine, and in the long run it is a weighing machine." Market prices are the result of an auction that we all participate in. On any given day millions of people decide the price of stocks and bonds by placing buy and sell orders. In the short term prices can move erratically as new information comes into the market that may conflict with forecasts and change opinions. In the long run the true economic impact of the news becomes clearer, which causes stock prices to adjust to a new forecast, and the cycle begins again.

"History may not repeat itself, but it rhymes," as the saying goes. To gain an understanding of the future potential of the stock and bond markets, we need to begin with the past data. Table 12–1 lists the nominal rates of return and historic price volatility of various financial markets. Subtracting the inflation rate from the nominal index return yields the real return. Since different indexes have different starting dates, there are three groups. The year 1950 was chosen for the return of major U.S. indexes. By focusing on the second half of the 20th century, we concentrate on the returns of "regulated" markets. In the early 1900s the stock market was only minimally regulated, and that had a large effect on the risk and return characteristics in the first half of the century. A start date of 1950 also takes us through two major bull markets and two major bear markets. Two complete market cycles are hardly an adequate statistical sample, but they are all we have to work with.

Risk as a Driver of Market Returns

Markets derive returns from a number of factors. *Risk* is certainly a major factor in the calculation of expected future returns. The most common measure for risk in the financial markets is standard deviation, written as the Greek symbol σ. Standard deviation is a mathematical formula that expresses the *average* amount of price volatility in a market. Standard deviation does not express the limit of market risk; it simply reports the "average miss," any given year a market has had from its historical average annual return.

TABLE 12–1

Historic Market Returns

Select US Indexes 1950–2001	Start Date	Nominal Return	Real Return	Annual Risk*
S&P 500 (Large Stocks)	1950	12.6	8.6	14.3
Small U.S. Stocks	1950	13.5	9.6	19.5
Long-Term Govt. Bonds	1950	5.9	1.9	8.9
Long-Term Corp. Bonds	1950	6.2	2.2	8.0
U.S. T-Bills	1950	5.1	1.1	0.8
Consumer Price Index	1950	4.0	NA	1.1
Select U.S. Sectors 1979–2001	**Start Date**	**Nominal Return**	**Real Return**	**Annual Risk***
Russell 3000 Value	1979	15.5	11.5	14.2
Russell 3000 Growth	1979	13.7	9.7	18.5
Wilshire REIT Index	1979	13.5	9.5	14.4
Select International Indexes—Various Dates	**Start Date**	**Nominal Return**	**Real Return**	**Annual Risk***
MSCI EAFE Index	1970	11.0	6.0	16.9
MSCI Emerging Markets	1988	11.3	6.3	24.2
JP Morgan Global Bond	1987	6.5	2.5	6.1

*Risk is measured by the annualized standard deviation of monthly returns.
Source: Russell, S&P, Federal Reserve Board, Bloomberg, Wilshire, MSCI

Figure 12–2 uses the data from Table 12–1. As you can see, the markets with the highest risk have generated the greatest long-term returns. Using historic risk numbers for each market and plugging them into a pricing model that also includes the current interest rate on Treasury bills, we can estimate expected future rewards for all markets.

The return of stocks and bonds varies from period to period. However, the risk of a market tends to be much more consistent and more predictable than its return. Since the risk of a market is fairly constant, we can use those data to forecast an expected reward for taking this extra risk. Stocks have more risk than Treasury bills (T-bills); therefore, by adding a "risk premium" to the return of T-bills,

FIGURE 12–2

Risk as a Driver of Expected Rewards

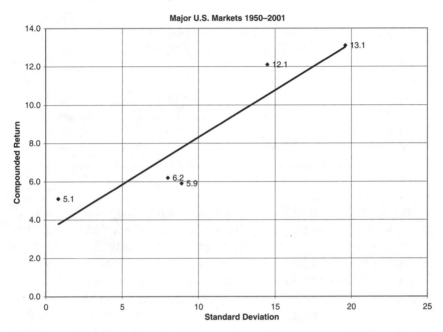

we can forecast an expected return for the stock market. The financial equation used to forecast expected market returns using risk as a factor is called the capital asset pricing model (CAPM).

I will spare you the details of the CAPM equation and just provide an overview. Table 12–2 lists the predicted returns of various markets based on the CAPM system. We know that the safest security you can own is a T-bill. The federal government has the power to print money and will pay off all T-bills. That makes the T-bill a risk-free investment. The return of T-bills can be forecasted to be 1.0 percent higher than the inflation rate during a long period of time. Since there is no investment as safe as a T-bill, you can estimate the return of other investments by adding an extra risk premium on top of the T-bill rate. The extra layer of return is directly related to the extra asset risk in the investment and is calculated in the CAPM equation (see Table 12–2).

You may be wondering why the expected returns are higher

TABLE 12–2

Projected Risk Premiums for Various Asset Classes

Asset Class	Historic Risk Premium over T-Bills	Forecast Risk Premium over T-Bills	Expected Return
T-bills	—	—	Inflation + 1.0%
Long treas. bonds	0.8	1.5%	T-bill rate + 1.5%
Corporate bonds	1.3	2.0%	T-bill rate + 2.0%
Large U.S. stocks	7.0	3.5%	T-bill rate + 3.5%
Small U.S. stocks	8.0	5.0%	T-bill rate + 5.0%

than the historic returns for bonds and lower than the historic returns for stocks. Bond prices have become more volatile since the 1950s due to increased volatility in the inflation rate. Since we must get paid more for taking more risk, the projected return of bonds is higher than the previous 50-year average. On the other hand, the return of stocks since 1950 reflects expanding valuation in the form of higher price-to-earnings ratios. Although the bear market of 2000–2001 has knocked down valuations some, they are still high relative to historic norms. I do not expect stock valuations to go back to 1999 levels, and they may even trend lower in the next 10 years.

Risk premiums make sense from a practical standpoint. Greater risk should yield greater returns. In addition to forecasting individual market returns, the CAPM is useful in determining the relationship of returns that should occur *between* markets and how mixing asset classes together actually reduces risk and increases return. The subject of asset allocation is explored in Chapter 13.

Economic Growth Drives Stock Prices

Until this point we have only used past market risk and returns to create a market forecast. A second method for calculating expected market returns is through the use of economic models. For example, using economic growth assumptions, we can forecast corporate earnings growth, which can be used to forecast stock returns. The formula looks like this: *Expected stock market returns = expected earn-*

ings growth + cash dividend yield + or − changes in the speculative pre-mium. That is a mouthful! To better understand this model, each part is explained next.

Earnings Growth

The primary driver behind stock prices is current earnings and projected earnings growth. The more money companies make and the more they are expected to make, the higher the stock market goes. To measure earnings growth potential in the stock market, you start with the growth in overall economic activity. Gross domestic product (GDP) is the single best measure of economic activity. GDP is the sum total of all goods and services produced in the United States during the year. There is a direct and consistent relationship between GDP growth and corporate earnings growth. Figure 12–3 illustrates that in the very long term, corporate earnings (the jagged line) follow GDP growth (the smooth line).

FIGURE 12–3

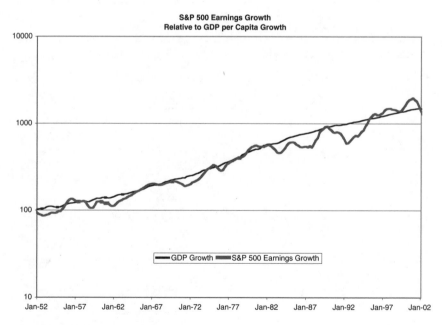

Source: S&P, U.S. Department of Commerce

Since it is the Federal Reserve's job to "adjust" the economy using monetary policy, they target GDP growth. In general, the Federal Reserve would like to see the economy grow by 3 percent per year adjusted for inflation. Because corporate earnings growth seems to follow GDP growth closely over time, we can forecast earnings growth to be about 3 percent per year adjusted for inflation.

Cash Dividends

The second part of the formula covers the cash payment of dividends. U.S. stocks currently pay about 1.5 percent per year in dividend yield as measured by the S&P 500 Index. That is historically a very low number. Dividend yields have dropped significantly since the 1950s, hitting a low of 1 percent in 1999 (Figure 12–4). One reason for the drop is that the number of companies paying dividends has fallen from approximately 70 percent to 20 percent. In addition, the percentage of earnings paid out in dividends is also at its lowest point. The payout rate of dividends is now only about 30 percent

FIGURE 12–4

S&P 500 Dividend Yields

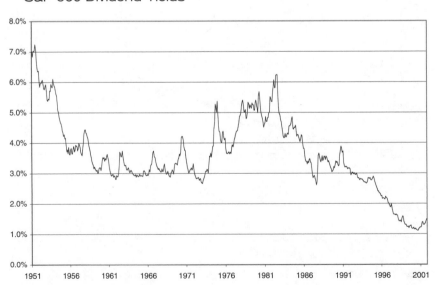

of earnings, whereas in the early twentieth century the payout rate was closer to 70 percent of earnings. As a result, dividends are not as large a part of the equation as they used to be, but they are still very important to your total return.

Speculation (PE Expansion and Contraction)

The third driver of total return is speculation. If most investors believe that corporate earnings will increase faster and greater than the average, the price of stock will increase in anticipation of the greater earnings forecast. This is exactly the reason Internet stocks kept going higher and higher in the late 1990s. The prices of those stocks were simply adjusting to the lofty earnings forecasts of investors. When real earnings became known, or no earnings in the case of most Internet stocks, value of the markets fell.

In a broad sense, speculation creates about 10 times more volatility in the market than actual earnings changes and about 100 times more volatility than dividend changes. If you have a crystal ball and can predict the mind of the masses, then you can make a lot of money on changing market valuation. Personally, I have never had any luck at it.

Figure 12–5 clearly illustrates the speculative booms and busts we have experienced in the stock market over the years. The S&P 500 price-to-GDP ratio is derived by dividing the price of the S&P 500 by gross domestic product per capita. This ratio is similar to the glorified price-to-earnings ratio (PE), only it is more stable. Using GDP in place of earnings in the ratio eliminates a lot of noise that market PE ratios create. In September 1981 the S&P 500 was trading at only 0.6 percent of GDP per capita, but by September 1999 it was trading at 3.2 percent of GDP per capita, over five times the 1981 level. In a good economy with low inflation, I believe a ratio of about 1.5 percent to 1.7 percent is appropriate. You can see how speculation radically changed the value of the stock market in the late 1990s, even though the level of economic activity in the United States remained fairly consistent (see Figure 12–3).

In the short run, speculation creates the volatility in stock price, but in the long run economic growth proves to be the real driver of returns. It is impossible to predict what investors will think about the value of the markets next week, next month, or next year, let alone 30 years from now. Speculation is not predictable, so there is

FIGURE   12–5

S&P 500 Speculative Premium

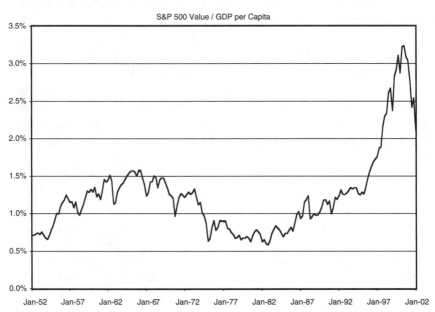

no sense trying to input that variable in a long-term forecast. For the following forecasts, we assume the price-to-GDP and PE ratios of the stock market are held constant at current levels, thereby eliminating speculative noise.

Inflation Drives Bond Returns

In the very long run, economic growth and dividends drive stock market returns. However, the bond market is different. There is a formula for calculating the expected long-term return of bonds, which is: *Expected bond return = interest payments + the reinvestment of interest + or − changes in inflation + or − changes in credit risk.* In the long term, the inflation rate drives the price of Treasury bonds, and the additional risk of default also drives the price of all other bonds.

There is a direct and inverse relationship between the inflation

Inflation and Its Effect on Bond Market Returns

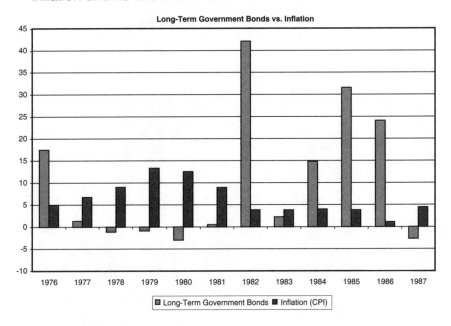

Long-Term Government Bonds vs. Inflation

■ Long-Term Government Bonds ■ Inflation (CPI)

rate and the price of all bonds. When inflation is rising, bond prices are falling, and when inflation is falling, bond prices are rising. Figure 12–6 illustrates the inverse relationship between inflation and bond market returns. The figure highlights one of the most volatile periods in U.S. bond market history. From 1976 through 1980, inflation soared to 15 percent, creating havoc in the Lehman Brothers Long-Term Government Bond Index. By 1982 inflation dropped like a rock, setting the Lehman index up for its best gain ever.

It is impossible to forecast the movement of the inflation rate. However, you can limit your risk by purchasing short-term bond index funds. The interest rates generally follow the inflation rate (Figure 12–7). If you purchase short-term bond funds, you will not experience the intense volatility of long-term bond funds. The bonds in short-term funds are much closer to maturity, so they exhibit less fluctuation in price. Although you earn extra interest from long-term bonds, the pickup in yield does not justify the added risk. His-

FIGURE   12–7

Treasury Note Yield and Inflation

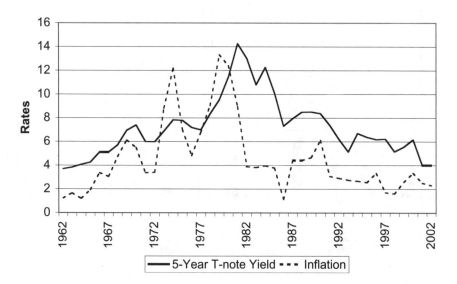

Interest Rates Follow Inflation

torically, there has been less than a 0.5 percent return advantage from long-term bond funds over short-term bond funds, while adding over 3 percent per year in extra risk (σ). See Chapter 9 for more information on bond indexes and bond index funds.

CREATING A FORECAST

We have analyzed four primary drivers of market returns: risk, inflation, earnings growth, and cash payments from interest and dividends. These factors are part of every valuation model. It would require a book much thicker than this one to detail all the alternative models used in forecasting expected stock and bond returns. I have drawn from a number of these models and present my best guess for the future. Table 12–3 is my median expected return for all of the major markets. These are 30-year numbers.

TABLE 12-3

30-Year Estimates of Bonds, Stocks, REITs, GDP, and
Inflation

Index	Nominal Forecast	Inflation Adjusted	Risk*
U.S. Treasury bills (1 year maturity)	4.0	1.0	2.0
U.S. Treasury notes (5 year maturity)	4.8	1.8	4.8
Govt. agency notes (5 year maturity)	5.3	2.3	5.3
Long-term U.S. Treasury bonds	5.5	2.5	8.0
Investment grade corporate bonds (5 yr)	6.0	3.0	5.5
Long-term invest. grade corp. bonds	6.5	3.5	8.5
High-yield corporate bonds (BB or less)	9.0	6.0	15.0
U.S. large stocks	8.0	5.0	15.0
U.S. small stocks	10.0	7.0	20.0
REITs (real estate investment trusts)	8.0	5.0	15.0
International developed country	8.0	5.0	17.0
International small country	10.0	7.0	22.0
International emerging country	12.0	9.0	25.0
Gross domestic product (Nominal & real rates)	6.0	3.0	2.0
Inflation (consumer price index)	3.0	—	1.5

*Risk is the standard deviation of annual returns.

CHAPTER SUMMARY

The market forecasts in this chapter are meant to be a guide for planning portfolios. No one knows what the actual returns of the markets will be over the next 30 years, but most people agree they will
certainly be less than in the past 30 years. We know there are consistent factors that contribute to market returns, and those factors are
likely to persist into the future. Most risk is reflected in price volatility, and it is clear that investments with greater price volatility demand higher returns. In addition, economic growth and inflation
drive stock and bond returns. By using government and private
forecasts of GDP, predicting market returns becomes more manage-
able, although the task is never easy and never totally accurate.

Although the future 30-year return of the markets cannot be known, I believe the relationship *between* the markets will be close to those predicted. In other words, small stocks should outperform large stocks, large stocks should outperform corporate bonds, and corporate bonds should outperform Treasury bills. With this information in hand, we will move on to the next step, which is to gain an understanding of asset allocation.

Since a "close" forecast is the best it gets, always try to err on the side of a conservative approach. It is wiser to plan for lower returns and be pleasantly surprised in a bull market than to rely on a rosy forecast and possibly run out of money later in life. Simply put, it is better to be safe than sorry.

CHAPTER 13

Asset Allocation

Key Concepts

- Diversifying a portfolio across several asset classes reduces risk and increases return.
- Rebalancing a portfolio at least once per year creates a positive effect.
- Ensure the investments you hold have a low correlation with each other.

Asset allocation is a modern way of saying "don't put all your eggs in one basket." The essence of the idea seems to be intuitive to all investors who have had long-term success in the markets. But prior to the 1970s, the science of making an asset allocation decision was foreign to all but a few academic researchers. To manage a portfolio of index funds effectively, you must develop a method for choosing among alternative stock and bond markets. This chapter covers the academics behind making those wise investment decisions.

The traditional view of diversification was simply to avoid putting all your money in one place. Investors who lived through the Great Depression have high resistance to putting all their money in one bank or brokerage house. When the financial system collapsed in the 1930s, many banks and brokerage firms became insolvent, and investors lost everything. Government regulation and insurance have made our financial institutions more secure, and there is little risk of a repeat of the Great Depression. However, proper diversification is still needed within an account to make your investment portfolio more secure. Asset allocation is the cornerstone of a solid, long-term investment plan.

MODERN PORTFOLIO THEORY (MPT)

In 1952 Harry Markowitz, a 25-year-old graduate student at the University of Chicago, wrote a revolutionary research paper entitled "Portfolio Selection." In short, the paper discussed the idea that financial risk is necessary in a portfolio to achieve a higher rate of return and that portfolio risk can be reduced through proper diversification. Now this was nothing revolutionary, and for that reason Markowitz's paper was not viewed as original research by many of his primary instructors. However, he did do something unique. Markowitz mathematically quantified the risk and return relationship in a stock portfolio and for the first time explained why combining different stock investments in the same portfolio lowered risk and increased return. Markowitz argued that the risk of an individual investment is not as important as how the entire portfolio fit together to achieve a positive result. After much deliberation in the economics department at the university, Markowitz's paper was submitted for publication in the *Journal of Finance*.

Initially, "Portfolio Selection" had little readership. Certainly, no one anticipated the small 14-page paper would eventually become the backbone of portfolio management over the next 50 years. The research began to leave its mark in 1959, when Markowitz published a book entitled *Portfolio Selection: Efficient Diversification of Investments*. That book earned Markowitz wide recognition and eventually the Nobel prize in economics in 1990.

In the 1970s portfolio management research expanded rapidly at universities, banks, and private money management companies across the country. Computing power was needed to do the long calculations, and it was finally becoming available at a reasonable cost. Using historic risks and returns, different amounts of stocks and bonds were mixed together and tested using computer simulations. The idea was to find the right allocation of assets from each asset class that achieved the "portfolio effect" of higher returns with less risk. This strategy of portfolio management became known as modern portfolio theory (MPT), and Harry Markowitz is often referred to as the father of MPT.

Today, nearly every institutional investor uses some form of MPT to invest in the financial markets. Abundant computing power crunches reams of market data nearly instantaneously in an attempt to find the most effective asset allocation mix. For individual investors index funds are an ideal way to reap the benefits of MPT. Creating an asset allocation of stock and bond index funds can reduce the portfolio risk and increase the portfolio return.

An Example of MPT

The best way to explain the benefits of MPT is through an example using two asset classes. By combining stocks and bonds in one portfolio, you will see how they can work together to increase the expected return of the portfolio and reduce the risk. Figures 13–1 and 13–2 illustrate the benefit of diversification using the S&P 500 Index

FIGURE   13–1

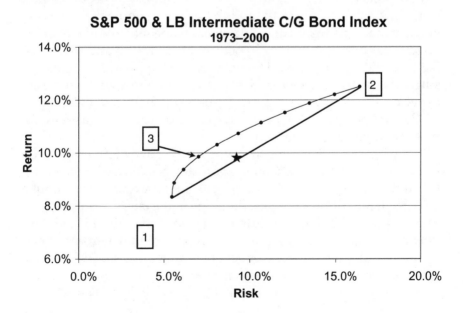

TABLE 13-1

Index Returns from 1973–2000	Annualized Return	Risk
100% Bond index (1)	8.3%	5.5%
100% S&P 500 (2)	12.5%	16.4%
Expected 70% bond and 30% stock mix (Star)	9.6%	8.7%
Actual 70% bond and 30% stock mix (3)	9.9%	7.0%
MPT advantage	0.3%	(1.7%)

and the Lehman Brothers Intermediate Corporate/Government Bond Index. Various mixes of the two investments are combined at 10 percent intervals, creating different points on Figure 13–1. Point 1 is 100 percent bonds, Point 2 is 100 percent stocks, and Point 3 is 70 percent bonds and 30 percent stocks.

The 100 percent stock portfolio has the highest return and the highest risk. The 100 percent bond portfolio has the lowest return and the lowest risk. A 70 percent bond and 30 percent stock mix would expect to have a return of 9.6 percent and a risk of 8.7 percent. This risk and return figure is based on a simple weighted average of market returns using 70 percent of the return and risk of the bond index and adding it to 30 percent of the return and risk of the S&P 500 Index. It is marked as a star on Figure 13–1. The actual result of the 70 percent bond and 30 percent stock mix was better than expected. The return during the period was 9.9 percent (3 in Figure 13–1), higher than the 9.6 percent expected. The risk was only 7.0 percent, lower than expected.

Figure 13–2 illustrates the return advantage of diversification in a different way. As we begin to add stocks to an all-bond portfolio, there is a large return advantage at first; however, after about a 20 percent allocation to stocks, the slope of the curve is not as steep, meaning the advantage of adding more stocks has diminished. This does not mean that you should not own more than 20 percent stocks; it simply states the portfolio effect of owning more stocks begins to diminish per extra unit of portfolio risk.

The MPT example assumes that the portfolio is *rebalanced* every

FIGURE 13–2

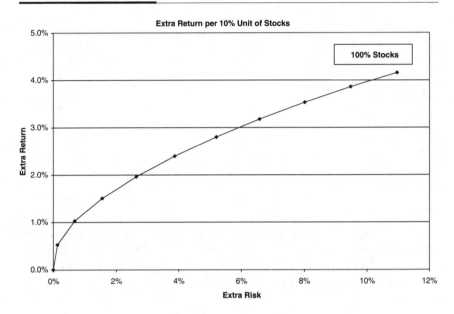

3 months to its original 70 percent bond and 30 percent stock mix. If the stock portion went down one quarter while the bond portion increased in value, the model assumes you sold bonds and bought stocks to bring the portfolio back to a 70 percent bond and 30 percent stock mix. Rebalancing often feels counterintuitive and does not always produce immediate gratification. However, applying a consistent rebalancing strategy over several years increases portfolio returns and significantly reduces risk.

Table 13–2 offers a mathematical explanation of why rebalancing works. Two hypothetical asset classes are created and tracked over a 2-year period. The risk and return of each asset class are identical, but an equally weighted portfolio holding 50 percent of each behaves very differently than the asset classes themselves.

Each asset class individually earned 8.0 percent over the 2-year period. A portfolio that held 50 percent in each asset class, with rebalancing after 1 year, eliminated all the volatility in the portfolio and resulted in a 2.25 percent higher return than either asset class measured separately. If you diversify across different investments

TABLE 13-2

	Year 1	Year 2	Total Return
Asset class 1	+20%	−10%	1.20 × 0.90 = 1.08
			1.08 − 1 = 8.0%
Asset class 2	−10%	+20%	0.90 × 1.20 = 1.08
			1.08 − 1 = 8.0%
50% /50% mix			
rebalanced after 1 year	5%	5%	1.05 × 1.05 = 1.1025
			1.1025 − 1 = 10.25%

and rebalance at regular intervals, you actually increase the return of the portfolio over time. The "free lunch" from asset allocation and rebalancing is the essence of modern portfolio theory, and the proof of this theory earned Harry Markowitz a Nobel prize.

CORRELATION EXPLAINED

The challenge of investment management is to lower the risk in a portfolio while not lowering the return. This goal can be accomplished by mixing asset classes together that have a low *correlation* with each other. If one asset class moves in perfect harmony with another, they have a perfect positive correlation. There is no benefit to diversifying into an index fund that has a high correlation with an index fund you already own. For example, it makes no sense to buy an index fund benchmarked to the S&P 500 Growth Index if you already own a fund benchmarked to the Russell 1000 Growth Index. The funds are highly correlated, and buying both does not add diversification to your portfolio. Many investors made this mistake in the 1990s by "diversifying" their retirement holdings into two or three aggressive growth funds. Although these people thought they were diversifying their assets, they were actually increasing the risk of a large loss. The bear market of 2000–2001 clearly pointed out their mistake.

Figure 13–3 illustrates a portfolio that is invested in two separate investments but is not diversified. Investment A and invest-

FIGURE 13–3

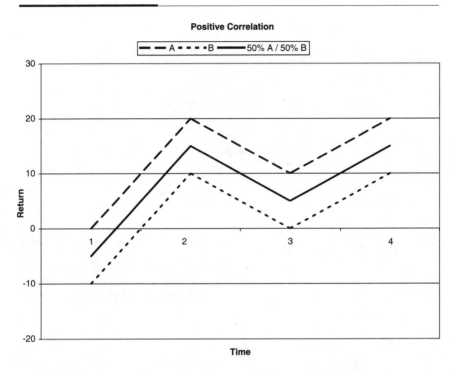

Positive Correlation

ment B have a high correlation with each other, so there is no risk reduction in a portfolio that invests 50 percent in fund A and 50 percent in fund B.

It is much better to invest in two mutual funds that have a negative correlation, no correlation, or a low positive correlation. Figure 13–4 shows that fund C and fund D frequently move in the opposite direction of each other. These investments are said to have a negative correlation. A portfolio of 50 percent fund C and 50 percent fund D, rebalanced at each interval, will result in a return that is much smoother than either of the two investments individually. This reduction in risk will increase the portfolio return in the long run. One last point: When two investments move randomly with each other and the performance of one has no effect on the performance of the other, they are said to be noncorrelated.

FIGURE   13–4

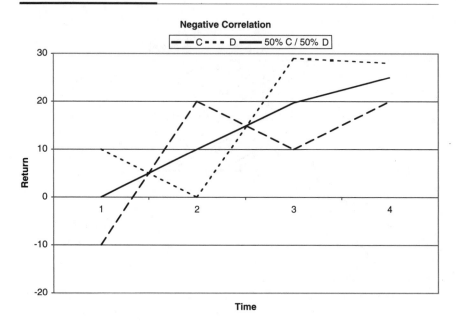

A matrix is used to show the correlation between investments. The matrix in Table 13–3 expresses the correlation between four asset classes from 1978 to 2000. The matrix compares large U.S. stocks (S&P 500), international stocks (EAFE Index), real estate investment trusts (Wilshire REIT), and bonds (Lehman Brothers Intermediate Term Government/Corporate Bond Index).

TABLE   13–3

Correlation 1978–2000	S&P 500 Index	EAFE Index	Wilshire REIT	LB Bond Index
S&P 500 Index	—	.48	.55	.29
EAFE Index	.48	—	.29	.20
Wilshire REIT	.55	.29	—	.24
LB Bond Index	.29	.20	.24	—

MULTIASSET CLASS PORTFOLIOS

The lower the correlation between indexes, the greater the benefit of holding those investments in a portfolio. Earlier you learned that adding an S&P 500 index fund to an intermediate-term bond index fund decreased the risk of a portfolio and increased the return. We can now go a step further. Adding a position in international stocks and REITs to the S&P 500/bond index portfolio also increases the portfolio return and reduces the risk. An asset allocation mix using four asset classes is more efficient than a portfolio consisting of only two. If we add a fifth asset class, the risk is reduced more and the return increases slightly above the old "efficient frontier" (Figure 13–5). The trick is to find several asset classes that have a low correlation with each other.

There are a number of books, Web sites, and computer programs that can assist you in learning about asset allocation. One of the best books on the market is William Bernstein's *The Intelligent Asset Allocator* (McGraw-Hill, 2000). In addition, Nobel laureate Bill Sharpe has an on-line service called Financial Engines (www.financialengines.com). This site can help you create and maintain an asset allocation of index funds for a nominal monthly fee.

F I G U R E   13–5

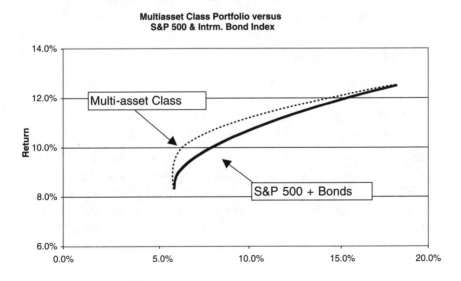

Whichever source of assistance you choose, there are a few points about asset class correlation you need to be aware of:

1. It is very difficult to find major asset classes that are non-correlated or negatively correlated with each other. The best you can hope for is to find a few asset classes that have a low positive correlation.

2. The correlation between asset classes can change. Investments that were once noncorrelated may become more correlated in a global marketplace. Past correlation should be viewed as a guide, not as an absolute.

3. During a time of crisis, the correlation between some asset classes actually increases. This is exactly the opposite of what you would like to see happen. When the World Trade Center was destroyed in September 2001, all stock markets around the world fell by more than 5 percent. Global diversification did not help during that horrific month.

4. Finally, don't expect absolute answers from any asset allocation model. The data used to create efficient frontiers and optimal portfolios are based on historic relationships and expected relationships. History is a nice guide, but the future can never be known. Asset allocation in the real world requires just as much common sense as it does quantitative number crunching.

CHAPTER SUMMARY

"My ventures are not in one bottom trusted, nor to one place;
Nor is my whole estate upon the fortune of this present year;
Therefore, my merchandise makes me not sad."

Antonio in The Merchant of Venice

To manage a portfolio of index funds effectively, you should forecast how those investments will act independently and how they will blend together as part of a well-diversified portfolio. Asset allocation is the cornerstone of every long-term investment plan and is the "science" of blending index funds together. You do not need

to be a Nobel laureate to benefit from the reduction in risk and increase in return that proper asset allocation and rebalancing deliver. Every long-term investor knows that buying, holding, and rebalancing a well-diversified portfolio is a much better strategy than
putting all your eggs in one basket.

CHAPTER 14

Defining Your Financial Goals

Key Concepts
- Estimate as closely as possible your future needs.
- Inventory your current savings and earning power.
- Assign an asset allocation to your required return.
- Stress test your stock and bond asset allocation.

We save and invest for many reasons. Most of us save to buy a car, a home, vacation property, pay for a child's education, retirement, and if there is any money left, pass it on to heirs or charity. Saving and investing effectively mean understanding when the major cash flows in life will occur and having a general idea of how much money you will need for each event, especially retirement. This chapter is all about calculating your financial needs so you can design an effective portfolio of index funds to meet those needs. Specifically, this chapter addresses the biggest financial hurdle in everyone's life: the need to save and invest for retirement.

Financial security is the most sought-after financial goal in everyone's life. Attaining financial security typically takes years of hard work and sacrifice. If you are still working and saving, this chapter will help answer questions revolving around how much money is enough to retire. If you are already retired, this chapter will help answer questions concerning the amount of money you can spend each year during retirement. We will also discuss changes to your index fund portfolio as you transition from working and saving, to preretirement, and to fully retired.

Attaining your goal means understanding your current financial situation and accurately forecasting your future obligations. In your planning you will need to address issues such as estate planning, health insurance, long-term care, and a multitude of other related subjects. Once you have a good handle on your current financial life, you will be ready to put together a sensible portfolio of index funds that addresses your needs in the future. Unfortunately, there is only limited space in this book, and we cannot go into details on subjects not directly related to investing. There are informative books in bookstores that can help you with many of the financial planning issues not addressed here.

Later in this chapter we will look at a technique for analyzing financial needs as they relate to managing an investment portfolio. That analysis will lead you to a simple stock and bond asset allocation, which will be expanded on in Chapter 15. Before we begin this analysis, there are a couple of points that need to be considered. We first need to look at the subject of risk and then to discuss the subject of control.

UNDERSTANDING RISK

Faithfully saving a percentage of your income each year is an important part of a secure retirement. Equally as important is the way you invest the money in your retirement accounts. Investing effectively means holding realistic expectations about market returns and having a solid understanding of the amount of risk you can personally handle. If you rely too much on high market returns or assume too much risk in a portfolio, there is a high probability that you will abandon your investment strategy prematurely. During severe market downturns, investors who are not emotionally prepared tend to reduce the risk in a portfolio at the wrong time, which weakens long-term performance.

It is always better to have a lower amount of risk in a portfolio than too much risk. If you have less risk, there is a very strong likelihood that you will hold onto the stocks in your portfolio during a bear market. By investing in a well-balanced portfolio and maintaining a level of risk at or below your pain threshold, you and your portfolio will be well prepared to face the uncertainties in the markets.

Risk tolerance means having an understanding of the maximum level of risk you can handle and not investing above that mark. *Risk avoidance* is a conscious decision to invest below your risk-tolerance level. Most investment questionnaires that are popular with insurance companies and brokerage firms try to push you into investing at your maximum risk level even if there is no need to do so. This is because those firms make more money if you take more risk (i.e., buy more stocks). That is the wrong approach to investing.

There is nothing wrong with avoiding risk if you do not need to take risk. At some point during your life, the financial freedom you are seeking will be realized. The money you need will be "in the bank," or at least you know you can get there by investing in low-risk investments. At that point in life, your world changes. You no longer need to take a lot of financial risk to achieve your goals. Thus, your portfolio should change from growth orientation to wealth preservation. Simply said, you have made the money, so don't lose it now. If there is one lesson I hope you take from this section of the book, it is that your portfolio should reflect a combination of investments based on what you need and what you are comfortable with, not what your maximum risk-tolerance level is.

I believe investors should reduce risk if they do not have a good reason for taking risk. However, that does not mean getting out of the stock market entirely. For example, if you have always been 60 percent in stocks and a secure retirement is now in sight, it is probably wise to reduce your exposure to 30 percent stocks. If you avoid risk when it is no longer necessary, you will save yourself a lot of aggravation. This simple strategy would have saved a lot of near retirees a lot of money in the 2000–2001 bear market.

CONTROL WHAT YOU CAN

The second item that needs to be discussed is "control," or rather the lack of it. There are many items in an investment plan that we can control, but much more that we cannot control. We can control portfolio risk (volatility) by allocating money between stock and bond index funds. The more bond index funds you have in a portfolio, the lower the risk. Although we can control portfolio risk, we cannot control the portfolio return. In the long run, the markets drive all investment performance, and there is nothing an individual can do to make the markets go up. So, paying a lot of money to hire the best investment adviser in the world is not going to make any difference. Even Warren Buffett cannot make the market go up.

We can control taxes in an account through various portfolio management techniques and estate planning, but we cannot control how Congress will change the tax laws in the future and how those changes will affect our wealth. We cannot control the tax rate we pay, but we can control when we pay the tax. There are many tax control issues relating to index fund investing discussed throughout the book.

Since there is so much we cannot control, it is important to focus your thinking on the investment planning items that you can control. This will increase your portfolio return. Do not worry about the ups and downs in the markets. That is what markets do. Only concern yourself with sticking to a long-term plan, and you will be successful.

INVESTING FOR RETIREMENT

> I would rather be certain of a good return than hopeful of a great one.
>
> *Warren Buffett*

This book uses a simple planning tool to help you make a very important investment decision. In fact, that investment decision is probably the most important one you will make in your lifetime. Once you make the decision, you should be prepared to stick by it for many years. In a sense you become married to your decision. If you break away from it prematurely, it will cost you more than any divorce. The investment decision is: How much money should you invest in the safety of bonds and how much should you risk in the stock market? This asset allocation decision will drive you crazy unless you approach it using a simple, yet sensible model.

A planning model should help you assess your current financial situation and project future needs. The retirement planning model presented in this book can be adapted to fit other financial goals such as a child's college education. The model includes a financial needs analysis and risk-tolerance test, and it results in a simple asset allocation mix between stocks and bonds. The simple stock and bond mix developed in this chapter will be expanded using more advanced portfolio management techniques in Chapter 15.

The amount of savings one person needs at retirement is always different from another. Most people find they need about 85 percent of their preretirement income. One reason the amount is less than preretirement income is due to lower income tax from the loss or reduction in pay. This chapter builds a model that attempts to quantify the amount you may need at retirement and begins to develop an investment plan to achieve that level of wealth.

A STARTING POINT

Investment planning starts by asking yourself: What do I want my money to do for me when I am alive, and what do I want my money to do for my heirs when I am dead? When asked these questions, most people have three common answers. First, we want financial security, which means we don't want to worry about running out of money while we are alive. Second, we want to live comfortably in retirement, which basically means living at a lifestyle that we have grown accustomed to. Third, we want to help our children, grandchildren, or other heirs get ahead in life and possibly help a favorite charity or two along the way.

If you agree with those answers, ask yourself: Is my investment portfolio set up to achieve these goals? Most people have no idea. Having reviewed thousands of portfolios over the years, I am saddened to report that most retirement accounts are a collection of unrelated stocks, bonds, and mutual funds gathered over the years as investors bounce from one brokerage firm to another. There is no real plan in most retirement accounts and certainly no "investment policy" in writing. I strongly recommend setting up a simple, workable investment plan and committing that plan to writing. An annual review of that document does wonders for keeping your ship on course.

The process of building an investment plan begins by putting dollar figures on subjective goals like how much money do you need to feel financially secure? How much money will you be spending each year in retirement? What is the maximum you should spend in retirement so that the money will last longer than you do? How much do you intend to gift to heirs or charity now, and how much would you like to leave them when you die? These important questions relate directly to the amount of money you will need to attain financial independence.

THE FIVE-STEP METHOD

When large corporations invest money in a company pension plan, they use a process called *liability matching*. This process matches the investments in a portfolio with the expected cash outflows of the pension plan over the years. If the cash flows are needed in the short term, a company invests in short-term investments with low risk. If cash flows are not needed for several years, a company can take more risk with a portion of the portfolio and potentially earn a higher reward. Under no circumstances should a pension committee allocate more to risky assets than is needed. The committee has a fiduciary responsibility to act prudently and control the risk in the pension fund.

Personal retirement accounts are no different from large pension funds. You have a fiduciary responsibility to act prudently and control the risk in your retirement account. If you design a portfolio to achieve a long-term investment objective based on future cash needs and the portfolio is within your risk tolerance, there is a strong likelihood that you will meet your retirement liabilities when they come due. In other words you will gain financial independence. The idea is to design a portfolio that fits your needs and follow the plan closely, without being swayed by market volatility, media hype, and the madness of the markets.

The five-step method is designed to help you decide your overall asset allocation between stocks and bonds. Before you buy any index funds in your account, you will need to know how much you are going to invest in stock index funds and how much in bond index funds.

1. Setting Goals

The largest financial liability we have in life is to build and maintain an adequate retirement fund. The size of the retirement fund will determine the quality of life you will live during the golden years and how much your heirs will receive when you are gone. So the obvious question is: How large of a nest egg do you need at retirement?

The minimum amount you will need at retirement depends in part on how much you spend each month prior to retirement. Most people do not increase the amount they spend after they retire, especially if all the children are out of the house. In fact, you may not need as much income because your taxes will be less. So, if you are still working toward retirement, calculate the amount you will need by analyzing your current monthly budget.

An Example
A 45-year-old couple has one 18-year-old child who is a freshman in college. The couple runs a small business. They plan to sell the business and retire in 20 years at age 65. The couple has accumulated $350,000 in a company profit-sharing plan and contributes $25,000 per year to their personal profit-sharing accounts. They spend about $5500 per month on living expenses, excluding college costs.

The $5500 per month budget is an after-tax figure, which means the couple needs about $8000 per month pretax to cover all federal, state, and social security taxes. When they retire, the couple will likely need the same amount to live comfortably, adjusted for inflation. If social security survives in some form, that would generate about $1500 per month in income at age 65. To get the pretax income back to $8000, the remaining $6500 per month would have to come from retirement savings. However, we will reduce the amount of monthly pretax income needed from the profit-sharing plan by $1000 because the couple will no longer pay social security tax and will pay less in federal and state tax. The bottom line is, the couple needs a distribution of $5500 per month ($66,000 per year) from the profit-sharing plan to maintain the lifestyle they have grown accustomed to.

Now that we know the profit-sharing distribution at retirement, we can work backward to determine the minimum value of the plan at retirement. I recommend people withdraw no more than 5 percent off of their retirement savings each year. That way you should not run out of money during retirement. This assumes that the financial markets cooperate and do not give us multiyear negative returns in both the stock and bond markets. The figure also assumes plowing back into the account any excess return over 5 percent for an inflation hedge.

For this couple to draw $66,000 per year out of their retirement fund, they would need a nest egg of $1,320,000 at retirement in today's dollars. To calculate that number, simply multiply the income needed by 20. The calculation is $66,000 × 20 = $1,320,000. To double-check that figure, multiply the nest egg amount by 5 percent. The calculation is $1,320,000 × 0.05 = $66,000.

The couple needs $1,320,000 at retirement in today's dollars to retire at a lifestyle they have grown accustomed to. Obviously, there are going to be other considerations that go into the nest egg figure, such as special needs of family members, health care concerns, future tax law changes, gifts made or received, inheritance, proceeds from the sale of a house, the sale of a businesses, or other assets, and so forth. These extra events could have major positive or negative effects on cashflow and should be considered when formulating a lump sum retirement amount. Unfortunately, there is not enough space in this book to cover all the contingencies, so I'll assume there are no other considerations in our example.

2. The Inflation Adjustment

A nest egg of $1,320,000 would suffice if our couple were to retire today; however, they are not going to retire for a number of years, so the figure needs to be adjusted for expected inflation. Assuming a 3 percent annual inflation rate over the next 20 years, the couple will need to withdraw $119,000 per year from the profit-sharing plan, which is $66,000 adjusted for inflation. Multiplying $119,000 by 20 equals a new nest egg target of $2,384,000, adjusted for inflation.

3. The Savings Plan and Required Return

Now that we know how much the couple needs at retirement, we can create a savings plan to get there. We have all the facts and figures, except a *required investment return*. What rate of return does the couple need on their retirement savings to reach $2,384,000 in 20 years?

There are four parts to this equation, and we already know three of the inputs:

1. The amount needed at retirement is $2,384,000.
2. The amount the couple has saved is $350,000.
3. The average amount the couple will save each year is $25,000.
4. What rate of return is needed to achieve their retirement goal?

Using a financial calculator or Microsoft Excel, you can calculate a required rate of return for the couple. Using an Excel spreadsheet, the commands are as follows:

1. Select the Function Key (*fx*) and select RATE under "Function Name."
2. Enter 20 in the NPER box. This is the number of years to retirement.
3. Enter the expected annual savings in PMT. Type −$25,000, a negative number.
4. Enter the amount the couple has saved under Pv. Type −$350,000, a negative number.
5. Enter the amount needed at retirement under Fv. Type $2,384,000, a positive number.
6. Press the OK button, and you should get a return of 7.0 percent. This is the *required return* that the couple needs to reach $2,384,000 in 20 years.

A 7.0 percent return is a reasonable expected return for a diversified investment portfolio. A mix of stock and bond index funds can be created that has a high probability of achieving a 7 percent return, but there is never a guarantee. Had the couple calculated a higher required return, such as 10 percent, then something would need to change in their retirement plan. A 10 percent return is simply not a realistic rate of return to use, and the probability of attaining that number is very low, especially after investment expenses. Consequently, the couple would need to either save more money each year, spend less in retirement, work longer, or leave a smaller inheritance to their child (my favorite option). For planning purposes, do not use more than 7.5 percent in any model.

TABLE 14-1

Stock, Bond, and Inflation Forecast

Index Return	Forecast 2002-2030
Large U.S. stock	8.0%
Corporate bonds (5 year)	6.0%
Inflation rate	3.0%
Source: Portfolio Solutions, LLC	

4. An Asset Allocation Decision

Now we finally get to the fun stuff: selecting a stock and bond mix. We know our couple needs a minimum return of 7.0 percent compounded over 20 years to meet the target goal of $2,384,000. Using forecasted returns from Chapter 12, we can piece together an asset allocation between stocks and bonds that is expected to deliver a 7 percent return (Table 14–1).

Using the estimates, a logical asset allocation for this portfolio would be 60 percent in a large U.S. stock index fund and 40 percent in an intermediate-term corporate bond index fund. This allocation is expected to earn about a 7.2 percent rate of return, which is slightly higher than the required return of 7.0 percent (Table 14–2).[1]

From a purely mathematical point of view, a 60 percent stock and 40 percent bond allocation is the correct answer. Most investors would accept this mix because the popular notion is that a 60 per-

TABLE 14-2

Portfolio Asset Allocation Recommendation

Index Funds	Allocation	Forecast	Return Contribution
Large U.S. stocks	60%	8.0%	4.8%
Intermediate corp. bonds	40%	6.0%	2.4%
Total	100%	na	7.2%

cent stock and 40 percent bond mix is "normal" or even "prudent." However, a more detailed analysis is warranted. There may be problems lurking beneath the surface.

One problem that emerges is the cost of implementation. The forecasted return of the markets is not the forecasted return of index funds. A small management fee must be paid to the index fund provider. That fee can vary based on the index fund you choose. A downward adjustment of 0.2 percent to 0.5 percent needs to be made to put the portfolio forecast in line. The cost of investing reduces the expected return of the 60/40 mix from 7.2 percent to about 7.0 percent. That return is right on top of what the couple requires.

Fees are one concern, but there is a deeper concern with the suggested allocation. Does the asset mix truly fit the personality of the investors? Is the portfolio within their risk tolerance?

5. Assessing the Risk

Up to this point we have taken a purely mathematical approach to discovering the best asset allocation for the couple. Now comes the hard part. Can the couple accept the risk in a 60 percent stock and 40 percent bond allocation that was determined to be technically correct, or will they feel the need to reduce their allocation of stocks during stressful times in the market? In other words, is the portfolio above the couple's risk-tolerance level? To find out we need to switch hats from financial engineer to behavioral psychologist.

We live in a capitalistic country, and taking financial risk is part of our national heritage. As a result, when people are asked how much risk they can handle, most tend to exaggerate. However, a look back in history shows that many people do not handle stock market declines very well. In fact, many self-proclaimed long-term investors duck out during and after bear markets. Individual investors were net sellers of stock after the crash of 1929, the deep bear market of 1973–1974, the "crash" of 1987, and people sold again in the bear market of 2000–2001. Despite a lot of brave talk, Joe and Jane average investor cannot handle a lot of market risk. All investors must do serious soul searching before deciding what level of risk is appropriate.

How can we determine if the mathematically correct 60 percent stock and 40 percent bond mix is at or below our couple's risk tolerance? Many financial advisers believe the answer to that question can be found by using a simple risk-tolerance questionnaire. These forms inquire about your age, time horizon, and ask a few "if-then" questions. The answers are fed into a computer, which spits out a risk profile and investment portfolio designed just for you. I believe this method of determining risk is nearly useless. Most of the questionnaires are too short, the questions are too vague, and there is little chance of capturing the essence of someone's risk tolerance.

One of the best methods to determine if an allocation of stock and bond index funds is acceptable is to run the portfolio through a *stress test*. This method of risk testing helps clients understand how they will react to losses in the portfolio during particularly difficult periods in the market. Most people react differently from anticipated when they start losing money month after month and year after year while getting closer and closer to retirement. The objective of a stress test is to simulate dollar losses from a chosen asset mix. If someone makes it through the test without saying "uncle," then the mix may be acceptable.

To conduct a stress test, it helps to use a recent period in market history. Prior to the 2000–2001 bear market, the stress test period I used was 1973–1974. That period was also particularly painful for stock investors. Most people who took the 1973–1974 stress test prior to year 2000 reduced their exposure to stocks by 20 to 40 percent. This reduction in stocks was not in anticipation of the upcoming 2000–2001 bear market. People reduced their allocation to stocks simply because they realized they had a lower tolerance for risk than they originally thought.

ASSET ALLOCATION STRESS TEST

The couple in our example needs a portfolio consisting of 60 percent in a large U.S. stock index fund and 40 percent in an intermediate-term corporate bond index fund to meet their retirement needs. Based on market forecasts, that allocation has a good chance of producing a 7.0 percent required return over the 20-year period. Let us assume it is the beginning of 1973, and our couple invests their $350,000 according to the 60–40 percent allocation. Here is the allocation at the beginning of 1973:

Initial Portfolio Allocation on January 1, 1973

Stock Index (60%)	Bond Index (40%)	Total Account
$210,000	$140,000	$350,000

In 1973 the stock market had a bad year and the bond market had so-so year. The stock market fell almost 15 percent and the intermediate-term corporate bond market gained about 3 percent. Our couple lost over $27,000. It was now time to add another $25,000 to their profit-sharing plan for this year's contribution and rebalance the portfolio. The couple is reluctant but decides to go along with the plan.

Portfolio Value on December 31, 1973

Stock Index	Bond Index	Total Account
$178,500	$144,200	$322,700
	Plus new cash	+25,000
	Balance 1/1/74	$347,700

New Portfolio Allocation for January 1, 1974

Stock Index (60%)	Bond Index (40%)	Total Account
$208,620	$139,080	$347,700

The year 1974 proved to be one of the worst in stock market history. Large-cap stocks fell over 26 percent, but bonds held on to a meager 1 percent gain. President Nixon resigned after taking the country off the gold standard. The value of the dollar tanked, and the Arab oil embargo was in full swing. The economy was flat on its back. The couple lost over $52,000 in 1974 and over $100,000 since starting the strategy. On January 1, 1975, it was now time for the couple to add another $25,000 to their profit-sharing plan and rebalance the portfolio back to 60 percent stocks and 40 percent bonds.

Portfolio Value on December 31, 1974

Stock Index	Bond Index	Total Account
$154,380	$140,470	$294,850
	Plus new cash	+25,000
	Balance 1/1/75	$319,850

New Portfolio Allocation for January 1, 1975

Stock Index (60%)	Bond Index (40%)	Total Account
$191,910	$127,940	$319,850

Stop the test! It's the end of the road! The couple is 2 years closer to retirement, their business is on the rocks because of the recession, and they are scared. They no longer want to have so much in stocks because they are losing more money then they are putting in. They now want safety, safety, *safety!* The couple may consider investing in a stock index fund when things get better but not now. The 60 percent stock and 40 percent bond portfolio did not pass the stress test.

A More Conservative Approach

Let's go back and rerun the 1973–1974 stress test using a more conservative portfolio. A portfolio of 40 percent stock and 60 percent short-term corporate bonds is created. The forecasted return on this portfolio is about 6.6 percent, less than the 7.0 percent needed to meet their retirement goal. As a result, the couple decided to increase their savings amount to $29,000 to make up for the potential shortfall in return. Here is the new allocations at the beginning of 1973:

Initial Portfolio Allocation on January 1, 1973

Stock Index (40%)	Bond Index (60%)	Total Account
$140,000	$210,000	$350,000

At the end of 1973, the portfolio was worth $335,300, a loss of $14,700.

Portfolio Value on December 31, 1973

Stock Index	Bond Index	Total Account
$119,000	$216,300	$335,300
	Plus new cash	+29,000
	Balance 1/1/74	$364,300

New Portfolio Allocation for January 1, 1974

Stock Index (40%)	Bond Index (60%)	Total Account
$145,720	$218,580	$364,300

Stocks in 1974 were worse than 1973. Large-cap stocks fell more than 26 percent, and bonds held a slight gain.

Portfolio Value on December 31, 1974

Stock Index	Bond Index	Total Account
$107,830	$220,760	$328,590
	Plus new cash	+29,000
	Balance 1/1/75	$357,590

New Portfolio Allocation for January 1, 1975

Stock Index (40%)	Bond Index (60%)	Total Account
$143,040	$214,550	$357,590

The couple is not happy with the fact that they lost slightly over $50,000 in the last two years, but they can live with the losses. They decide to stick with the plan because they think the market will eventually turn around. The portfolio passed the stress test. A 40

percent stock index fund and a 60 percent bond index fund allocation worked for the couple because it was not beyond their risk tolerance.

Stocks were up 37 percent in 1975 and up 24 percent in 1976.
Corporate bonds had strong years as well. As a result, the couple
would be further ahead with a conservative 40 percent stock and 60
percent bond portfolio rather than a 60 percent stock and 40 percent
bond portfolio because they stayed invested. If a more aggressive
portfolio were pushed on the couple, they would have reduced their
allocation to stocks at precisely the wrong time. The best performing portfolio is not the one with the largest allocation to stocks; it is
the one with a controllable level of stocks that an investor feels comfortable with *during all market conditions.*

IMPORTANT POINTS TO REMEMBER

The 60 percent stock and 40 percent bond allocation was the mathematically correct asset mix for the couple in the example. However, it would have proved too volatile during a steep downturn in the
stock market, and the couple would have likely sold most of their
stocks at the bottom of the next bear market. The stress test revealed
that the couple needed a more conservative asset mix.

Once the changes were in place, we ran the stress test again.
This time the couple stayed with the allocation during the entire
1973–1974 period and rebalanced the account at the end of each
year. This put them in an ideal position to benefit from a strong ral-
ly in the stock and bond markets that occurred from 1975–1976. The
moral of the story is that the best asset allocation is the one that you
can maintain during all market conditions.

MORE IDEAS ABOUT INVESTMENT PLANNING

Should you always reduce your exposure to risk once you have met
your investment goal, as we discussed at the beginning of the chapter? For most people the answer is "yes" if you saved only enough
to retire. On the other hand, the answer is "no" if you have accumulated significantly more wealth beyond your needs. People who
have accumulated more wealth than they need to live on for the rest
of their lives are actually investing for the benefit of their heirs. The

portion of wealth that will not be needed by the investor has a different time horizon; therefore, it warrants a different asset mix than the rest of the portfolio. This chapter was written with the first level of wealth in mind: retirement money. However, the model can be adapted to different levels of wealth, including multigeneration estate plans.

CHAPTER SUMMARY

"You can't always get what you want. But if you try sometimes, you just might find, you get what you need."

The Rolling Stones

Understanding your financial needs is not a 1-minute subject, and there are many items to think about. When constructing an investment plan, the asset allocation mix is the most important decision you will make because it determines the level of risk in a portfolio. The true essence of investment planning is to develop a mix of stocks and bonds that satisfies your return objectives, while keeping the risk at or below your risk-tolerance level. Investors who maintain a comfortable and consistent asset allocation to stocks during all market conditions will perform better than investors who take too much risk and ultimately sell stocks at the wrong time.

Risk tolerance is an understanding of the maximum level of loss you can handle in a portfolio before changing your allocation. Risk avoidance is a conscious decision to invest below your risk-tolerance level. Risk avoidance is a well-planned decision that is made with no emotion. At some point during your life, you financial goals will be realized. At that time you should reduce the risk you are taking in a portfolio and concentrate on conserving wealth.

NOTES

1. The actual expected return is higher than 7.2 percent due to the "portfolio effect" of mixing two different assets classes together in one account. Chapter 13 details this benefit of diversification.

CHAPTER 15

Designing Your Index Fund Portfolio

Key Concepts

- ◆ Taxable portfolios are managed differently from nontaxable portfolios.
- ◆ A simple portfolio is best in a taxable account.
- ◆ More complex strategies can be used in a nontaxable account.
- ◆ The right portfolio for you is the one you are comfortable with.

If you have followed along in Part III of this book, it should be clear that building and maintaining a portfolio of index funds involves a multistage process. It starts with an inventory of your financial goals and risk tolerance, builds on realistic market expectations, and results in a well-balanced portfolio of stock and bond index funds that matches your needs. In addition, tax planning plays an important role in the selection and management of a taxable account. In this chapter we finally start to consider actual index funds and how a portfolio of index funds fits together.

Developing an appropriate index fund portfolio requires time. It is unlikely that your first mix of funds will be correct because you probably have not gathered enough information. That is fine because you have to start someplace. The model portfolios presented in this chapter are a good place to start. As you learn more about index funds and the markets, you can adjust the portfolio to your specific needs. At some point you will become satisfied with the portfolio and stop tinkering with it, even during poor market conditions. That will be the ideal index fund portfolio for you. This chapter cannot tell you what the best portfolio should be; it can only guide you in a direction of self-discovery.

Your ideal portfolio will be unique. It can be a simple two-fund mix or a complex multiasset class portfolio. A complex portfolio is not better than a simple one, especially if it is not fully understood by you. Warren Buffett's philosophy is that if you invest within your sphere of competence, you will be much happier with your investments and will accumulate more wealth. There is no guarantee that a complex portfolio will generate higher returns than a simple two-fund portfolio, so you shouldn't not invest in one just because other people are.

REGROUP AND ADVANCE

The most important decision you will make in a portfolio is the overall mix between stock and bond index funds. This decision accounts for more than 90 percent of the portfolio's performance over time.[1] These asset allocation studies assume that an investor maintains the same weight in both the stock and bond index funds for a very long time. Thus, it is very important to select a good one right from the start.

First, here is a quick review of where we have been and a snapshot of where we are going. Several details of the portfolio management process have been discussed in earlier chapters. Those chapter numbers are indicated in parentheses.

1. Understand the historic relationship between risk and return and have realistic expectations of what the financial markets can achieve in the future (Chapter 12).

2. Analyze your current financial situation and determine the amount needed to achieve your financial goals. Calculate a minimum return needed on an investment portfolio to attain your goals (Chapter 14).

3. Create a simple asset allocation using forecast stock and

bond returns that match your required return. Use a stress test to ensure that the selected mix is not above your risk-tolerance level. Make adjustments to the stock and bond mix as needed (Chapter 14).

4. Using information from this chapter, enhance the initial asset allocation with additional asset classes based on your income needs and personal convictions. Select index funds that are benchmarked to those asset classes. For a review of individual index funds, see Part II of this book.

ASSET LOCATION

Asset "location" decisions are an interesting subject. If you are going to build a portfolio using two separate accounts, such as a tax-deferred IRA and a taxable personal account, should you own stock index funds in one account and bond index funds in the other or use the same balance in all accounts? There are many opinions on this issue, and I have mine. I believe most people should hold the same mix of stock and bond index funds in all their portfolios regardless of the type of account or tax status. The reason is to avoid focusing on the performance of one account over another. If stocks are placed in one account and bonds in another, people tend to compare the performance of the two accounts against each other rather than view them as one combined portfolio.

Focusing on the performance of one account over another can have major consequences. Although there might be a slight tax advantage to placing stocks in one type of account and bonds in another, it increases the psychological burden on investors. It is very difficult for most people to hold an all-stock account in a very bad market, even though it may be part of an overall balanced portfolio involving bonds in another account. Chances are much higher that individuals will reduce their equity position in the all-stock account during a bear market than if they had spread the stock funds evenly among all accounts. The result of emotionally selling stocks in a stock-heavy account will reduce the chances of meeting a financial goal. Unless you are extremely disciplined and always focused on your entire portfolio, it is wise to use the same asset allocation across all of your accounts.

MODEL PORTFOLIOS

The remainder of this chapter examines various model portfolios. These models are examples of index fund portfolios rather than recommended portfolios. There are an infinite number of portfolios that can be created using the index funds discussed in Part II. In addition, some actively managed "almost" index funds are included when there are no low-cost index fund available in certain asset classes. The models do not include individual municipal bonds, Treasury bonds, Treasury inflation protection securities (TIPS), or other individual bonds that may be appropriate for your personal situation. You will have to substitute on your own.

All the models are based on a balance of 50 percent bonds and 50 percent stocks. The asset allocation in stocks and bonds is also for illustration purposes only. Your actual percentage in each asset class should include an analysis of your long-term goals as discussed in Chapter 14.

There are important differences between managing taxable accounts and nontaxable accounts. For that reason this section is divided into two parts: one for managing taxable accounts (personal, joint, trusts, and UGMA accounts) and the other for managing nontaxable accounts (IRA, 401k, and charitable accounts). The nontaxable section builds on the taxable section, so it is important to read the taxable section first.

Managing Taxable Accounts

The overall asset allocation between stocks and bonds is the most important determinant of portfolio performance. However, in a taxable account, the second most important determinant of performance is tax efficiency. If you can defer taxable gains and reduce taxable dividends and interest, then the performance of your account on an after-tax basis is increased. By creating a low tax portfolio, you will pay less in taxes, which automatically increases your wealth.

There are several strategies you can use to reduce taxes in a portfolio. First, select only investments that are tax efficient. Check the prospectus of an index fund for its tax efficiency. The SEC mandates that all mutual funds report after-tax performance as well as pretax performance. In addition, Morningstar gives each mutual fund a tax-efficiency rating, which is also useful. Morningstar mutual fund reports are free from most public libraries or can be obtained from the company for an annual fee.

Some open-end index funds are "tax managed," which means the fund manager uses special trading strategies to make the fund as tax friendly as possible. This involves holding on to winning stocks and "harvesting" losses in losing stocks. It may also involve buying only stocks that pay low dividends or no dividends. Exchange-traded funds (ETFs) by their design are more tax efficient than most open-end index funds. The redemption and creation feature of ETFs allow fund managers to pass most capital gains onto the institutional investors who redeem shares, thus helping individual investors save on taxes (see Chapter 4).

A strategy individual investors can use to reduce taxes is called *tax swapping*. This strategy involves harvesting tax losses as they occur in your index fund portfolio and simultaneously rolling into a similar index fund; thus, you are never out of the market. The tax losses can then be used to offset realized capital gains and can offset up to $3000 per year in ordinary income. A detailed explanation of tax swaps can be found in Chapter 5.

The Bond Portion of a Taxable Account

Deciding which type of bond fund to use in a taxable account is almost done for you. First, dig out your most recent tax return and look for the line on your 1040 Form labeled "Taxable income." The amount on this line will guide you into a taxable bond index fund or tax-exempt municipal bond fund. The decision to go into a taxable bond fund or tax-exempt bond fund is driven by your projected tax status.

Generally, if your taxable income was below $50,000, then you should invest in a taxable bond index fund and pay the taxes on the interest. This will give you the highest after-tax return because your income tax rate is below 30 percent. On the other hand, if your taxable income was more than $150,000, you may be better off investing in a tax-exempt bond fund. Although the interest rate is lower in a tax-exempt bond fund than a taxable one, the interest income is free from all federal tax. This means your after-tax cashflow may be higher. If you make more than $50,000 but less than $150,000, your best strategy may be to invest some of your money in a taxable bond fund and the remainder in a tax-exempt fund. Place enough in the taxable bond fund so that the taxable interest brings your taxable income up to the next tax bracket; then place the remaining amount in a tax-exempt bond fund. This split strategy gives you the best after-tax return, but is a little messy. If you do not know which way to go, ask the person who prepares your tax returns.

<u>Select Bond Mutual Funds for Taxable Accounts</u>   It is wise to keep your taxable portfolio very simple. The fewer investments the better because it makes your account tax efficient and easy to manage. There are a variety of taxable bond index funds to choose from and several tax-exempt municipal bond funds that are "almost" index funds (see Chapter 9 for details). There is no reason for most people to have more than one or two bond funds in a taxable account. Fewer 1099 Forms mean less of your CPA's time is spent filling out paperwork during tax season, and that saves you money.

Depending on your tax bracket, one or two of the following funds should suffice:

Taxable Index Funds

◆ Vanguard Short-Term Government / Credit Index Fund (VBISX)

◆ Schwab Short-term Bond Market (SWBDX)

◆ Vanguard Total Bond Market Fund (VBMFX)

◆ Vanguard Intermediate-Term Index Fund (VBIIX)

◆ iShares Government / Credit Index ETF

Tax-Exempt "Almost" Index Funds

◆ Vanguard Limited-Term Tax-Exempt Bond Fund (VMLTX)

◆ Vanguard Intermediate-Term Tax-Exempt Bond Fund (VWITX)

◆ USAA Tax-Exempt Short-Term Bond Fund (USSTX)

The Stock Portion of a Taxable Account

Developing a simple index fund strategy on the stock portion of your account can be reduced to one or two index funds. A total U.S. stock market index fund covers the entire U.S. stock market, and some people believe this is the only stock fund you will ever need. John Bogle, founder of the Vanguard Group, is one of those who believe in the one-fund concept. If you take Bogle's advice, you will buy one bond index fund and one total U.S. stock market index fund. There is absolutely nothing wrong with this approach.

Personally, I like to use a two-stock fund approach. This idea simply adds a slice of a total international stock index fund to a total U.S. stock market index fund. This two-fund mix provides global diversification, solid return potential, risk control, and great tax management.

We rely on modern portfolio theory (MPT) to determine an appropriate mix between a U.S. stock index fund and an international stock index fund. In Chapter 13 we learned that the correlation between the U.S. stock market (S&P 500) and the international stock market (EAFE) was about +0.5, a moderately positive number. According to MPT, if two different index funds have a correlation less than +1.0, then mixing those two funds in a portfolio provides hidden benefits. Together, low-correlated asset classes reduce the risk in a portfolio and increase the return. Using various mixes of U.S. and international stocks, we find that an asset allocation of about 70 percent U.S. and 30 percent international seems to generate the greatest portfolio effect, meaning it is the lowest risk portfolio. Again, refer to Chapter 13 for an explanation of these terms.

Select Stock Funds for Taxable Accounts   The next step is to select appropriate U.S. stock index funds and international stock index funds to purchase in the portfolio. A simple solution is to place 70 percent in an S&P 500 Index fund and 30 percent in a EAFE Index fund. That matches our model exactly. However, while an S&P 500 Index fund and EAFE Index fund make good choices, there are better ones. The S&P 500 Index does not include most small- and mid-cap stocks, and the EAFE Index does not include emerging countries. Thus, a portfolio using only an S&P 500 Index fund and an EAFE Index fund does not represent the entire global marketplace. A better choice may be to use "total market" index funds. These funds offer complete depth of both the U.S. and international marketplace. The following list has a variety of total U.S. market index funds and one international index fund:

Total U.S. Stock Market Index Funds

◆ Vanguard Total U.S. Stock Market (VTSMX)

◆ Fidelity Spartan Total Market (FSTMX)

◆ Vanguard Total U.S. Stock Market ETF (VTI)

◆ iShares Russell 3000 ETF (IWV)

◆ iShares Dow Jones Total Stock Market ETF (IYY)

Total International Stock Market Index Fund

◆ Vanguard Total International Index Portfolio (VGTSX) is the only all-inclusive fund; however, you lose the foreign tax exclusion (see Chapter 8).

Since there are no tax credits available on the Vanguard Total International Index Portfolio, here are a few more diversified developed country index funds that do pass through a foreign tax credit. [The Vanguard Developed Markets Index Fund (VDMIX) is not listed because it is also a "fund of funds" and does not qualify for the foreign tax credit.]

Developed International Market Index Funds

◆ Fidelity Spartan International Index Fund (FSIIX)

◆ Schwab International Index Fund (SWINX)

◆ iShares MSCI EAFE ETF (EFA)

One way to reduce the tax burden in a portfolio is to utilize tax-managed index funds offered through Vanguard and other index fund providers. Tax-managed funds use several internal trading mechanisms that reduce year-end taxable distributions to shareholders. Should you invest in a tax-managed fund? It is not necessary. First, investing in an index fund labeled "tax-managed" may also be a moot point for a few years because the bear market of 2000–2001 has left many mutual funds with large tax losses on their books. It will take several years for many mutual funds to work off the tax losses before distributing capital gains to shareholders. Second, most total stock market index funds are extremely tax efficient due to their low turnover of stocks in the fund each year. Third, ETFs are even more tax efficient than open-end funds due to their unique operating structure (see Chapter 4). Finally, Vanguard tax-managed funds have a redemption fee attached to them, which makes tax swapping more expensive. Despite their setbacks, here are a few tax-managed funds for you to research.

Tax-Managed U.S. Stock Index Funds

- Vanguard Tax-Managed Growth & Income* (VTGIX)
- DFA Tax-Managed Market Wide Value Portfolio[†] (DTMMX)

Tax-Managed International Stock Index Funds

- Vanguard Tax-Managed International Fund* (VTMGX)
- DFA Tax-Managed International Value Portfolio[†] (VTMIX)

The Total Taxable Portfolio

When you are finished choosing a bond index fund, a total U.S. stock market index fund, and a broad international index fund, you will have a very simple, yet complete portfolio (Figure 15-1). This approach offers broad diversification, low fees, tax efficiency, and ease of maintenance. It will serve you well in both good markets and bad.

<u>Enhancements for Increasing Current Income</u>   If you desire more current income from a taxable portfolio, you can add these income enhancements without changing the original stock and bond mix. Two ways to increase current income in a taxable account is to include a real estate investment trust (REIT) index fund as part of the stock portion, and a high-yield corporate bond index fund and the Vanguard GNMA fund to the bond portion. There is one exception. There is no need to add the GNMA fund if you already own the Total Bond Market Fund, because the Total Bond Fund already includes mortgage-backed securities. These investments generate higher income than their representative asset classes. High-yield bond funds typically generate about 3 percent more income than investment-grade corporate bond funds and GNMA funds add about 1 percent extra return over intermediate-term Treasury bonds. On the stock side, REITs generate about 7 percent in dividend income per year from rental income, with the added benefit that a small part of the dividend is nontaxable because it reflects de-

---

*Vanguard tax-managed funds are only available through direct purchase from Vanguard.
[†]Dimensional Fund Advisors (DFA) are only available through a qualified investment adviser.

FIGURE 15-1

The Three-Index Fund Portfolio Mix

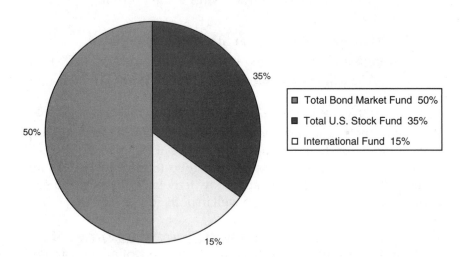

Simple Index Fund Portfolio
Using a 50% Bond and 50% Stock Mix

▣	Total Bond Market Fund 50%
■	Total U.S. Stock Fund 35%
▢	International Fund 15%

preciation in the properties held in the REITs. But these gains do not come without risk. High-yield bond funds are much more volatile than short-term investment grade funds, and the higher income from REITs is at the expense of potentially long-term capital gains.

Despite the added risks of high-yield bonds and the lower growth prospects of REITs, investors who place a small portion of each fund in their account will increase their current income. You could invest up to 10 percent of your total portfolio value in a REIT index fund and 10 percent in a high-yield bond fund.

YIELD-ENHANCING ADDITIONS
GNMA Fund
- ◆ Vanguard GNMA Fund (VFIIX)

High-Yield Bond Funds
- ◆ Vanguard High-Yield Corporate (VWEHX)
- ◆ TIAA-CREF High-Yield Bond Fund (TCHYX)

FIGURE 15–2

High-Income Portfolio Using REITs and High-Yield Bonds

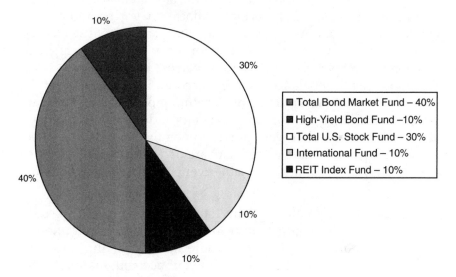

**High-Income Portfolio
Using a 50% Bond and 50% Stock Mix**

- ■ Total Bond Market Fund – 40%
- ■ High-Yield Bond Fund –10%
- □ Total U.S. Stock Fund – 30%
- □ International Fund – 10%
- ■ REIT Index Fund – 10%

REIT Index Funds

- ◆ Vanguard REIT Index Fund (VGSIX)
- ◆ AON REIT Index Fund (AREYX)
- ◆ iShares Cohen & Steers Reality Majors REIT Index ETF (ICF)

Using a 50 percent stock and 50 percent bond account and placing the maximum 10 percent of the total portfolio in a high-yield bond fund and 10 percent in a REIT index fund would create the high-income mix in Figure 15–2.

The portfolios illustrated in this section assume a 50 percent bond and 50 percent stock mix. Your overall stock and bond asset allocation may be quite different. To create a new portfolio using a different stock and bond asset allocation, simply maintain the weightings of each fund within its asset class and adjust the asset class weight in the portfolio.

<u>Rebalancing a Taxable Account</u>   As markets go up and down, the value of the asset classes in your account also shifts. Inevitably, a portfolio will get so far out of kilter that it will need to be adjusted back to its original asset allocation. This process is called *rebalancing*. I believe that when the overall stock and bond mix is off by 10 percent or more from its target allocation, you should consider rebalancing. For example, a portfolio that is 55 percent stocks and 45 percent bonds would be looked at for rebalancing if the target allocation was 50 percent stocks and 50 percent bonds.

One way to rebalance a taxable account is to sell some of the index funds that are up and purchase more of funds that are lagging. Unfortunately, selling a portion of the index fund that went up and buying a fund that went down do not always make sense because it creates a taxable gain. There are better ways to rebalance a taxable account to minimize taxable events. Consider the following methods:

1. Do not automatically reinvest mutual fund income. Let all income distributions flow into your cash account rather than automatically buying more shares of an index fund. Once cash has accumulated in your account, manually invest it in the index fund where it is needed. Taking dividends and interest in cash also allows you to maintain control over the cost basis of your index funds, whereas automatically reinvesting mutual fund distributions can create a tax accounting nightmare.

2. When adding new money to a taxable account, use the opportunity to rebalance the portfolio.

3. If you have a tax loss carry forward or can offset a capital gain through tax swapping (Chapter 5), use the loss to offset the gain from selling the index fund that went up in value. Then use the cash from the sale to rebalance your account.

4. If one asset class moves significantly higher than another and your asset allocation is off by a wide margin, sell only those shares that have been in your account for more than 1 year. It is better to pay a lower long-term capital gain tax rate than to pay the higher short-term capital gain rate. If no shares have been held for more than 1 year, then wait

until they have been held for more than 1 year before selling.

Rebalancing in a taxable portfolio does not have to take place on a regular basis to be effective. It is better to wait for an appropriate time and circumstance than to pay a heavy tax bill.

Managing Nontaxable Accounts

The strategy behind managing a nontaxable account builds on the ideas presented in the taxable account section. In many ways developing and managing a nontaxable index fund portfolio are much easier than a taxable portfolio because taxes do not get in the way of decision making. This gives you the freedom to add many different asset classes to an account and allows rebalancing to take place when needed. In addition, mutual fund dividends can and should be automatically reinvested in the fund that paid the distribution. There is no benefit to accumulating cash and then purchasing different tax lots. Finally, the average cost method of mutual fund accounting works well in a nontaxable account, which is easier to maintain.

Although you have more freedom to choose between different index funds in a nontaxable portfolio, there is no reason one of the simple index fund portfolios outlined in the taxable section cannot be used, less the tax-exempt bond funds. An IRA account that holds only a total bond market index fund, total U.S. stock market index fund, and total international index fund is perfectly fine. In fact, a simple portfolio is preferred over a complex one for investors who do not want to get too involved in managing their accounts.

The Bond Portion of a Nontaxable Account

Managing the bond portion of a nontaxable account is very similar to a taxable account. You should start with a well-diversified total bond market index fund or a short-term corporate/government index bond fund and add a small segment of a high-yield corporate bond fund if desired. Obviously, there is no need for a tax-exempt bond fund in the portfolio because the interest income in a nontaxable account is already tax-free. An appropriate mix between an investment grade bond index fund and a high-yield corporate bond fund is about 80–20 percent, respectively. I do not recommend investing more than 10 percent of your total portfolio value in a high-yield bond fund.

The Stock Portion of a Nontaxable Account

Managing the stock side of a nontaxable account can be as simple or as complex as you would like it to be. You can maintain one or two stock index funds in a portfolio, similar to a taxable account, or you can cut the stock portfolio into several pieces and allocate across market sectors. Whichever method you choose, there are no guarantees that a complex stock portfolio will produce better returns than a simple stock portfolio.

There are three major stock asset classes that I use in complex allocation of stock index funds. They are the U.S. stock portion, international stock portion, and REIT index funds. Each of these three asset classes has a fairly low correlation with each other, allowing us to apply modern portfolio theory.

In general, the allocation between U.S. index funds, international index funds, and REIT funds should be about 65, 25, and 10 percent, respectively. You can place up to 20 percent of your stock allocation in REIT index funds and reduce your U.S. stock and international stock portion; however, I do not recommend placing over 10 percent of the total value of your portfolio in REIT index funds. For example, if you decide on an asset allocation of 60 percent stocks and 40 percent bonds, your REIT allocation should be no more than 6 percent.

The U.S. Stock Portion   Buying a total U.S. stock market index fund based on the Wilshire 5000 or Russell 3000 is the easiest and simplest way to participate in the U.S. stock market. You literally own thousands of stocks in one index fund, and it will perform right in line with the broad U.S. index. A second avenue to a total market approach is to reconstruct the total market using different index funds from the same index provider. For example, using the Standard & Poor's U.S. stock methodology, you can create a total stock market portfolio by investing approximately 70 percent in an S&P 500 index fund, 22 percent in an S&P 400 mid-cap index fund, and 8 percent in an S&P 600 small-cap index fund. Reconstruction can also take place using Russell or Dow Jones index methodologies as outlined in Chapter 6.

<u>Small-Cap and Value Tilts</u>   A total market approach also re-quires very little time and effort to maintain; however, it is about as exciting as watching grass grow. Personally, I like watching grass grow, but some people want to do more with the U.S. stock index fund portion. There are a few "tilts" you can use that may increase the rate of return in the portfolio, while at the same time lowering risk and increasing excitement.

One advantage of creating your own total market portfolio is the ability to tilt the index to increase or decrease small-cap expo-sure. In late 1999 the large-cap portion of the U.S. stock market grew to over 80 percent of the total index, but there have also been times when large-cap stock made up only 60 percent of the total market index. Historically, large-cap stocks have represented about 70 per-cent of broad U.S. market averages, and the rest is comprised of mid- and small-cap stocks. By piecing together your own total stock market portfolio, you can tilt the portfolio to include more large-cap index funds or small- and mid-cap index funds. If you want to cre-ate a portfolio that has a higher expected return than the broad U.S. market, you would tilt that portfolio to smaller stocks. A portfolio with 60 percent in large-cap U.S. index funds and 40 percent in small- and mid-cap index funds creates an expected return that is higher than a total stock market index, but with more risk. The risk and return characteristics of small-cap stocks are presented later in this chapter.

In addition to size factors, the U.S. stock market is divided by fundamental factors into value stocks and growth stocks. All index providers divide the total stock market into value and growth in dif-ferent ways; that is, S&P measures value differently than Dow Jones, which differs from Russell and Wilshire (see Chapter 6). When the indexes are divided by size and value, all U.S. stocks end up in one of four general categories: large-cap growth, large-cap value, small-cap growth, and small-cap value (mid-cap is included in small-cap for this discussion).

Figure 15–3 shows that the average mix between large compa-ny stocks and small company stocks is about 70 percent to 30 per-cent, and the mix between value stocks and growth stocks is about 50 percent to 50 percent. The mix can vary during the year depend-ing on market conditions and the index provider. Research by Eu-gene Fama, Kenneth French, and other academics finds that over the long term, investors earned extra returns by investing in small

FIGURE 15–3

Historic U.S. Market by Size and Valuation

Historic U.S. Stock Market Breakdown

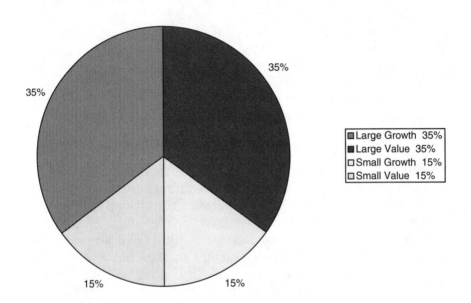

Large Growth 35%
Large Value 35%
Small Growth 15%
Small Value 15%

stocks and value stocks, but at the price of more risk.[2] Table 15–1 highlights the historic risk and return of small-cap stocks and value stocks compared to the total stock market.

As you can see, both small stocks and value stocks have beaten the total market over the very long term. However, they have done so with more risk. The small-cap and value premium does not occur every year. In fact there have been many long periods of time when small stocks and value stocks did not beat the general market. Some of those periods have occurred in the recent past.

A challenge for investors is how to capture the small-cap and value premium in the marketplace without incurring a greater risk. Referring to Table 15–2, if you would have invested in the Russell 2000 Small-Cap Index from 1985 through 2000, you would have

T A B L E   15–1

Index Comparison 1928–2000*	Return	Risk	Excess Return	Excess Risk
Total stock market	10.5%	19.1%		
All growth stocks	9.8%	20.1%	−0.7%	1.0%
All value stocks	13.1%	28.0%	+2.6%	8.9%
Large-cap index—S&P 500	10.7%	19.7%		
Large-cap growth	10.0%	20.0%	−0.7%	0.3%
Large-cap value	12.4%	27.5%	+1.7%	7.6%
All small-cap index	11.7%	28.0%		
Small-cap growth	9.4%	33.2%	−2.3%	5.2%
Small-cap value	14.2%	32.3%	+2.5%	4.3%

Source: Ibbotson 2001 Yearbook, Dimensional Fund Advisors
*Value and growth indexes are based on Fama/French methodology

been disappointed in every period except 1992–1994. The Russell 3000 Value Index stocks beat the Russell 3000 Growth Index in three of five periods but still performed slightly less than the broad Russell 3000 Index. During the 1985–2000 period, there was no extra reward for taking small-cap and value risk. In fact, depending on your small-cap exposure, your portfolio may have underperformed significantly. The moral of the story is: If you are going to tilt a portfolio to small-cap or value, use moderation and be prepared to wait.

T A B L E   15–2

Period	Russell 3000	Russell 3000 Growth Index	Russell 3000 Value Index	Russell 1000 Large-Cap	Russell 2000 Small-Cap
1998–2000	11.6%	11.9%	9.4%	12.3%	4.6%
1995–1997	30.0%	28.9%	31.0%	30.9%	22.4%
1992–1994	6.7%	3.7%	10.2%	5.8%	11.4%
1988–1991	17.8%	20.5%	15.1%	18.1%	14.3%
1985–1987	16.3%	16.4%	16.0%	17.1%	8.1%
1985–2000	16.3%	16.3%	16.0%	16.7%	12.1%

Source: Bloomberg

TABLE 15-3

Russell Index Strategies Compared

1979–2000	Return	Risk
Russell 3000 Index	16.2%	15.3%
50% Russell 3000 Growth and 50% Russell 3000 Value	16.1%	15.3%
Source: Russell		

There is one more point about value investing that you need to be aware of. Many people think they are capturing the value premium by splitting their U.S. stock portfolio between growth index funds and value index funds. However, that does not add any value. Refer to Table 15–3. If you place 50 percent of your U.S. stock money in a Russell 3000 Value Index Fund and 50 percent in a Russell 3000 Growth Index Fund and rebalance that mix every year back to its original 50 percent value and 50 percent growth allocation, the net result is a wash (before transaction fees). A value tilt is obtained by investing a portion of your U.S. stock allocation in a value index and the rest in total market index funds.

TABLE 15-4

Portfolios with a Small-Cap and Value Tilt

Index Fund	Percent
Russell 3000 Index Fund	75%
Russell 3000 Value Fund	15%
Russell 2000 Index Fund	10%
Index Fund	**Percent**
S&P 500 Index Fund	55%
S&P/Barra 500 Value Index Fund	10%
S&P 400 Mid-Cap Index Fund	20%
S&P 600 Small-Cap Index Fund	10%
S&P/Barra 600 Value Small-Cap Index	5%

Using Russell and S&P index funds, the following two portfolios are constructed with about a 15 percent tilt to value and a 10 percent tilt to small-cap (Table 15–4). If you are not using index funds benchmarked to the Russell or S&P indexes, see Chapter 6 for details on Wilshire and Dow Jones Small and Value Index Funds and style funds.

For more information on using small-cap and value factors in your portfolio, read *What Wall Street Doesn't Want You to Know: How You Can Build Real Wealth Investing in Index Funds*, by Larry E. Swedroe. The book does a great job explaining the nuances of small-cap and value investing. In addition, Swedroe provides several model portfolios.

International Stock Portion You can envision the international stock market as comprised of several geographical sectors: the Pacific region, the European region, the Americas (ex-US), and emerging markets. All of these sectors are captured in the Vanguard Total International Stock Index Fund. So, the easy solution to international stock investing is to buy this fund.

Another alternative is to piece together a total international index portfolio using two or more index funds. There are several developed market index funds available on the market. Many of those funds are benchmarked to the MSCI EAFE Index, which unfortunately does not include an emerging market component (see Chapter 8). If you purchase an international index fund that does not have emerging market exposure, then the first order of business is to find an emerging market index fund and place about 20 percent of your international allocation into it. The 20 percent allocation is roughly the correct amount based on the optimal risk and return point using modern portfolio theory (Chapter 13).

Emerging Market Index Funds
- Vanguard Emerging Market Stock Index Fund (VDMIX)
- DFA Emerging Markets Fund* (DFEMX)

There is another way to slice the international portion of your portfolio. As mentioned earlier, only developed markets are in the

---

*Dimensional Fund Advisors (DFA) funds are only available through a qualified investment adviser.

TABLE 15–5

International Index Fund Portfolio

Recommended Vanguard International Index Fund Mix	Percent	Symbol
Vanguard Pacific Stock Index	40%	VPACX
Vanguard European Stock Index	40%	VEURX
Emerging Markets Index Fund	20%	VEIEX
International ETF Mix	**Percent**	**Symbol**
iShares S&P Europe 350 Index	40%	IEV
iShares S&P TOPIX/150 (Japan)	25%	ITF
iShares MSCI Pacific ex-Japan	15%	EPP
iShares Latin America 40	20%	ILF

MSCI EAFE Index. This index consists of large stocks from the Pacific Rim and Europe. Morgan Stanley places no restriction on regional weights in the index. That means the weighting of stocks in the index can swing dramatically between Pacific Rim stocks and European stocks. For example, in 1970 Japan was only 10 percent of the EAFE, and Europe was the major region. By 1990 Japan dominated the EAFE Index by capturing over 60 percent of the value. However, by 2000 everything had reversed again. Japan fell to only 20 percent of the index and Europe flourished.

If you do not feel comfortable with the way the EAFE shifts back and forth between the Pacific Rim and Europe, you can create a stable international index that holds fixed regional weights. For example, an international stock allocation may consist of 40 percent in the European market, 40 percent in the Pacific Rim, and 20 percent in emerging markets. This regional mix is easily created using Vanguard index funds or exchange-traded funds. With the iShares portfolio, you can adjust the weighting in Japan to a fixed amount (Table 15–5).

<u>Putting a Nontaxable Portfolio Together</u>   The model portfolio for a nontaxable account incorporates many of the tilts we have

TABLE 15-6

Model Nontaxable Account

Bond Funds	50%
Total bond index fund	30%
Short-term govt. fund	10%
High-Yield bond fund	10%
U.S. Stock Funds	**30%**
S&P 500 Index Fund	17%
S&P 400 Index Fund	5%
S&P 600 Index Fund	3%
S&P/Barra 500 Value Index Fund	3%
S&P/Barra 600 Value Index Fund	2%
REIT Index Fund	**5%**
International Stocks	**15%**
Pacific stock index fund	6%
European stock index fund	6%
Emerging market index fund	3%

discussed in this section. This portfolio is not an ideal mix for all investors, nor is it likely to be the mix you should use. It is simply a guide to a few of the ways you can tilt an index fund portfolio. The model represents a complex portfolio mix, but I am certainly not suggesting that all investors use a complex strategy in a nontaxable account. A simple portfolio consisting of a total bond market index fund plus a total U.S. stock market index fund may be the best choice for many people. Use what works for you.

The model portfolio is split between 50 percent bonds and 50 percent stocks, and it has several tilts (Table 15-6). On the fixed-income side, the portfolio is titled toward high-yield bonds for added income. On the U.S. stock side, the portfolio is titled toward small-cap stocks, value stocks, and REITs. In the international stock portion, the portfolio is in a fixed mix of regional and emerging market funds.

<u>Rebalancing a Nontaxable Account</u>   As the markets go up and down, so will the index fund values in your portfolio. For all the asset classes to work together properly in your account, it is a good idea to rebalance at least annually, especially if the mix between stocks and bonds is off by 5 percent or more. For example, rebalance when market forces cause a 50 percent stock and 50 percent bond portfolio to be a 53 percent stock and 47 percent bond portfolio. Since there are no tax consequences to rebalancing, the only disadvantages are your time and any commission cost. If there are commissions to trade your index funds, you will have to weigh the cost of the commission against the advantage of rebalancing.

Remember the key to long-term portfolio returns is the asset allocation between stock and bond index funds. As long as the stock and bond mix is within your risk-tolerance level, then rebalancing is not necessary. However, if the risk of the portfolio moves outside your threshold for pain, I recommend rebalancing immediately.

CHAPTER SUMMARY

Managing taxable and nontaxable index fund accounts can be as simple or as complex as you want to make it. A simple two-fund portfolio may be all you need to accomplish your investment objectives. After deciding the appropriate amount to invest in stock and bond index funds based on your objective, the rest is tailoring the portfolio to fit your preferences and tax situation.

You will need to separate taxable accounts from nontaxable accounts. They need to be managed differently for tax reasons. The accounts may hold different index funds, and the tax status of a portfolio will affect rebalancing decisions. It is wise to place tax-inefficient index funds in a tax-sheltered account and tax-efficient index funds in a taxable account. This would mean placing most REIT funds, junk bond funds, and U.S. value funds in a tax-sheltered account and placing total market funds and tax-managed funds in a taxable account. Common sense needs to be applied when deciding which account should hold a particular fund.

Finally, you are a unique person, and your investment portfolio will also be unique. Developing an appropriate index fund mix requires time. It is likely that your first index fund portfolio will not be a perfect fit because you have not gathered enough information.

As you continue to read, study, and understand, the right portfolio will reveal itself.

NOTES

1. Gary P. Brinson, L. Randolph Hood, and Gilbert L. Beebower,. "Determinants of Portfolio Performance," *Financial Analysts Journal*, Vol. 51, No. 1 (January/February 1995): 133–138.
2. James Davis, Eugene Fama, and Kenneth French, "Characteristics, Covariances, and Average Returns: 1929–1997," *Journal of Finance*, Vol. 55, No. 1 (February 2000).

CHAPTER 16

Tips on Account Operations

Key Concepts

- ◆ Decide which accounts will be indexed.
- ◆ Choose a custodian for your index funds.
- ◆ Look for brokerage firms with access to all fund companies.
- ◆ Hiring an investment adviser makes sense for many people.

Congratulations! You have decided to join the rational and savvy investors of the world and convert to an index fund strategy. Sound logic has convinced you that index funds make sense from all aspects. You have spent time formulating an investment plan and have designed an index fund portfolio that fits your needs. Now it is time to open an account and put the plan into action. So, what do you do?

This chapter discusses the mechanics of opening and managing an index fund account. It highlights the advantages and disadvantages of working directly with a mutual fund company or purchasing index funds through a brokerage firm. Tips for transferring assets into an account are also discussed. Although the topic of opening an account and transferring assets may seem dull, a delay in processing your paperwork can cost you time and money.

The topic of professional management is also introduced. If

you are not inclined to do your own planning, paperwork, and port-folio management, an investment manager can be hired to do it all for you at a nominal fee. Hiring a manager saves you time and keeps you on track.

STEPS TO OPENING AN ACCOUNT

Before you can buy index funds, you need to open an account some-place that is index fund-friendly and then fund that account with cash or securities. Five basic steps are involved in opening and fund-ing an account. These steps are listed here, and then discussed in more detail.

1. Decide which type of account or accounts will use an index fund strategy (i.e., IRA, personal, custodial).
2. Select a custodian for your account. You can either invest directly with a mutual fund company or buy index funds through a brokerage firm.
3. Request a new account application for the type of account you are opening (IRA, personal). Also request a transfer form if you are moving stocks, bonds, or mutual funds from a different custodian.
4. Complete and return the forms to the mutual fund company or brokerage firm.
5. Track the process of paperwork to ensure the account is opened correctly and the transfer takes place.

Step 1

The first step toward managing an index fund portfolio is to decide which account or accounts you are going to commit to an indexing strategy. You may be looking at several accounts, which is good be-cause it is my sincere belief that 100 percent of your money should be in index funds. Within that mix of accounts, an IRA will likely be under consideration. In fact the easiest account to convert to index-ing is an IRA because there are no tax consequences when selling the investments you already own.

Some of your accounts may not be eligible for indexing. For ex-ample, you may work at a company that has a 401(k) plan managed by a bank, insurance company, or brokerage firm. Many of these turnkey programs have large imbedded fees attached to their mutual funds, so they do not offer low-cost index fund options. If that is the case at your company, you need to talk to the plan administrator at your firm about adding a few index funds to the 401(k) selection.

Variable annuity accounts may also be nontransferable. Many variable annuities have a back-end sales charge that can linger for up to 10 years. If you recently purchased a variable annuity through a brokerage firm or insurance salesperson, there is a good chance you are subject to a horrendous back-end fee. There is no way of getting around this fee unless you die, which is not an option. On the other hand, if the back-end load period is over, I recommend contacting the Vanguard Group and inquiring about their Variable Annuity Plan. Vanguard offers a very low-cost annuity that has many index fund options. There is no cost or tax consequence to do a 1035 transfer into the Vanguard plan.

Step 2

The next step in the process is to decide which investment firm will hold your index fund account. You can go directly to a mutual fund company, such as Vanguard or State Street, or you can operate through a brokerage firm that has access to all major index fund companies. There are advantages and disadvantages to each, and there is not a perfect solution.

Going directly to a mutual fund company has the advantage of low cost and the disadvantage of limited flexibility. A likely choice using the direct method is Vanguard. They have the largest variety of index funds on the market. There is no cost to buy index funds directly through Vanguard, but there is a $10 per year charge on accounts below $10,000. You can easily exchange from one fund to another within the Vanguard family, although there are a few funds that have a back-end redemption fee. The disadvantage of Vanguard, and other mutual fund providers, is limited access. You cannot buy Schwab index funds through Vanguard. Nor can you buy exchange-traded funds (ETFs) or any other investment except Vanguard mutual funds. The same goes for other direct mutual fund providers.

Vanguard has solved some of the problems of limited flexibility by offering brokerage services through an independent company. Vanguard Brokerage Service, VBS®, has teamed up with an independent broker/dealer Pershing® to offer traditional brokerage services to Vanguard customers. Through Pershing, you are able to buy virtually any stock, bond, or mutual fund on the market. Of course, there will be a commission or fee to pay when buying non-Vanguard mutual funds, and there is always a commission and market spread to buy ETFs, stocks, and bonds.

Discount brokerage firms such as Charles Schwab and Fidelity offer access to thousands of mutual funds and all stocks and bonds. In fact, Schwab originated the concept of the mutual fund supermarket in the early 1990s. This made managing a portfolio of index funds from different fund companies very convenient. The disadvantage is cost. Every time you buy a non-Schwab or non-Fidelity mutual fund, there is a commission cost or imbedded 12b-1 fee (higher internal fund expense). In addition, not all index funds are available through mutual fund supermarkets. For example, Vanguard does not distribute its Tax-Managed Growth & Income or Tax-Managed International Fund through other firms.

If you are considering using one of the full-service brokerage firms, you may be fighting an uphill battle. There are a few firms that offer most index funds, including Vanguard index funds; however, a vast majority of full-service brokers do not have a sales agreement with the Vanguard Group. The reason most full-service brokers shun Vanguard is because the company refuses to pay commissions or 12b-1 fees. A 12b-1 fee is an annual fund charge that is paid to the broker. It basically doubles the cost of an index fund.

All things considered, I recommend using Vanguard Brokerage Service, Charles Schwab, or Fidelity Investments. You will have access to most index funds through their mutual funds supermarkets and can also buy ETFs at a reasonable commission rate. If you decide to invest with a full-service broker, find one that allows you to invest in the Vanguard family of index funds.

Step 3

After deciding on a custodian for your account, call that company or visit their Web site and request a new account application and transfer form. If you are simply wiring a check to the account, there is no need to ask for a transfer form. Make sure you get the right application. If you are opening an IRA account, ask for an IRA application. Many accounts have been held up because the wrong paperwork was sent in. If you are not sure, it is best to call and ask.

People who live near a major city may have a Schwab or Fidelity brokerage office nearby. If that is your situation, make a face-to-face appointment with a customer representative, and they will be happy to help you. They will also provide all the necessary paperwork and help complete it. This is a free service for customers.

Step 4

If you do not meet with a brokerage representative directly, the fourth step is completing the new account application and transfer form and putting them in the mail. Make sure you fill in all the blanks on the forms. Many times people leave off important information like social security numbers and IRA beneficiaries. You should not be worried about providing personal financial information to the custodian. These firms are required by law to have that information, and they are legally bound to hold the information confidential.

If you are transferring assets from an old account at a different firm, you have to make some decisions when you complete the transfer form. For example, should you liquidate the investments at your old firm and transfer cash? Or should you transfer securities to the new firm and liquidate the securities when they get there? If you are transferring to a brokerage firm, such as VBS, Schwab, or Fidelity, you can transfer cash or securities. However, if you are investing directly with a mutual fund company (not VBS), you are only allowed to deposit cash. Therefore, all investments must be liquidated at the old firm.

There are two items to consider when making the decision to transfer cash or securities. They are commissions and taxes. You need to calculate what the commission cost of selling at the old firm would be and compare it to the cost of selling at the new custodian. If you are moving stocks from a full-service broker to one of the lower cost brokers mentioned earlier, it usually makes economic sense to transfer the securities "in kind" and pay a lower commission rate to sell the stocks at the new firm. However, if you are moving mutual fund shares, it usually makes economic sense to liquidate the funds at the old firm and transfer cash. The reason is that full-service brokerage firms do not charge a commission to liquidate mutual funds they sold to you; however, Schwab, VBS, and Fidelity may charge you a commission to sell. The second consideration is taxes, and this only applies to a taxable account. If you will incur a realized capital gain by selling a security, and the security is getting close to the 12-month minimum hold period for the lower long-term capital gains tax rate, then it may be best to wait until 12 months before liquidating.

Step 5

Watch your transfer. Although modern communications allow for most transfers to proceed flawlessly, there are occasional problems. Make sure you monitor the opening of the account and the transfer of assets. After mailing in the new account forms, it takes about 1 week to get an account number and then another 3 weeks before the transfer is complete. If you are selling stocks or mutual funds at the old firm, make sure you initiate those trades before submitting a transfer request to the new firm. You cannot trade an account during the middle of a transfer, and if old trades have not settled, it will hold up the process. Feel free to call the new custodian at any time for an update on your account.

When your assets arrive at the new firm, contact the company again and do a complete inventory. If securities or cash are missing, ask the broker to "status" the account, and they will run a broker-to-broker check. Sometimes a small amount of cash gets stuck at the old firm, and the new custodian can request a "residual sweep." That should take care of the problem. When the entire transfer is complete, you will be well prepared to enter index fund nirvana!

The Enemy within Us

Completing and returning the new account application are the most difficult steps in the account opening process. This is not because the paperwork is difficult to complete. It is because the paperwork does not get done. A hidden enemy lurks in paperwork piles. That enemy has a name. It is called *procrastination*. Despite good intentions many account applications sit on a desk in a pile of paperwork collecting dust. The longer it sits, the more money you waste. Millions of dollars have been lost because of procrastination. Don't procrastinate.

HIRING AN INVESTMENT ADVISER

Some people are better off hiring an investment adviser to do most of the dirty work for them. Investment advisers are paid a management fee for designing, implementing, and managing an investment portfolio. The right hired help will get the process moving in the right direction.

Many investment advisers have access to institutional index fund shares. These are lower cost index funds, or funds that individual investors do not have access to. For example, an adviser may be authorized to purchase Dimensional Fund Adviser (DFA) funds. DFA offers several unique small-cap and value funds that are only available through qualified fee-only investment advisers.

The problem with hiring an investment adviser is that they come in all shapes, sizes, and levels of competence. You will definitely need to do some homework. I suggest contacting the Vanguard Group and asking for a free copy of "How to Select a Financial Adviser." The booklet is available online at www.Vanguard.com, or it can be obtained by mail by calling 1-800-662-7447. Another place to shop for a knowledgeable investment adviser is through the www.Indexfunds.com Web site. This site is where many index fund advisers converse with each other and pass along new information. You are welcome to ask questions on the message boards or contact the advisers directly.

Contrary to popular belief, good investment advisers do not try to convince you that they can predict the next bull market or pick the next Microsoft. They exist to help you formulate a plan and implement it in a reasonable time. When you find a good adviser, hiring one may make good economic sense. Not only will an adviser ensure that the paperwork gets done, but he or she also provides many ongoing services. Here is a partial list of those services.

1. **Help tailor an investment plan:** Many people need help formulating an investment plan and developing the cor-

rect asset allocation for their needs. They may already have a general idea of where they want to go financially but do not have the tools or expertise to put a complete plan together. A competent adviser will help clients understand how their needs can be met through index fund investing and help them implement and manage the complete investment plan.

2. **Offers consistency of strategy:** People switch investment strategies about every 3 years on average (as measured by the Investment Company Institute mutual fund turnover statistics). Three years ago people could not buy enough growth stocks, now everyone is moving to value stocks, and three years from now it might be international stocks. Advisers are (or should be) more consistent. This consistency of management style will help achieve higher lifetime returns.

3. **Creates a human circuit breaker:** Sometimes, when investors wake up in the middle of the night because they dreamed the markets collapsed, advisers are there to act as a psychologist. This usually means calming investors' nerves and talking them out of making emotional investment decisions.

4. **Places someone on duty 24/7/365:** Believe it or not, there will come a time in your life when you just do not want to deal with this investment stuff anymore, or can't deal with it for health reasons. Advisers are there to do the investment chores for you day in and day out.

As an investment adviser, I believe we best serve our clients by acting in an administrative function, not in a guru function. It is not my job to forecast the markets; however it is my job to understand the risks of the markets and help clients design the right mix of investments for their needs and tolerance for risk. Then it is my job to implement the plan and keep the portfolio and the client focused. For these services we are paid a small annual fee.

CHAPTER SUMMARY

Index fund investing should be the most rewarding investment experience of your life. To ensure success you need to be prepared for success. It is important to choose the right index funds for your needs, and it is equally important to choose the right custodian for those funds and the right people to help you manage the process. Compare the advantages and disadvantages of each brokerage firm or mutual fund company you are considering as a custodian of your wealth. They should offer access to a wide variety of index funds at a reasonable cost.

Hiring an investment adviser to help manage your investment portfolio makes a lot of sense. Advisers can help formulate a plan for your needs, implement the plan, and manage your account on an ongoing basis. Make sure you choose an experienced fee-only adviser who is knowledgeable about index funds.

Appendixes

- ◆ Appendix A: Low-Cost Index Fund Providers
- ◆ Appendix B: Recommended Resources

Low-Cost Index
Fund Providers*

Index Fund Providers	Phone Numbers
American Century Investments	800-345-2021
AON Funds	800-266-3637
Armada Funds	800-342-5734
Barclays Global Investors	800-474-2737
Bridgeway Funds	800-661-3550
California Investment Trust Group	800-225-8778
Deutsche Asset Management	800-730-1313
Dreyfus	800-373-9387
E*TRADE Funds	800-786-2575
Eclipse Funds	770-631-0414
Fidelity Group	800-544-8888
Financial Investors Trust	800-298-3442
Galaxy Funds	800-628-0414
Harris Insight Funds	800-982-8782
Merrill Lynch Investment Managers	609-282-2800
Nationwide Funds	800-848-0920
Schwab Funds	800-435-4000
Scudder Funds	800-621-1048
State Street Global Advisors	800-843-2639
Strong Funds	800-368-1030
TD Waterhouse Funds	800-934-4448
T. Rowe Price Funds	800-638-5660
Transamerica Premier Funds	800-892-7587
USAA Group	800-382-8722
Vanguard Group	800-662-7447
Vantagepoint Funds	800-669-7400
Wachovia Funds	800-994-4414
Wilshire Target Funds	888-200-6796

*Mutual fund companies with index fund fees less than 0.50 percent and no sales load.
Courtesy of www.Indexfunds.com "Fund Screener."

Recommended Resources

RESEARCH WEB SITES

Investment Advice Sites

Indexfunds.com
Independent index investing and index commentary; providing comprehensive returns, definitions, and tracking of worldwide indexes and index funds. A clearinghouse of information about index funds.

Morningstar.com
Providers of news and analyses on markets, stocks, and mutual funds, for the individual investor. The *VANGUARD DIEHARDS* conversation board is a great place to find information and ask questions.

Vanguard.com
Besides one of the best places to shop for index funds, Vanguard's Education, Planning, and Advice section is one of the best on the Web. There is lots of good information in the Plain Talk® Library.

EfficientFrontier.com
William J. Bernstein and Susan F. Sharin edit *Efficient Frontier: An Online Journal of Practical Asset Allocation*. Bernstein's quarterly online journal is a must read for all serious index fund investors.

Dfafunds.com
Dimensional Fund Advisors offers unique index funds through investment advisers. Their three-factor approach to portfolio construction is gaining acceptance worldwide.

iShares.com
Learn about exchange-traded funds and use the helpful portfolio management tools on Barclay's iShares Web site.

Ssga.com
State Street Global Advisers manages many exchange-traded funds around the world. Their site offers tools and information.

PSinvest.com
The Web site of Portfolio Solutions, LLC, a leading investment adviser specializing in index fund management.

Index Information Sites

Spglobal.com

Standard & Poor's offers comprehensive analyses and commentary of all their global indexes.

Barra.com

Barra is a leading provider of index data on the U.S. equity market. They have teamed up with S&P to provide many of the popular growth and value index fund benchmarks.

DowJones.com

Dow Jones offers lots of great information on the markets and a wonderful historical section featuring charts that include major economic and world events.

MSCI.com

Morgan Stanley Capital International (MSCI) market covers the globe with their Web site. It includes methodology and analysis.

Russell.com

Comprehensive information about all the Russell indexes and methodology.

Wilshire.com

Wilshire indexes are considered the most complete U.S. equity benchmarks covering over 6500 U.S. companies.

BOOKS ABOUT INDEX FUND INVESTING

Common Sense on Mutual Funds by John C. Bogle. Index fund icon shares his views in this must-read book for any index investor.

Winning the Loser's Game by Charles Ellis. Classic book outlines how investors can increase returns and decrease risk by buying the market.

A Random Walk Down Wall Street by Burton G. Malkiel. A comprehensive look at today's market and what is driving it.

The Intelligent Asset Allocator by William J. Bernstein. Comprehensive analysis of sensible asset allocation for advanced investors.

Serious Money, Straight Talk About Investing for Retirement by Richard A. Ferri, CFA. States the virtues of low-cost index investing in meeting financial goals.

Exchange Traded Funds by Jim Wiandt and Will McClatchy. IndexFunds.com comprehensive overview of ETFs: when, why, and how to use them.

The Only Investment Strategy You'll Ever Need: Index Funds and Beyond—The Way Smart Money Invests Today by Larry Swedroe. A detailed case for index funds and how to use them in a portfolio.

What Wall Street Doesn't Want You to Know: How You Can Build Real Wealth Investing in Index Funds by Larry Swedroe. Learn how to use risk and diversification to your advantage.

Outpacing the Pros by David Blitzer. Learn about indexing from the S&P 500 committee head.

The Coffeehouse Investor by Bill Schultheis. Investment strategy for those who don't want to waste their time on research.

Mutual Funds: Profiting from an Investment Revolution by Scott Simon. An investment adviser shares his views on indexing.

100 Ways to Beat the Market by Gene Walden. Book's title belies its message, which is that index funds are your best bet.

GLOSSARY

12b-1 fee   An annual fee charged by some mutual funds to pay for marketing and distribution activities. The fee is taken directly from fund assets, which reduces a shareholder's total return.

active management   An investment strategy that seeks to outperform the average returns of the financial markets. Active managers rely on research, market forecasts, and their own judgment and experience in selecting securities to buy and sell.

alternative minimum tax (AMT)   A separate tax system designed to assure that wealthy individuals and organizations pay at least a minimum amount of federal income taxes. Certain securities used to fund private, for-profit activities are subject to the AMT.

annualize   To make a period of less than a year apply to a full year, usually for purposes of comparison. For instance, a portfolio turnover rate of 36 percent over a 6-month period could be converted to an annualized rate of 72 percent.

asked price   The price at which a security is offered for sale. For a no-load mutual fund, the asked price is the same as the fund's net asset value per share. Also called offering price.

automatic reinvestment   An arrangement by which the dividends or other earnings from an investment are used to buy additional shares in the investment vehicle.

average coupon   The average interest rate (coupon rate) of all bonds in a portfolio.

average effective maturity   A weighted average of the maturity dates for all securities in a money market or bond fund. (The maturity date is the date that a money market instrument or bond buyer will be repaid by the security's issuer.) The longer the average maturity, the more a fund's share price will move up or down in response to changes in interest rates.

back-end load   A sales fee charged by some mutual funds when an investor sells fund shares. Also called a contingent deferred sales charge.

benchmark index   An index that correlates with a fund, used to measure a fund manager's performance.

beta   A measure of the magnitude of a portfolio's past share-price fluctuations in relation to the ups and downs of the overall market (or appropriate market index). The market (or index) is assigned a beta of 1.00, so a portfolio with a beta of 1.20 would have seen its share price rise or fall by 12 percent when the overall market rose or fell by 10 percent.

bid-ask spread   The difference between what a buyer is willing to bid (pay) for a security and the seller's ask (offer) price.

blue-chip stocks   Common stock of well-known companies with a history of growth and dividend payments.

book value   A company's assets minus any liabilities and intangible assets.

broker/broker-dealer   An individual or firm that buys or sells mutual funds or other securities for the public.

capital gain/loss   The difference between the sale price of an asset—such as a mutual fund, stock, or bond—and the original cost of the asset.

capital gains distributions   Payments to mutual fund shareholders of gains realized during the year on securities that the fund has sold at a profit, minus any realized losses.

cash investments   Short-term debt instruments—such as commercial paper, banker's acceptances, and Treasury bills—that mature in less than one year. Also known as money market instruments or cash reserves.

certified financial planner® (CFP®)   An investment professional who has passed exams administered by the CFP Board of Standards on subjects such as taxes, securities, insurance, and estate planning.

certified public accountant (CPA)   An investment professional who is state licensed to practice public accounting.

chartered financial analyst (CFA)   An investment professional who has met competence standards in economics, securities, portfolio management, and financial accounting as determined by the Institute of Chartered Financial Analysts.

closed-end fund   A mutual fund that has a fixed number of shares, usually listed on a major stock exchange.

commodities   Unprocessed goods such as grains, metals, and minerals traded in large amounts on a commodities exchange.

consumer price index (CPI)   A measure of the price change in consumer goods and services. The CPI is used to track the pace of inflation.

cost basis   The original cost of an investment. For tax purposes the cost basis is subtracted from the sales price to determine any capital gain or loss.

country risk   The possibility that political events (a war, national elections), financial problems (rising inflation, government default), or natural disasters (an earthquake, a poor harvest) will weaken a country's economy and cause investments in that country to decline.

coupon/coupon rate   The interest rate that a bond issuer promises to pay the bondholder until the bond matures.

credit rating   A published ranking, based on a careful financial analysis, of a creditor's ability to pay interest or principal owed on a debt.

credit risk   The possibility that a bond issuer will fail to repay interest and principal in a timely manner. Also called default risk.

currency risk The possibility that returns could be reduced for Americans investing in foreign securities because of a rise in the value of the U.S. dollar against foreign currencies. Also called exchange rate risk.

custodian Either (1) a bank, agent, trust company, or other organization responsible for safeguarding financial assets or (2) the individual who oversees the mutual fund assets of a minor's custodial account.

declaration date The date the board of directors of a company or mutual fund announces the amount and date of its next dividend payment.

default A failure to pay principal or interest when due.

depreciation A decrease in the value of an investment.

derivative A financial contract whose value is based on, or "derived" from, a traditional security (e.g., a stock or bond), an asset (e.g., a commodity), or a market index (e.g., the S&P 500 Index).

discount broker A brokerage that executes orders to buy and sell securities at commission rates lower than a full-service brokerage.

distributions Either (1) withdrawals made by the owner from an individual retirement account (IRA) or (2) payments of dividends and/or capital gains by a mutual fund.

dividend reinvestment plan The automatic reinvestment of shareholder dividends in more shares of the company's stock.

dividend yield The annual rate of return on a share of stock, determined by dividing the annual dividend by its current share price. In a stock mutual fund, this figure represents the average dividend yield of the stocks held by the fund.

dollar-cost averaging Investing equal amounts of money at regular intervals on an ongoing basis. This technique ensures that an investor buys fewer shares when prices are high and more shares when prices are low.

earnings per share A company's earnings divided by the number of common shares outstanding.

efficient market The theory—disputed by some experts—that stock prices reflect all market information that is known by all investors. Also states that investors cannot beat the market because it is impossible to determine future stock prices.

enhanced index fund An index fund that is designed to generally track an index but also to outperform it through the use of leverage, futures, trading strategies, capital gains management, and other methods.

equivalent taxable yield The yield needed from a taxable bond to give the same after-tax yield as a tax-exempt issue.

exchange privilege The shareholder's ability to move money from one mutual fund to another within the same fund family, often without an additional charge.

exchange-traded fund   An exchange-traded fund is an index fund that trades on the stock market. Some common ETFs are the Nasdaq-100 Index Tracking Stock (QQQ), which tracks the Nasdaq-100, and Standard & Poor's Depositary Receipts (SPY), which tracks the S & P 500.

ex-dividend date   The date when a distribution of dividends and/or capital gains is deducted from a mutual fund's assets or set aside for payment to shareholders. On the ex-dividend date, the fund's share price drops by the amount of the distribution (plus or minus any market activity). Also known as the reinvestment date.

expense ratio   The percentage of a portfolio's average net assets used to pay its annual expenses. The expense ratio, which includes management fees, administrative fees, and any 12b-1 fees, directly reduces returns to investors.

Federal Reserve   The central bank that regulates the supply of money and credit throughout the United States. The Fed's seven-member board of governors, appointed by the president, has significant influence on U.S. monetary and economic policy.

fee-only adviser   An arrangement in which a financial adviser charges a set hourly rate or an agreed upon percentage of assets under management for a financial plan.

first in, first out (FIFO)   A method for calculating taxable gain or loss when mutual fund shares are sold. The FIFO method assumes that the first shares sold were the first shares purchased.

front-end load   A sales commission charged at the time of purchase by some mutual funds and other investment vehicles.

full faith and credit   A pledge to pay interest and principal on a bond issued by the government.

fund family   A group of mutual funds sponsored by the same organization, often offering exchange privileges between funds and combined account statements for multiple funds.

fundamental analysis   A method of examining a company's financial statements and operations as a means of forecasting stock price movements.

futures/futures contracts   A contract to buy or sell specific amounts of a specific commodity (e.g., grain or foreign currency) for an agreed upon price at a certain time in the future.

global fund   A mutual fund that invests in stocks of companies in the United States and foreign countries.

gross domestic product (GDP)   The value of all goods and services provided by U.S. labor in a given year. One of the primary measures of the U.S. economy, the GDP is issued quarterly by the Department of Commerce. Formerly known as the gross national product (GNP).

hedge   A strategy in which one investment is used to offset the risk of another security.

high-yield fund   A mutual fund that invests primarily in bonds with a credit rating of BB or lower. Because of the speculative nature of high-yield bonds, high-yield funds are subject to greater share price volatility and greater credit risk than other types of bond funds.

indexing   An investment strategy to match the average performance of a market or group of stocks. Usually this is accomplished by buying a small amount of each stock in a market.

index providers   Companies that construct and maintain stock and bond indexes. The main providers are Standard & Poor's, Dow Jones, Lehman Brothers, Morgan Stanley, Russell, and Wilshire.

inflation risk   The possibility that increases in the cost of living will reduce or eliminate the returns on a particular investment.

interest rate risk   The possibility that a security or mutual fund will decline in value because of an increase in interest rates.

international fund   A mutual fund that invests in securities traded in markets outside of the United States. Foreign markets present additional risks, including currency fluctuation and political instability. In the past these risks have made prices of foreign stocks more volatile than those of U.S. stocks.

inverse index fund   An index fund designed to go in the opposite direction of the stock or bond market.

investment adviser   A person or organization that makes the day-to-day decisions regarding a portfolio's investments. Also called a portfolio manager.

investment grade   A bond whose credit quality is considered to be among the highest by independent bond-rating agencies.

junk bond   A bond with a credit rating of BB or lower. Also known as high-yield bonds because of the rewards offered to those who are willing to take on the additional risks of a lower quality bond.

large-cap   A company whose stock market value is generally in excess of $10 billion, although the range varies according to the index provider.

leveraged index fund   An index fund that is designed to move more than the market, but in proportion to the market. A leveraged S&P 500 fund that has a 2-to-1 ratio will go up or down twice as much as the S&P 500 index.

liquidity   The degree of a security's marketability; that is, how quickly the security can be sold at a fair price and converted to cash.

load fund   A mutual fund that levies a sales charge either when shares are bought (a front-end load) or sold (a back-end load).

long-term capital gain   A profit on the sale of a security or mutual fund share that has been held for more than 1 year.

management fee   The amount a mutual fund pays to its investment adviser for the work of overseeing the fund's holdings. Also called an advisory fee.

market capitalization   A determination of a company's value, calculated by multiplying the total number of company stock shares outstanding by the price per share. Also called capitalization.

maturity/maturity date   The date when the issuer of a money market instrument or bond agrees to repay the principal, or face value, to the buyer.

median market cap   The midpoint of market capitalization (market price multiplied by the number of shares outstanding) of the stocks in a portfolio. Half the stocks in the portfolio will have higher market capitalizations, and half will have lower.

mid-cap   A company whose stock market value is between $2 billion and $10 billion, although the range varies according to the index provider.

municipal bond fund   A mutual fund that invests in tax-exempt bonds issued by state, city, and/or local governments. The interest obtained from these bonds is passed through to shareholders and is generally free of federal (and sometimes state and local) income taxes.

National Association of Securities Dealers (NASD)   An organization of brokers and dealers designed to protect the investing public against fraudulent acts.

net asset value (NAV)   The market value of a mutual fund's total assets, minus liabilities, divided by the number of shares outstanding. The value of a single share is called its share value or share price.

no-load fund   A mutual fund that charges no sales commission or load.

nominal return   The return on an investment before adjustment for inflation.

open-end fund   An investment entity that has the ability to issue or redeem the number of shares outstanding on a daily basis. Prices are quoted once per day, at the end of the day, at the net asset value of the fund (NAV).

operating expenses   The amount paid for asset maintenance or the cost of doing business. Earnings are distributed after operating expenses are deducted.

option   A contract in which a seller gives a buyer the right, but not the obligation, to buy or sell securities at a specified price on or before a given date.

payable date   The date when dividends or capital gains are paid to shareholders. For mutual funds the payable date is usually within 2 to 4 days of the record date. The payable date also refers to the date on which a declared stock dividend or bond interest payment is scheduled to be paid.

portfolio transaction costs The expenses associated with buying and selling securities, including commissions, purchase and redemption fees, exchange fees, and other miscellaneous costs. In a mutual fund prospectus, these expenses would be listed separately from the fund's expense ratio. Does not include the bid/ask spread.

premium An amount that exceeds the face value or redemption value of a security or of a comparable security or group of investments. It may indicate that a security is favored highly by investors. Also refers to a fee for obtaining insurance coverage.

price-to-book (P/B) ratio The price per share of a stock divided by its book value (i.e., net worth) per share. For a portfolio the ratio is the weighted average price-to-book ratio of the stocks it holds.

price-to-earnings (P/E) ratio The share price of a stock divided by its per-share earnings over the past year. For a portfolio, the weighted average P/E ratio of the stocks in the portfolio. P/E is a good indicator of market expectations about a company's prospects; the higher the P/E, the greater the expectations for a company's future growth in earnings.

prospectus A legal document that gives prospective investors information about a mutual fund, including discussions of its investment objectives and policies, risks, costs, and past performance. A prospectus must be provided to a potential investor before he or she can establish an account and must also be filed with the Securities and Exchange Commission.

proxy Written authorization by a shareholder giving someone else (e.g., fund or company management) authority to represent his or her vote at a shareholder meeting.

quantitative analysis In securities, an assessment of specific measurable factors (e.g., cost of capital, value of assets) and projections of sales, costs, earnings, and profits. Combined with more subjective or qualitative considerations (e.g., management effectiveness), quantitative analysis can enhance investment decisions and portfolios.

real estate investment trust (REIT) A company that manages a group of real estate investments and distributes to its shareholders at least 95 percent of its net earnings annually. REITs often specialize in a particular kind of property. They can, for example, invest in real estate such as office buildings, shopping centers, or hotels; purchase real estate (an equity REIT); and provide loans to building developers (a mortgage REIT).

real return The actual return received on an investment after factoring in inflation. For example, if the nominal investment return for a particular period was 8 percent and inflation was 3 percent, the real return would be 5 percent (8 percent − 3 percent).

record date   The date used to determine who is eligible to receive a company or fund's next distribution of dividends or capital gains.

redemption   The return of an investor's principal in a security. Bond redemption can occur at or before maturity; mutual fund shares are redeemed at net asset value when an investor's holdings are liquidated.

redemption fee   A fee charged by some mutual funds when an investor sells shares within a short period of time.

registered investment adviser (RIA)   An investment professional who is registered—but not endorsed—by the Securities and Exchange Commission (SEC) who may recommend certain types of investment products.

reinvestment   The use of investment income to buy additional securities. Many mutual fund companies and investment services offer the automatic reinvestment of dividends and capital gains distributions as an option to investors.

return of capital   A distribution that is not paid out of earnings and profits. It is a return of the investor's principal.

risk tolerance   An investor's ability or willingness to endure declines in the prices of investments while waiting for them to increase in value.

R-squared   A measure of how much of a portfolio's performance can be explained by the returns from the overall market (or a benchmark index). If a portfolio's total return precisely matched that of the overall market or benchmark, its R-squared would be 1.00. If a portfolio's return bore no relationship to the market's returns, its R-squared would be 0.

sector diversification   The percentage of a portfolio's stocks from companies in each of the major industry groups.

sector fund   A mutual fund that concentrates on a relatively narrow market sector. These funds can experience higher share-price volatility than some diversified funds because sector funds are subject to issues specific to a given sector.

Securities and Exchange Commission (SEC)   The agency of the federal government that regulates mutual funds, registered investment advisers, the stock and bond markets, and broker-dealers. The SEC was established by the Securities Exchange Act of 1934.

Sharpe ratio   A measure of risk-adjusted return. To calculate a Sharpe ratio, an asset's excess returns (its return in excess of the return generated by risk-free assets such as Treasury bills) are divided by the asset's standard deviation. Can be calculated versus a benchmark or an index.

short sale   Sale of a security or option contract not owned by the seller, usually to take advantage of an expected drop in the price of the security or option. In a typical short sale transaction, a borrowed security or option is sold, and the borrower agrees to purchase replacement shares or options at the market price on or by a specified future date. Generally considered a risky investment strategy.

short-term capital gain   A profit on the sale of a security or mutual fund share that has been held for 1 year or less. A short-term capital gain is taxed as ordinary income.

small-cap   A company whose stock market value is less than $2 billion, although the range varies according to the index provider.

spread   For stocks and bonds, the difference between the bid price and the asked price.

standard deviation   A measure of the degree to which a fund's return varies from its previous returns or from the average of all similar funds. The larger the standard deviation, the greater the likelihood (and risk) that a security's performance will fluctuate from the average return.

style drift   When a fund moves away from its stated investment objective over time.

swap agreement   An arrangement between two parties to exchange one security for another, to change the mix of a portfolio or the maturities of the bonds it includes, or to alter another aspect of a portfolio or financial arrangement, such as interest rate payments or currencies.

tax deferral   Delaying the payment of income taxes on investment income. For example, owners of traditional IRAs do not pay income taxes on the interest, dividends, or capital gains accumulating in their retirement accounts until they begin making withdrawals.

tax swapping   Creating a tax loss by the simultaneous sale of one index fund and the purchase of a similar fund.

taxable equivalent yield   The return from a higher paying but taxable investment that would equal the return from a tax-free investment. It depends on the investor's tax bracket.

tax-exempt bond   A bond, usually issued by municipal, county, or state governments, whose interest payments are not subject to federal, and in some cases, state and local income tax.

total return   A percentage change, over a specified period, in a mutual fund's net asset value, with the ending net asset value adjusted to account for the reinvestment of all distributions of dividends and capital gains.

transaction fee/commission   A charge assessed by an intermediary, such as a broker-dealer or a bank, for assisting in the sale or purchase of a security.

Treasury security   A negotiable debt obligation issued by the U.S. government for a specific amount and maturity. Income from Treasury securities is exempt from state and local tax but not from federal income tax. Treasury securities include Treasury bills (T-bills 1 year or less), Treasury notes (T-notes 1 to 10 years), and Treasury bonds (T-bonds over 10 years).

turnover rate   An indication of trading activity during the past year. Portfolios with high turnover rates incur higher transaction costs and are more likely to distribute capital gains (which are taxable to nonretirement accounts).

unit investment trust (UIT)   An SEC-registered investment company that purchases a fixed, unmanaged portfolio of income-producing securities and then sells shares in the trust to investors, usually in units of at least $1000. Usually sold by an intermediary such as a broker.

unrealized capital gain/loss   An increase (or decrease) in the value of a security that is not "real" because the security has not been sold. Once a security is sold by the portfolio manager, the capital gains/losses are "realized" by the fund, and any payment to the shareholder is taxable during the tax year in which the security was sold.

volatility   The degree of fluctuation in the value of a security, mutual fund, or index. Volatility is often expressed as a mathematical measure such as a standard deviation or beta. The greater a fund's volatility, the wider the fluctuations between its high and low prices.

wash sale rule   The IRS regulation that prohibits a taxpayer from claiming a loss on the sale of an investment if that investment, or a substantially identical investment, is purchased within 30 days before or after the sale.

Yankee dollars/bonds   Debt obligations, such as bonds or certificates of deposit bearing U.S. dollar denominations, issued in the United States by foreign banks and corporations.

yield curve   A line plotted on a graph that depicts the yields of bonds of varying maturities, from short term to long term. The line or "curve" shows the relationship between short- and long-term interest rates.

yield to maturity   The rate of return an investor would receive if the securities held by a portfolio were held to their maturity dates.

INDEX

About the Author

Richard A. Ferri earned a Bachelor of Science degree in business administration from the University of Rhode Island in 1980. He then served 8 years as an officer and fighter pilot in the U.S. Marine Corps. Ferri left active duty in 1988 and began working as a stockbroker with a major Wall Street firm.

In 1995 Ferri earned the designation of chartered financial analyst (CFA) offered through the Association of Investment Management and Research (AIMR). He also holds a Master of Science degree in finance from Walsh College in Troy, Michigan, where he currently serves as an adjunct professor of finance.

In 1999 Ferri founded Portfolio Solutions, LLC, an independent investment firm in Troy, Michigan. The firm manages individual accounts for high net worth families, foundations, and corporate pension plans. Ferri specializes in low-cost, low-tax investment strategies using index mutual funds and municipal bonds. Portfolio Solutions currently manages over $150 million in assets for 75 clients.

In March 2000 Ferri published his first book, *Serious Money, Straight Talk About Investing for Retirement*. The book carefully maps out the steps required to develop a successful approach to navigating the minefields of Wall Street. He also writes for several investment magazines and online investment sites.

AM7067-2
2   CA